ORGANIZING IMMIGR

Organizing Immigrants

The Challenge for Unions in Contemporary California

Edited by Ruth Milkman

ILR PRESS

an imprint of

CORNELL UNIVERSITY PRESS

Ithaca and London

First published 2000 by Cornell University Press
First printing, Cornell Paperbacks, 2000

Printed in the United States of America

Library of Congress Cataloging-in-Publication Data

Organizing immigrants: the challenge for unions in contemporary California / edited by Ruth Milkman.
    p. cm.
   Includes bibliographical references and index.
   ISBN 0-8014-3697-4 (cloth)—ISBN 0-8014-8617-3 (pbk.)
   1. Alien labor—Labor unions—Organizing—California.   I. Title: Challenge for unions in contemporary California.   II. Milkman, Ruth, 1954–

HD6490.O72 U657 2000
331.6'2—dc21

                                                 99-050221

Cloth printing   10 9 8 7 6 5 4 3 2 1

Paperback printing   10 9 8 7 6 5 4 3 2 1

Contents

Acknowledgments

This volume had its origins in a conference held at UCLA in May 1998, which I co-organized with Roger Waldinger, then Director of the UCLA Lewis Center for Regional Policy Studies. My heartfelt thanks to Roger for his ongoing support and practical advice, which helped transform a vague idea floated in a casual e-mail into a palpable reality. The other person who contributed immeasurably to this project is Kent Wong, director of the UCLA Labor Center, who offered innumerable suggestions and helped involve the local labor community in the conference, greatly enriching both the discussions held there and ultimately the contents of this volume.

In addition to the seed money provided by the Lewis Center, I am grateful to the many conference co-sponsors: the California Policy Seminar, UC Mexus, the UCLA Center for Social Theory and Comparative History, the UCLA Division of Social Sciences, the UCLA Associate Vice Chancellor for Academic Affairs, and the Office of the President of the University of California. The administrative support of Margaret Johnson, Belinda Vigil, and Luis Escala Rabadan was also essential to making the conference a success. Thanks also to David Gutiérrez, Sanford Jacoby, Peter Olney, and Paul Johnston, who served as commentators at the conference, stimulating valuable discussions and offering insightful comments on earlier versions of the chapters appearing in this volume.

Fran Benson at Cornell University Press was enthusiastic about this book from the outset and offered consistent encouragement at every step in the publication process. Dan Clawson and Elissa McBride provided supportive and incisive comments on the conference proceedings that were extremely helpful in shaping the final version of the book. Thanks also to Laura Robinson for expert technical assistance in the final stages of preparing the manuscript for publication.

RUTH MILKMAN

Los Angeles, California

ORGANIZING IMMIGRANTS

Introduction

Ruth Milkman

$\mathbf{A}$t the end of the twentieth century, the challenge of recruiting immigrant workers into union ranks has become increasingly central to the larger project of rebuilding the United States labor movement, which has been in a downward spiral for decades. Today only about one in ten private sector workers, and only 15 percent of the workforce as a whole, are union members—less than half the level of union density forty years ago. When legal changes sparked a resurgence of mass immigration to the United States after 1965, union membership levels and influence were already waning; and in the decades since, labor movement decline has accelerated even as the immigrant population has swelled. Today, recent immigrants are even less likely than native-born workers to be unionized. Yet in some regions, among them the major metropolitan areas of California, immigrants today comprise a majority of those employed in manual jobs with limited educational requirements—the very jobs that were once key strongholds of union organization. Thus recruiting immigrants is an increasingly urgent imperative for the besieged labor movement.

There are some hopeful portents on the horizon. In the 1990s, a series of dramatic immigrant organizing successes—many of them documented in these pages—demonstrated the potential for bringing foreign-born workers into the orbit of organized labor. At the same time, a new group of progressive leaders has taken command of the American Federation of Labor–Congress of Industrial Organizations (AFL-CIO) and

I am grateful to Michael Burawoy, Paul Johnston, Roger Waldinger and especially Dorothy Sue Cobble for their critical comments on an earlier version of this introduction.

some of the major unions affiliated with it have begun pouring resources into organizing on a scale not seen for decades. Immigrant workers are a crucial focus in these new efforts, especially in California, the nation's single largest magnet for immigrants and a key arena in the struggle for labor movement revitalization.

Are immigrant workers fundamentally different from their native-born counterparts when it comes to union organizing? Does the fact that most immigrants who come to the United States today are from Latin America and Asia make their propensity to unionize (or lack of it) different from that of the earlier wave of European immigrants in the late nineteenth and early twentieth century? Are temporary sojourners more or less "organizable" than long-term residents who have no intention of returning to their home countries; more generally, are there differences between the orientations of settled immigrants and newcomers? How does the legal status of immigrants affect the situation—do naturalized citizens, legal residents, and undocumented immigrants differ in regard to their interest in unionization? Once organized, do foreign-born workers have different needs than their native-born counterparts, shaping a distinctive pattern of consolidating unionism, once it is established? How much does the political and cultural background of immigrants matter—are politicized Central American refugees, say, more likely to organize or be recruited into unions than *campesinos* from rural Mexico or impoverished migrants from Thailand? And how do all these variations among workers play out in the context of the dramatic structural transformations that have been underway since the mid-1970s? Is there any relationship between immigration and the bold anti-union offensives on the part of employers and the state in this period? What about the rapid growth of inequality in income and wealth that has accompanied economic restructuring? How does the newly intensified polarization between rich and poor affect foreign-born workers and the prospects for bringing them into the labor movement? In short, what are the social, political, and economic conditions that facilitate, and those that impede, immigrant unionization?

These are among the questions the contributors to this volume explore, drawing on newly collected evidence on immigrants and unions in late twentieth-century California. The chapters include broad overviews of immigrant employment and unionization patterns in the nation's most populous state, as well as studies of particular organizing campaigns, strikes, and immigrant-employing industries in a variety of urban settings, with cases from both northern and southern California. Most of the emphasis is on Latinos, who constitute the bulk of the state's working-class immigrants, although some chapters explore the situation of Asian immigrants as well.

There have been few previous efforts to document and analyze the relationship of immigrants to unionism in the contemporary United States, but the basic issues involved here are hardly new. Indeed, the historical literature on immigrants and the labor movement offers some useful insights that can help make sense of the current scene. For the American working class always has been comprised overwhelmingly of immigrants and their offspring. From the outset, there were many instances in which "ethnic bonds...served to cement labor organization" (Brody 1993, 108). On the other hand, the diversity of nationalities within the United States was a challenge for union organizers from the earliest period. In order to forge durable labor organizations, "a multi-ethnic working-class subculture of opposition had to be created," historian Richard Oestreicher (1986) notes in one influential formulation of the problem. "New institutions had to be created, and a new moral code developed that convinced workers that they owed the same kinds of loyalties to workers of other nationalities that they owed to people of their own nationality" (61).

This task was never easy, and in the unions affiliated with the American Federation of Labor (AFL), which by the end of the nineteenth century was the nation's hegemonic labor organization, all too often it was not even attempted. Many of the craft unionists of northern and western European origins that dominated the AFL were openly hostile toward more recent immigrants from southern and eastern Europe, whom employers freely exploited as strikebreakers and who dominated the ranks of the unskilled. Although in the 1880s and 1890s the AFL had made some serious efforts to incorporate these "new immigrants" into their organizations, by the turn of the century most trade union leaders had come to see them as "unorganizable" and to favor restrictions on new immigration (Greene 1998). The most extreme exclusionary impulses were directed at non-European migrants—the case of Chinese workers in California is especially infamous—and pervaded even the most progressive unions and labor organizations (Mink 1986). In some AFL affiliates, the "new immigrants" organized themselves or were recruited into de facto industrial unions, but this effort produced lasting results in only a few industries—most importantly, clothing and coal mining. Otherwise, except in such short-lived organizations as the Industrial Workers of the World, they remained unorganized until the mass industrial-union drives of the 1930s.

The problem was not lack of interest in unionization on the part of the "new immigrants" themselves, however. When the opportunity arose to organize, they responded with marked enthusiasm. Economist Issac A. Hourwich wrote in 1912 that "immigrants from Southern and Eastern Europe are the backbone of some of the strongest labor unions" (34). In the unionization drive in the steel industry during World War I, "the great initial response came from the immigrant steelworkers. They were the first to crowd the mass meetings and sign up for membership," David Brody notes (1960, p. 223). "In contrast, the natives were, according to all reports, an unenthusiastic lot." In meatpacking, too, "organizers found the foreign-born much easier to organize than the native-born" (Barrett 1987, 195). Similarly, in the needle trades, especially among left-wing east European Jews, "it was within the immigrant working-class community that the roots of labor militance took hold and spread" (Glenn 1990, 178). Both for the largely Slavic immigrants in steel and meatpacking and for the Jewish garment workers—as for English and German immigrants half a century earlier (see Brody 1993, 110–11)—receptivity to unionization efforts was often linked to prior experiences with strikes and labor organization in Europe (Hourwich 1912, 349–51; Glenn 1990, 178–85). Of course, not all "new immigrants" had this kind of background, and ethnic parochialism and fragmentation among workers could be an obstacle to unionization in some contexts. But on the whole, what held back immigrant labor organizing in the early twentieth century was not antipathy toward unionism among the foreign-born themselves. Rather, the key difficulties were intensive, state-supported employer resistance on the one side, and on the other, the structural limitations of the craft-dominated AFL, for whose leaders the idea of recruiting within the ranks of the unskilled, where the new immigrants were so highly concentrated, was anathema.

Only with the triumph of industrial unionism in the 1930s were these workers fully welcomed into the house of labor, along with the long-marginalized African American working class. As Lizabeth Cohen has argued, the homogenizing effects of mass popular culture in the 1920s, along with the highly deliberate efforts a decade later by the Congress of Industrial Organizations (CIO) to build a "culture of unity" that preempted ethnic fragmentation, yielded powerful results when economic and political conditions shifted in a direction favorable to union-building in the New Deal era. Now union leaders aimed "to meet workers on their ethnic, or racial, ground and pull them into a self-consciously common culture that transcended those distinctions" (1990, 339), and unskilled first- and second-generation immigrants from southern and eastern

Europe became the core of the newly revitalized labor movement. Whereas earlier unionizing efforts among this population, even when successful, had failed to build lasting organizations, the new industrial unions (both those in the CIO and the many AFL unions that transformed themselves into industrial organizations in this period) soon were consolidated into vast bureaucratic empires that would endure for decades. As such they offered opportunities to those first- and second-generation immigrants with the requisite leadership skills to become career union officials; at the same time the CIO's institutional success brought rank-and-file foreign-born workers squarely into the economic mainstream, often for the first time.

Paradoxically, then, the putatively oppositional industrial union movement was a vehicle of immigrant assimilation. It is probably significant in this regard that the birth of the CIO came a full decade after the flow of immigrants from Europe was cut off by legal restrictions on entry to the United States, when the foreign-born population had largely stabilized. The fragmentary evidence available indicates that second-generation immigrants predominated among CIO activists (Cohen 1990, 324–25; see also Friedlander 1975). Indeed, Michael Piore has suggested that the unionism of the 1930s "can be understood in large measure as a part of the process through which ethnic communities coalesced and the second-generation communities expressed their resentment against the job characteristics that the parental communities, with a different motivation and a different attitude toward the labor market, had come to accept" (1979, 156–57).

Cultural assimilation went hand in hand with economic integration. Not only did their entrance into industrial unions bring economic stability and a measure of dignity for those first- and second-generation immigrants who directly shared in the material gains the CIO extracted on behalf of their members. But also, the CIO's success helped transform the nation's overall economic structure in a more egalitarian direction, raising wages (and later, extracting fringe benefits) for blue-collar workers—among whom immigrants and their children were disproportionately represented—who had previously eked out a marginal existence. Levels of inequality in income and wealth stabilized in this period, and from the end of World War II through the early 1970s, with U.S. hegemony at its height, living standards for the working class as a whole rose dramatically while poverty levels fell to their lowest point ever (Levy 1988). Although industrial unionism was hardly the only factor shaping this process, it played an important role (Freeman 1993).

In California and the Southwest (and on a smaller scale, in Chicago as well), the CIO helped further assimilation and Americanization among Mexican Americans in much the same way as it did for those from southern and eastern Europe. There had been extensive immigration from Mexico in the 1910s and 1920s, and Mexican Americans were by far the largest Latino immigrant group (Portes and Bach 1985, 76–83). Unionism now brought large numbers of *Mexicanos*, both those born in the United States and immigrant newcomers, substantial improvements in economic status. A number of Mexican American union leaders emerged in this period as well. Even when it had a distinctively left-wing character, as was the case more often than not, labor activism among Mexican Americans in this period "involved at its core an attempt by the children of the immigrant generation and those who had arrived in the United States as youngsters to integrate themselves into American society," historian George Sánchez (1993, 249) writes in his study of Los Angeles. "Ironically, such [left-wing] labor and political activity often served as the greatest 'Americanizing agent' of the 1930s and 1940s."

But there were limits to Americanization in this case. As the southern and eastern Europeans who dominated the early twentieth-century foreign-born population were incorporated into the economic mainstream with the help of industrial unionism, they also became "white," shedding their previously racialized status. By contrast, like African Americans, Mexican Americans and other Latinos not only continued to be classified racially (despite the wide variation in their actual skin color) and subjected to systematic discrimination in many public settings, but they also remained economically disadvantaged relative to non-Hispanic whites. Still, in the postwar boom years, thanks in large part to the direct and indirect effects of large-scale unionization, Mexican Americans made substantial gains in income, occupational status, and educational attainment, narrowing the gap with the white majority (Gutiérrez 1998, 312).

The public image of Mexican American unionism in the postwar era is strongly associated with the United Farm Workers (UFW), thanks to its high-profile boycott efforts and the stature of its key leader, Cesar Chavez, in the 1960s. However, as had been the case with previous efforts to build agricultural unionism, the UFW's collective bargaining achievements proved fleeting (see Martin 1996). The UFW nonetheless became a key symbol of the potential of unionism for the Mexican American community, especially in California, and provided a crucible of organizing experience for Latino labor activists that would be an important resource in later unionization efforts. Although they never achieved the UFW's national visibility, in the 1960s Mexican Americans also engaged in labor organizing efforts in urban settings, where settled immigrants were more likely to be employed (in contrast, farmworkers were disproportionately newcomers). Both the UFW and other union-building efforts attracted the energies of a new generation of Latino political activists influenced by the Civil Rights movement and the New Left—a group that included the college-educated children of blue-collar workers who had been unionized in the CIO era (Gutiérrez 1995, chap. 6).

Just as this wave of ethnic political activism was emerging among Mexican Americans, the 1965 amendments to the nation's immigration law set the stage for a massive influx of newcomers that would soon enlarge and transform the Latino community. Immigrants poured in from Mexico, and later, Central America as well, and many came without the benefit of legal documents. Most were poor and had little education—in contrast to the more diverse and often more prosperous population of Asian immigrants who were arriving at the same time. California, especially southern California, was the destination of choice for the new immigrants, and this phenomenon was amplified by patterns of chain migration. Most of the Latino newcomers clustered at the bottom of the state's labor market, in low-wage manual jobs with limited educational requirements.

Whereas the postwar boom had opened up opportunities for immigrants and their descendants to improve their lot, the post-1965 immigrants entered an economy where such opportunities were becoming more constricted. Deunionization and economic restructuring combined to create an increasingly polarized social structure, with the masses of working-class immigrants concentrated in low-level blue-collar factory and service jobs as well as a wide variety of positions in the informal sector where subminimum wages, homework, child labor, and other illegal practices are widespread. Although for many, even the bottom of the labor market in the United States represented a vast economic improvement over what they had left behind at home, future prospects for these immigrants and their children may be quite different from those of earlier cohorts. As David Gutiérrez (1998, 321) has written, "whereas ethnic Mexicans and their children in most areas in the postwar years had a reasonable chance of moving from entry-level, low status, unskilled and semiskilled occupations into higher-paying, higher status, skilled blue-collar occupations, in recent years Mexican immigrants have tended to enter the...bottom of the economy—and to stay there." The same is true for other working-class Latino immigrants (and some Asian groups as well), although for most of them there is no settled comparison group of the same nationality.

Could unionism once again serve as the vehicle for lifting the new immigrants out of poverty and into the economic and cultural mainstream, as it did for the last wave of mass immigration half a century ago? One issue that differentiates the current situation from that of earlier periods is the presence of large numbers of illegal, undocumented immigrants—a category which simply did not exist before the imposition of restrictions on immigration in 1924. Because of their vulnerability to deportation, one might expect the undocumented to be more fearful about the risks involved in union organizing, particularly when confrontations with state authority are likely. Yet this may be less of an obstacle to union mobilization than is generally presumed. "Undocumented workers' fear of the 'migra' [U.S. Immigration and Naturalization Service] did not make them more difficult to organize than native workers or immigrant workers with papers employed in the same industries," Héctor Delgado (1993, 61) concluded from his pioneering study of a factory unionizing drive involving immigrants, most of them undocumented, in Los Angeles during the mid-1980s.

> Workers reported giving little thought to their citizenship status and the possibility of an INS raid of the plant. . . . A forklift driver at Camagua [pseudonym for the company] claimed that he had never been afraid of the INS, adding, "I've never seen them here. Only in Tijuana." . . . [Another worker] said that he had a better chance of "getting hit by a car"—and he didn't worry about either. . . . In response to the prospect of deportation, . . . workers responded that if deported they would have simply returned (in some cases, "after a short vacation"). Julia Real [pseudonym], a sewer, commented, "They're not going to kill you! The worse [*sic*] thing they [the INS] can do is send me home, and I'll come back." (61, 63)

To be sure, recent efforts to tighten restrictions on immigration and renewed initiatives to deport the undocumented may have altered the climate in the years since Delgado did his fieldwork. Yet, despite the large numbers of undocumented immigrants among them, there is survey evidence, albeit fragmentary, suggesting that foreign-born workers'—and especially Latinos'—attitudes are generally more favorable toward unions than are those of native-born workers, even though immigrants often have difficulty securing work in the unionized sector of the economy (See DeFreitas 1993). In the 1998 referendum on the anti-union Proposition 226 in California, which would have required unions to obtain members' permission to spend any of their dues on politics, 75 percent of the heavily immigrant Latino voting population opposed the measure, compared to only 53.5 percent of voters overall (Bailey and Shogan 1998).

One reason for their more pro-union views may be that many of today's immigrant Latinos—especially those from Central America—have some positive experiences of unionism in their home countries. Although this transnational influence is less extensive than it was for their early twentieth-century European predecessors, it is striking that many of the new rank-and-file immigrant union leaders have a history of union activism or left-wing political ties in their native lands. While many immigrant workers are from rural backgrounds, a substantial number arrive in the United States far more acquainted with the idioms of unionism and class politics than their native-born counterparts. Among the workers involved in the Justice for Janitors campaign in Los Angeles, for example, organizers reported a "high level of class consciousness," as well as a willingness to take the risks involved in organizing that was palpably shaped by experiences back home. "There, if you were in a union, they killed you," one organizer explained in discussing the Salvadorans' role in this effort. "Here...you lost a job at $4.25" (Waldinger et al. 1998, 117).

The shared ordeal of immigration itself and the persistently high degree of stigmatization that foreign-born workers are forced to endure in their new home may also enhance the appeal of union organization. And, crucially, the strong social networks among immigrants—in marked contrast to the atomized communities typical of the native-born workforce in contemporary California—also facilitate organizing, as the Los Angeles janitors as well as other cases illustrate (see Delgado 1993; Milkman and Wong, this volume). Interest in unionism seems to be strongest among the growing number of immigrants who have been in the United States longer, and who plan to remain here (precisely those who voted against Proposition 226), whereas newcomers presumably have a different orientation.

Immigrant workers, undocumented or not, seem ripe for organizing. The major impediment is not a lack of interest in unions on their part, but rather the intensely anti-labor environment which makes organizing workers of any type difficult in the late twentieth century. National Labor Relations Board (NLRB) representation elections—once the primary means of recruiting new members— had become a cruel charade by the 1980s, as employers learned to manipulate the system to subvert even the minority of elections that unions were able to win. Unfair labor practice complaints filed against employers with the NLRB skyrocketed in the 1970s and 1980s (Freeman 1988). Among other things, illegal firings of pro-union workers are now a routine practice, as workers themselves are only too aware. "The fear of losing jobs, not the fear of being apprehended and deported by the 'migra,' was [workers'] principal concern" in the union organizing drive that Delgado studied (1993, 57). Employers have increasingly petitioned to decertify existing unions by means of NLRB elections as well.

Even in workplaces where unions have been able to maintain a presence, there was a massive power shift from labor to management in the 1980s. Unions in one industry after another made dramatic concessions and "givebacks," eroding pay rates, benefits, job security, and what little worker control over the labor process they had managed to obtain in earlier years. Emboldened employers went on the offensive on every front starting in the late 1970s, and even where they failed to avoid or eliminate unions entirely, they drastically reduced labor's legitimacy and influence. In the political arena, unions found themselves increasingly marginalized and isolated from potential allies in other social movements, as public support for unionism plummeted. Meanwhile, workers' real wages stagnated, income inequalities soared to levels not seen since World War II, and employment insecurity became pandemic.

The decline in organized labor's power and influence turned what had been a gradual process of erosion of union density into a rout, and by the 1980s union membership levels were in a free fall. The trend in California was similar to that in the United States as a whole: in 1961, over a third (34.5 percent) of all nonagricultural wage and salary workers in California were unionized; by 1987 the figure had dropped to only 19.1 percent (California Department of Industrial Relations 1989, 3). Private sector union density had fallen to a postwar low of 10.0 percent in the United States by 1996, and to 10.4 percent in California (Hirsch and Macpherson 1997, 26). Although this precipitous decline was primarily due to the anti-union offensive launched by employers starting in the 1970s (Freeman 1988), it did not help matters that unions devoted minimal resources to new organizing efforts in the postwar period (Voos 1984).

In the 1990s, as the crisis deepened to the point where its very survival was threatened, the labor movement finally began to reorient itself. The turning point was John J. Sweeney's October 1995 victory in the first-ever contested election for the AFL-CIO presidency, bringing a dedicated and savvy group of young, progressive unionists into key positions in the AFL-CIO bureaucracy. Sweeney has made a strong commitment to diversifying the nation's labor leadership and has initiated a dynamic union revitalization program as well. He has devoted considerable financial resources to new organizing—30 percent of the overall AFL-CIO budget—and is encouraging unions to build on recent experiments with new organizing tactics that a few innovative union locals have undertaken (see Sherman and Voss, this volume).

In California, more than anywhere else in the United States, meeting the larger challenge of rebuilding the labor movement inherently demands an effort to reach out to the vast and growing population of working-class immigrants. In many of the state's industries and occupations (including the janitorial and drywall cases analyzed in this volume), as wages and working conditions deteriorated after employers successfully eliminated or weakened unions, native workers simply exited and were subsequently replaced by immigrants. Thus even recapturing formerly unionized territory—much less making inroads into newer sectors that have never been organized, where foreign-born workers also have a huge presence—requires the labor movement in California to confront the issue of immigration head-on. There have been some promising developments on this score, especially in the state's southern region, where the influx of Latino immigrants into the labor force has been particularly dramatic, and where they suddenly emerged as a core source of union militancy in the early 1990s. Latinos have recently risen to prominent positions in the regional labor movement, most notably with the 1996 election of Miguel Contreras as the head of the Los Angeles County Federation of Labor, the first non-Anglo ever to hold that position (Sipchen 1997). And in February 1999, a stunning 74,000 Los Angeles County home-health-care workers, many of them Latino immigrants, voted to unionize after an eleven-year campaign by the Service Employees' International Union—the single largest organizing success anywhere in the United States since the 1930s (Greenhouse 1999). The future of the labor movement in California may depend on whether it can build on this groundwork to recruit the vast numbers of low-wage immigrant workers in the state into its ranks. The following chapters explore the prospects for that occurrence from a variety of perspectives.

We begin with a broad overview of the role of foreign-born workers in California's economy, which has been disproportionately affected by recent immigration. Nearly one-fourth of the state's population is foreign-born, compared to less than one-tenth of the United States population as a whole. David Lopez and Cynthia Feliciano's analysis highlights the intense concentration of Latino immigrants, most of whom are from Mexico and Central America, in California's low-level manual jobs. Foreign-born Latinos are 17 percent of California's total workforce, but they constitute 36 percent of its service workers, 42 percent of its factory operatives, and fully 49 percent of its laborers. At the other extreme, immigrant Latinos account for only 5 percent of the state's professional and technical workers. The situation of Asian immigrants, who make up 10 percent of the state's workforce, is quite different: they are much more evenly distributed through the occupational structure, thanks to higher levels of education and far greater diversity in class background. Lopez and Feliciano also examine employment patterns in the state's two most important metropolitan areas, greater Los Angeles and the San Francisco Bay Area. Latino immigrants constitute 19 percent of the workforce in the Los Angeles region, more than triple their share in the Bay Area (6 percent), where foreign-born Asians comprise a larger proportion of the workforce (11 percent). It is also striking that the relatively small Latino immigrant population in northern California has higher educational, occupational, and income levels than its southern counterparts—perhaps because unions have historically been stronger in the Bay Area than in Los Angeles.

Lopez and Feliciano pose the question whether the state's Latino immigrants will, like past generations of European immigrants, ultimately move into the economic mainstream, or whether they are more likely to become a castelike group stuck at the bottom of the occupational hierarchy. To explore this vital issue, they assess recent data on the educational and early job market experiences of the emerging population of second-generation Latinos. The results are not especially encouraging. In contrast to their Asian counterparts, whose educational and employment levels are actually ahead of native whites', Latinos are lagging behind. "The Latino second generation will certainly experience social mobility in contrast to their parents, from the bottom to the middle rungs," Lopez and Feliciano conclude, assuming that new immigrants continue to fill the bottom rungs. "But changes in the economy, plus the vastly greater size of the new second generation, make it difficult to predict that they will end up even as well off as today's Chicano working class."

Arguably, the fate of these second-generation Latino immigrants hinges largely on the degree to which the current efforts to revive the labor movement in California succeed. The optimistic scenario would be a reprise of the CIO era, when a burgeoning union movement served as the vehicle for second-generation immigrants to move up economically and simultaneously to assimilate into the mainstream of American culture. In the second chapter of this volume, however, Roger Waldinger and Claudia Der-Martirosian present a more pessimistic outlook, based on their analysis of unionization patterns among immigrants and native-born workers in the United States as a whole and in California. They deploy Current Population Survey (CPS) data for this purpose, using a combined four-year sample from the mid-1990s. Such an analysis was not possible until recently, as the CPS began asking about respondents' place of birth only a few years ago.

Waldinger and Der-Martirosian show that immigrants are underrepresented among union members nationally, and to an even greater extent in immigrant-rich California. They suggest several possible explanations for this. At the high end, for professionals and other highly educated middle-class immigrants, who constitute a greater proportion of the foreign-born today than in the early decades of this century, economic security and high incomes often can be achieved without union protection. At the other end of the class spectrum, unionization—especially if it involves short-term sacrifices—may have little appeal to low-wage "target earners" who are part of circular migration streams, even if they are the most exploited members of the foreign-born workforce, since their standard of comparison is to wages in their home countries, to which they plan to return.

A key finding from this analysis is that recent immigrants (those arriving in 1990 or later) are the least likely to be unionized, whereas those who have been in the United States the longest (arriving before 1980) have unionization levels roughly double those of newcomers, and in California over four times as great. Although these cohort differences are reduced in size once controls for other variables are included in the analysis, they remain the most striking finding of this chapter. In fact, for the nation's most settled immigrants, union membership is as likely—and for most subgroups, more likely—as for native workers. In California, however, even foreign-born workers who arrived in the United States before 1980 are less likely to be unionized than natives, in contrast to the national pattern. Still, the cohort effect is powerful in California too, with a far greater gap between the unionization levels of natives and recent arrivals than between those of natives and long-settled immigrants.

As Waldinger and Der-Martirosian recognize, it would be misleading to draw inferences from these findings about the attitudes or propensities of different groups in relation to unionism, for in the twentieth-century United States what determines whether a given worker is a union member is not his or her personal preferences but rather whether she or he is employed in a workplace where a union exists. Recent immigrants are often effectively excluded by language limitations or citizenship requirements from public sector employment—the one sector where unionization levels are high. Given this, together with the fact that nine out of ten private sector jobs are nonunion, it is hardly surprising that newcomers would be less likely than natives or more settled immigrants to find unionized jobs, which pay more than nonunion jobs and offer superior benefits.

Waldinger and Der-Martirosian conclude on a pessimistic note that "immigration is unlikely to add a silver lining to the dark clouds facing American labor." Although they make a compelling case for the claim that recruiting immigrant newcomers into union ranks is a formidable task indeed, the dramatic differences they reveal among immigrant cohorts nonetheless may augur well for the longer-term prospects of unionizing the foreign-born population. If Lopez and Feliciano's predictions prove correct, that the new second generation will face serious obstacles to economic mobility, the prospects for recruiting them into the labor movement in future years may be enhanced still further.

Whether the optimistic or pessimistic views about the labor movement's future ultimately prove to be correct may depend on the extent to which some of the successful new organizing tactics with which a few innovative unions have been experimenting in recent years are adopted more widely, and on whether they can be used to expand union recruitment of immigrant workers in particular. This is the focus of Rachel Sherman and Kim Voss's chapter, which draws on fieldwork in northern California to analyze the conditions under which local unions deploy such new tactics and to assess their effectiveness when applied to predominantly immigrant workforces. Their starting point is the observation that, despite evidence that the aggressive rank-and-file strategies recently adopted by a few leading-edge unions have proven highly effective, most unions have continued to use traditional methods. By comparing three groups of local unions, which they label "full innovators," "partial innovators," and "mandated innovators," they identify the conditions under which the new organizing strategies are most likely to be adopted. They also assess the impact of innovation on local unions' ability to organize immigrant workers.

The focus on local unions here is salutary, since the success of the new AFL-CIO leadership's efforts to revitalize the labor movement ultimately will depend on what happens within its various affiliates, especially at the local level where organizing efforts are concentrated. Extending the revolution that has occurred at the top of the labor federation into these long-established structures is among the most difficult tasks that lie ahead. Thousands of mid-level union officers and staff members remain loyal to entrenched internal political machines, and many are hostile to Sweeney and his allies. As Sherman and Voss point out, even shifting from the familiar emphasis on "servicing" existing members to an approach that puts new organizing at the center is experienced as threatening by many traditional union leaders.

The locals that are "full innovators" commit extensive resources to new organizing and to campaigns that involve a high level of rank-and-file participation, a focus on issues of dignity and justice in the workplace, and aggressive, confrontational tactics vis-à-vis management, such as civil disobedience. These locals often pursue "corporate campaigns" that attack an employer's public image. Rather than simply going after "hot shops" where worker militancy has already erupted and where a desire for union representation is apparent—the only organizing which more traditional unions engage in at all—these locals use strategic targeting in choosing organizing sites. They also adopt various novel techniques to avoid the pitfalls of the traditional NLRB election process.

Sherman and Voss identify three key conditions that, in combination, facilitate such innovative organizing: (1) a crisis of survival for the local union, usually precipitated by serious membership losses in its historical jurisdiction; (2) support from the International union with which the local is affiliated—often involving a top-down process of introducing tactical innovation rather than one emerging from the grass roots; and (3) the presence on the local union's staff of activists from other social movements, such as veterans of the 1960s, schooled in more militant and participatory mobilization tactics than those in labor's conventional arsenal. Foreign-born organizers on the staffs of these locals, similarly, often can draw on political experience in their home countries that facilitate the innovation process.

Sherman and Voss argue that the full innovators are the locals most likely to succeed in organizing immigrants, partly because their leaders tend to be more sensitive to the needs of rank-and-file workers generally. When they target immigrant-employing workplaces, these locals are more likely than others to hire bilingual organizers and to integrate issues of specific concern to immigrants into their campaigns. Yet the full innovators seldom seek to organize immigrants qua immigrants, that is, to the exclusion of native-born workers. These locals choose organizing targets for strategic reasons, and if those targets are found to employ significant numbers of immigrants, as many in California inevitably do, the full innovators' rank-and-file orientation leads them to respond more effectively than other locals to the specific needs of such workers and often to frame their campaigns around issues of immigrants' rights as well. In short, the full innovators are more effective than other locals at organizing generally, and this makes them more effective at organizing immigrants in particular.

Complementing Sherman and Voss's overview of organizational and tactical innovation is Miriam Wells's case study of a single local union, Local 2 of the Hotel Employees and Restaurant Employees (HERE), which has long represented workers in the San Francisco hotel industry. This is an example of a unionized industry where the workforce has undergone dramatic shifts in composition, from a predominantly native-born population in 1970 to one in which immigrants (mostly Chinese, Filipino, and Salvadoran) made up 48 percent of the workers in 1990. In response to this transformation, Local 2 has successfully adapted, by effectively reaching out to its new foreign-born members. Although this case involves internal organizing rather than new recruiting, it does fit Sherman and Voss's model to some extent. The local union recruited onto its staff community activists and others with experience in social movements outside of organized labor, many of them bilingual, with support from the International HERE. This recruitment enabled the local union to preempt an internal crisis (Sherman and Voss's third condition for full innovators), although a major strike in 1980 did threaten to become just such an occasion.

Wells analyzes the occupational distribution of immigrants within the San Francisco hotel industry, demonstrating that they are overrepresented in "back-of-the-house" jobs such as food preparation and room cleaning, although they have made some inroads into the industry's better jobs as well. She finds that most occupations, even within a single hotel, usually include workers of more than one nationality, so that "individuals with cultural differences also shared economic interests." Wells emphasizes that the great diversity within the local union's membership led it to avoid focusing on the needs of any one ethnic or national group, but rather to mobilize around the unifying experience of work. At the same time, Local 2 has actively sought to meet the specific needs of its foreign-born membership, including providing assistance with immigration-related problems.

A major contribution of this chapter is its analysis, based on extensive interviews with union staffers, of the variations among immigrants of different nationalities in receptivity to the union's efforts. Wells suggests that Asians, with the exception of Filipinos, generally have a less positive view of unions than Latinos, especially Central Americans. She attributes these differences to workers' experiences (or lack thereof) with labor organizations in their home countries, and in particular to the "dangerous authority-challenging struggles" in which many foreign-born Latinos engaged in the course of the immigration process itself. Wells reports that despite the variation among immigrants, as a group they are generally more responsive to the union's efforts than native-born whites. (African Americans, in contrast, are strongly pro-union, but they make up only a tiny part of Local 2's membership today.)

The geographic context for both Sherman and Voss's empirical analysis and Wells's case study is the San Francisco Bay Area, the part of California where unions have historically been strongest—although with the deunionization of the 1970s and 1980s, the regional gap has narrowed somewhat. In 1961, according to data collected by the state of California, 46 percent of nonagricultural wage and salary workers in the San Francisco–Oakland area were unionized; a figure that had dropped to 26 percent by 1987. In Los Angeles–Long Beach, by contrast, union density was always lower, declining from 32 to 20 percent over the same period (California Department of Industrial Relations 1963 and 1989). By 1996, according to CPS data, the gap between these two areas was even smaller: in the Los Angeles–Riverside–Orange county area, 15.4 percent of the workforce were union members (slightly higher than the national figure of 14.5 percent), while in the area including San Francisco, Oakland, and San Jose, the figure was 18.9 percent—a figure that may be somewhat misleading since unions were never as strong in San Jose as in San Francisco and Oakland (Hirsch and Macpherson 1997, 51, 55). San Francisco is distinctive in another important dimension: as Waldinger and Der-Martirosian note (see table 2.4, this volume), the gap in unionization levels between immigrants and native-born workers is much smaller there than in the rest of the state.

In southern California the dilemmas involved in immigrant unionization are especially stark. Not only have unions historically been weaker there than in the north, but also, as Lopez and Feliciano show, the immigrant influx into the workforce has been far more extensive than in the northern part of the state, particularly among Latinos. There have been numerous immigrant organizing efforts in southern California—some successful, some not— which are the subjects of the remaining chapters in this volume. An extreme example is the case of the garment industry, the largest surviving manufacturing industry in the region, which is the focus of Edna Bonacich's chapter. This industry, which accounts for nearly a fifth of all manufacturing employment in Los Angeles, represents the very bottom of the labor market for immigrants, attracting mostly female, often undocumented, recent arrivals who earn substandard wages and labor under notoriously poor conditions.

Because garment-making is a prototypically global industry, with much of its production long since shifted offshore, downward pressures on labor costs are especially intense, and employers' resistance to unions

is fierce. The industry was once centered in New York, where the relatively few garment workers who remain are still highly unionized. But in
Los Angeles, which today has more garment industry employment (over
120,000 workers) than any other part of the United States, only a few
hundred of the industry's workers are unionized, despite ongoing efforts
by the Union of Needletrades, Industrial and Textile Employees
(UNITE) to recruit them. In view of the recent successful efforts to
unionize immigrants in Los Angeles in other industries on the one hand,
and the history of unionism in the garment industry (which has long relied heavily on immigrant labor) in other times and places, why has organizing proved so difficult?

Bonacich points out that many of the recent immigrant organizing
successes in southern California involve work that is not geographically
mobile, such as janitorial services and construction. By contrast, garment
factories threatened with unionization can readily shift production offshore. As for the poorly paid immigrant women from southern and eastern Europe who did manage to unionize in early twentieth-century New
York, against great odds, Bonacich suggests that the sophistication of the
manufacturers and the ease with which they can relocate production on a
global scale is far greater today than it was then. She emphasizes that the
problem is not a lack of interest in unionization among rank-and-file garment workers but rather their knowledge that organizing is likely to lead
to job losses and that the chances of victory are slim.

The traditional route to union representation, namely NLRB elections, is virtually irrelevant under current conditions in this industry,
which relies heavily on subcontracting. Any factory in which UNITE wins
an NLRB election is simply avoided by the manufacturers, and is therefore likely to go out of business, as has occurred many times already in
Los Angeles. Faced with this grim reality, UNITE has recognized the need
to target manufacturers rather than subcontractors, or even better, to try
to organize an entire sector of the industry at once. The current corporate campaign against Guess, Inc. is an example of this type of targeting,
although thus far the company has resisted the union's efforts fiercely. As
Bonacich points out, such large-scale organizing drives involve a huge
commitment of resources, which UNITE may be reluctant to make given
the enormous obstacles to success.

Yet organizing immigrants in the globalized manufacturing sector is
not completely impossible, as Carol Zabin's chapter shows. She analyzes a
wildcat strike that erupted in the summer of 1990 among the twelve hundred workers at the American Racing Equipment (ARE) wheel factory in
Los Angeles, which led to union recognition the following year. Although

the company does have a plant in Mexico, where a great deal of auto parts production has been moving in recent years, it also has some good reasons to continue production in Los Angeles, so that the threat of plant relocation or closure in response to unionization is less dire than in the apparel case. The workforce at this plant is quite different from that in the garment industry, even though both are comprised almost entirely of Latino immigrants: unlike the female newcomers who dominate the apparel workforce, most of the ARE workers are long-settled male immigrants—confirming Waldinger and Der-Martirosian's finding that immigrants of the longest vintage are more likely to be unionized.

Zabin emphasizes the fact that the ARE strike and the union recognition campaign that it galvanized were traditional in character. Although some of the innovative tactics that Sherman and Voss discuss were employed, this was a prototypical "hot shop." A previous attempt to unionize the plant two years before had failed, but now rank-and-file workers, infuriated by technological and organizational changes, organized on their own. Their three-day wildcat strike came to the attention of the labor movement only after it was reported in the *Los Angeles Times*, at which point a number of local unions made overtures to the workers. The ensuing union drive took a traditional form, organized around the goals of winning an NLRB representation election and, subsequently, a first contract.

The International Association of Machinists and Aerospace Workers (IAM), which emerged the victor in the interunion competition to take up the organizing opportunity that the wildcat strike presented, by all accounts conducted an exemplary campaign. It rented an office near the plant that was open twenty-four hours a day, assigned several bilingual Latino organizers to the effort, and developed a rank-and-file workers' committee which was integral to the NLRB election campaign. Tactics included house calls, barbeques, and generally promoting the idea that the workers themselves "owned" the campaign. Despite the fact that ARE hired an anti-union "labor consultant," the union won the election in a close vote in December 1990. Next came a nine-month campaign for a first contract, an effort which included extensive worker education and training and a variety of in-plant shows of force to maintain pressure on the company. The first contract brought fairly minimal benefits (as is often the case), but since that time the union has improved its terms significantly, and management seems to accept the union at this plant as a fact of life.

Two of the most talented rank-and-file leaders who emerged in the ARE strike were hired as Machinists' Union staffers, although not for some years after the strike. Yet as Zabin emphasizes, the union failed to take the other logical follow-up step to its victory at ARE, namely to attempt to organize the rest of the wheel industry in the region. Among twenty-five wheel plants in greater Los Angeles, only two (including ARE) are unionized—and even ARE has a second, nonunion plant in the area. Despite talk of an industry-wide campaign, this has yet to be seriously attempted. Still, the ARE case suggests that immigrants in the manufacturing sector can, at least under certain conditions, be successfully unionized.

Just as the union at ARE was securing its first contract, an even larger organizing effort was emerging among southern California's immigrant workers. As Ruth Milkman and Kent Wong's chapter recounts, thousands of Mexican drywall hangers, squeezed by wage cuts during the severe residential construction slump of the early 1990s, began a union organizing effort in late 1991, culminating the following year in a successful five-month strike that shut down housing construction in six southern California counties. As in the ARE strike two years earlier, the initiative in the drywallers' strike came from the grass roots. Workers began to organize entirely on their own, and indeed their effort met with considerable skepticism by the Carpenters' union that had represented residential drywallers prior to the trade's deunionization in the late 1970s and early 1980s. Although the Carpenters did allow the strikers to use their halls for meetings, there was no official union involvement until the strike's end, when the Carpenters negotiated a settlement and contract, under which 2,400 drywall hangers ultimately became union members.

The strike was partly built on the basis of social networks among the immigrant workforce: most of the leaders and many others who participated in the campaign's early stages were from the same small village in Mexico. Once the strike was underway, the organized labor movement rose to the occasion and provided extensive financial support as well as legal assistance. There was enormous community support for the effort as well, with Latino immigrant organizations and church groups providing food and other forms of support. The California Immigrant Workers' Association (CIWA), sponsored by the AFL-CIO, played a crucial role also, mainly through its legal work. Yet all of these support efforts were stimulated by the rank-and-file's own mobilization efforts.

Ultimately legal issues became central to the strike's success, and at the same time limited the scope of the victory. On the positive side of the ledger, what finally induced the contractors to sign an agreement settling the strike and recognizing the union was a series of CIWA-funded lawsuits alleging violations of the overtime provisions of the Fair Labor Standards

Act (FLSA). Labor practices of dubious legality had become widespread in the residential drywall industry during the 1980s, after the union had been eliminated, and the employers proved extremely vulnerable to the FLSA suits, which were dropped in exchange for union recognition at the end of 1992. Meanwhile, however, a group of San Diego drywall employers, who refused to become part of the strike settlement, opened a second legal front to counterattack the Carpenters' union, filing suit against it under the Racketeer Influenced and Corrupt Organizations Act (RICO), which has increasingly been used against labor unions in recent years. This suit, which accused the union of orchestrating the strike and of responsibility for various acts of violence allegedly associated with it, was eventually settled out of court in the employers' favor for an undisclosed sum.

The drywallers' strike, like the ARE case, demonstrates the potential for large-scale organizing among the Latino immigrants who increasingly dominate the manual labor force of southern California, even under the inhospitable conditions that unions face today. In both these cases success was predicated on the combination of bottom-up organizing among immigrant workers themselves, partly rooted in immigrant social networks, on the one hand, and the labor movement's willingness to commit extensive financial and legal resources to supporting the effort, on the other. Yet again, in both cases, organized labor failed to build on the momentum of these struggles. Just as the Machinists' union made no serious effort to organize the other wheel factories in the area after the ARE strike, so too there was hardly any follow-up on the drywallers' victory in terms of new organizing among the vast numbers of nonunion residential construction workers—many of them Latino immigrants as well—in other trades. Worse still, since the 1992 strike victory, the Carpenters' union has actually lost ground within the drywall industry, as nonunion contractors have taken over an increasing share of the market.

The problem of union consolidation in the aftermath of organizing success is the focus of the chapter by Catherine Fisk, Daniel Mitchell, and Christopher Erickson. The janitors' Los Angeles organizing drive, which culminated in a strike in 1990 that led to a pathbreaking contract settlement, was initiated by the Service Employees' International Union (SEIU), which was headed at that time by current AFL-CIO President John Sweeney. In contrast to the ARE and drywaller strikes, it began as a top-down effort, although the campaign did involve extensive ground-level mobilization among immigrant janitors themselves as well. The story of the organizing, recapitulated briefly by Fisk, Mitchell, and Erickson, has been told in detail elsewhere (see Waldinger et al. 1998;

Savage 1998). This chapter's main contribution is its analysis of the aftermath of the effort, examining the critical issue of sustaining the initial achievements of the organizing campaign and building a durable union structure.

In the immediate aftermath of the 1990 victory, the SEIU local with which the janitors were affiliated became mired in factionalism, pitting those who wanted to put resources into continued organizing against others who wanted instead to concentrate resources on servicing the existing membership—a dilemma that many unions face after major organizing victories. The internal turmoil ultimately led the International union to put the local into trusteeship. In addition, the local union confronted challenges on a number of fronts.

One involves maintaining the hard-won union share of the office building cleaning market, which is continually threatened by the possibility that union-cleaned buildings will revert to nonunion status and by the emergence of new nonunion buildings as the regional market expands. So far the union has held on to its market share (in contrast to the drywallers, who have already suffered serious decline in this respect), but the potential for erosion is ever present. As Fisk, Mitchell, and Erickson note, assuming economic growth continues in the region, protecting its existing membership ultimately will require the Los Angeles janitors' union to embark on aggressive new organizing just to maintain its current market share.

This prospect, in turn, demands that the union confront a number of legal challenges that have emerged since the 1990 contract victory in Los Angeles. Recent court decisions have limited the kinds of tactics that SEIU—known for its creative and highly confrontational "in-your-face" style of militancy—will be permitted to employ in future janitorial organizing. Most important are concerns involving the delicate issue of long-prohibited secondary boycotts (actions targeting not the immediate employer, which in the case of janitors is an office cleaning contractor, but other businesses such as building owners or tenants). Recent case law limits the union's right to engage in picketing as a way of mobilizing public sympathy and pressuring employers, as previous janitors' campaigns often did. Such issues have not become particularly salient in southern California thus far, simply because the janitors have done little in the way of new organizing since their 1990 victory, but they are potentially important concerns for the future.

In 1990 the janitors won a union contract, as did the ARE workers the following year. Then came the 1992 drywallers' strike and victory. These struggles together brought several thousand of southern California's im-

migrant workers into the union fold in rapid succession, creating a sense
of momentum that many in the regional labor movement hoped would
be the beginning of a massive wave of immigrant organizing. Yet since
1992 there have been few new breakthroughs, and none involving such
large numbers of workers as these three key campaigns did. If these ex-
amples served to liquidate any lingering notions that immigrant workers
are "unorganizable," they also indicate that enormous resources are
needed to carry out such efforts. What they all shared was a dynamic
rank-and-file mobilization effort and a major material and moral commitment from existing unions—in the janitors' and drywallers' cases
amounting to millions of dollars. Even with such vast outlays, consolidating unionism in the aftermath of organizing success and continuing to recruit new members on the foundation these victories established has
proven extremely problematic.

In the moment of hopefulness that these three success stories produced, in the early 1990s a group of veteran Los Angeles–based labor organizers conceived of a new endeavor, which they called the Los Angeles
Manufacturing Action Project (LAMAP). Héctor Delgado's chapter,
the last in this volume, analyzes the trajectory of this effort and the reasons for its ultimate abandonment only three years after it was officially
established in 1994. The key LAMAP concept was strategically targeted,
industry-wide organizing campaigns in Los Angeles' vast manufacturing
sector, which employs about 700,000 workers, most of them Latino immigrants. The project included a substantial research component, with assistance from faculty members in the UCLA Urban Planning program as
well as numerous students. From the outset, links to ethnic and community groups were also central to the project, which explicitly targeted immigrant workers.

LAMAP envisioned multiunion campaigns, with financial contributions pooled from a wide array of labor organizations. The original no-
tion was that any workers who were recruited through these efforts would
become part of a new entity, rather than affiliating with individual
unions, but this idea was soon abandoned in the face of resistance from
some of the unions involved. As Delgado emphasizes, the traditional organizational culture of unionism in this respect proved incompatible with
the more collective, movement-building vision LAMAP tried to promote.
In any case, a necessary condition of the project's success was a serious
financial commitment on the part of multiple unions. Though the project did receive seed money from a number of unions, when the time
came to make a more serious financial commitment, almost all of them
backed off.

Unfortunately, the timing of the effort coincided with the internal revolution within the AFL-CIO that culminated in the election of John Sweeney to the presidency in 1995. Despite the fact that LAMAP's ideas about organizing were almost perfectly congruent with those of the new leadership, the turmoil within the AFL-CIO's affiliates precipitated by Sweeney's ascent created new obstacles to bringing the project to fruition. That LAMAP had been conceived during the previous AFL-CIO administration, which even had provided it with some preliminary support, tainted it in many eyes as being associated with the "old guard." In addition, the project now could be seen as competition for the organizing efforts the Sweeney regime itself wanted to undertake. Ironically, these concerns ultimately led the AFL-CIO to decline to support it. In the end, only the International Brotherhood of Teamsters was willing to make a serious financial commitment, and though this did lead to some small-scale organizing efforts, it was insufficient to allow LAMAP's talented organizing staff to even attempt to carry out their original, highly ambitious plans. Not long after, the Teamsters themselves became embroiled in internal turmoil with the result that in 1997, even their support was cut off. Thus the most explicit effort to build on the lessons of the immigrant organizing successes in the early 1990s proved abortive.

Nonetheless, LAMAP had an important impact on the thinking of labor movement activists in southern California, and to some extent nationwide, who absorbed both the vision of multiunion, citywide organizing that it embodied, as well as the lessons of its sad demise in the context of internal labor movement politics. One can only hope that if and when the new labor movement overcomes its growing pains, other attempts will emerge to pursue the immigrant organizing agenda defined by LAMAP and some of the other organizations whose efforts are documented in these pages. If this volume helps in that effort, even in a small way, it will have amply fulfilled its purpose.

1

Who Does What? California's Emerging Plural Labor Force

David Lopez and Cynthia Feliciano

In the past twenty-five years immigrants have increased threefold as a proportion of California's workforce, and now constitute at least one-third of the total. Immigrant workers are among the most exploited of employees in California, they are the majority of workers in many settings that seem ripe for organizing, and they may carry with them a spirit of worker solidarity that has largely died out among U.S. workers. At the same time, they pose the traditional challenges to labor organization of any desperate and abundant labor force, and many face the special challenges of illegal status. This chapter provides an overview of the role that immigrants play in California's labor force.[1] We begin with a review of the remarkable demographic changes the state is experiencing, and the implications for the future. Then we trace the growth of the immigrant workforce and look at its ethnic composition in particular occupations and industries. Finally, we pose questions about the future economic role of the children of recent immigrants, the emerging second generation.

The very phrase "immigrant *workers*" is ambiguous. About half of all immigrants in the workforce are manual workers falling into the laborer,

1. Our statistical data are drawn largely from two sources: the decennial U.S. Censuses and, for the most up-to-date information, the Census Bureau's Current Population Surveys done in March 1995, 1996, and 1997. Decennial Census data for 1970–90 are derived from analysis of the Integrated Public Use Microdata Sample (IPUMS), the compilation of census data from 1850 through 1990 that eases the burden of making comparisons over time. Some census data come from published reports by the Bureau of the Census, as specified in each table. We have combined the nonduplicated respondents to the March 1995, 1996, and 1997 Current Population Surveys to provide one unified sample, which we refer to as the 1996 CPS.

operative, and service occupational categories, and these are the focus of our attention in this chapter. But conversely half hold white-collar or comparatively well-paying craft jobs. In fact, one of the distinctive characteristics of immigration today is its considerable socioeconomic diversity, particularly among immigrants from Asia. Indian physicians, Taiwanese engineers, and Mexican professors have arrived in the United States recently, along with Salvadoran peasants and Chinese factory workers. A comprehensive understanding of the role that immigrants play in California's economy must consider all of these, as well as the immigrant entrepreneurs and managers under whom immigrant workers often toil. But our focus here is on those at the lower end of the occupational spectrum: semiskilled and unskilled factory workers, laborers, and service workers, and we shall reserve the term "worker" for them. Such jobs constitute a small and declining proportion of the California job market, which is nearly two-thirds white-collar. There are almost four times more managerial, professional, and technical employees in the state than factory workers. But immigrants are disproportionately found in the humbler jobs, and they also make up larger and larger proportions of all manual workers in the state.

The racial/ethnic dimension of immigration is fundamental to understanding California's changing demographics and especially the composition of the state's army of manual workers.[2] Over 70 percent of California's immigrant manual workers are Latino, overwhelmingly from Mexico and Central America. In many specific occupations immigrant Latinos now constitute one-third or more of all workers. Within thirty years immigrant Latino workers and their children will almost certainly comprise the majority of California's semi- and unskilled workers. This transformation has already occurred in the state's agricultural regions, and it is also nearly complete in the Los Angeles area. In the San Francisco Bay Area the Latino immigrant presence is less striking; there are nearly twice as many Asian immigrants in the labor force. Will ethnic concentration enhance worker solidarity and facilitate labor organizing? Or

2. Throughout this chapter our use of racial/ethnic terms follows conventional usage in California, which corresponds to U.S. Census categories: Asian American, African American, white (the "non-Hispanic White" census category) and Latino ("Hispanic Origin"). The first two are technically "racial" terms according to the Census Bureau, and the last is a unique sort of "ethnic" category, used only with reference to Latinos. Each term is based on a host of complex and contradictory "racial" and "ethnic" meanings and are umbrella terms covering a wide variety of subgroups. These four terms are also the most commonly used racial and ethnic labels and categories used in California, past and present, and are therefore the best to use in broad analyses such as that presented in this chapter. "Other" races amount to less than one percent of California's population.

will its primary effect be to increase animosity and ethnic tensions? What-ever the result, we are certain that the salience of ethnicity will increase in the economy, as it will in all sectors of life in California.

Like most newcomers to the United States throughout its history, im-migrants and migrants from other states have usually been relegated to the bottom rungs of the occupational ladder in California. Most Euro-American and Asian American subgroups have reached rough parity within a generation or two, in contrast to African Americans who con-tinue to have markedly lower rates of upward mobility (Blau and Duncan, 1967). What about Latinos? Thirty years ago, in their massive study *The Mexican-American People*, Grebler, Moore, and Guzman (1970) argued that the future of Mexican Americans might go in either of two directions: they might proceed along a somewhat delayed path of assimilation and increased economic equity, like Italians and other Euro-American ethnic groups; or they might share the castelike fate of African Americans.[3] The answer was to be found in the future, as third- and fourth-generation Mexican Americans became the majority of the group's population.

What Grebler and his associates did not foresee was the great revival of immigration that has taken place in the past thirty-five years. Today Mexican and Central American immigrants and their young children have overwhelmed the state's older Mexican American population. This demographic transformation has greatly complicated the question posed by Grebler and his associates, and the immigration of poorly educated Latinos concentrated in low-paying manual jobs has contributed to the appearance of a castelike status for Latinos and growing ethnic stratifica-tion for the state as a whole. But even a minimal definition of "castelike" requires that low socioeconomic status be passed on from generation to generation. The social progress of third generation and subsequent Lati-nos in California and the United States generally is itself a complicated and contentious topic, but the balance of evidence suggests that they are not approaching parity with Euro-Americans.[4] Whatever the fate of these older generations, the "place" of Latinos in California society is increas-ingly determined by the large and growing population of immigrant workers and their children. There is little doubt that immigrants will con-

3. The term "castelike" here refers to groups or societies in which occupational and social status are strongly correlated with ethnicity, from one generation to the next. We use the term descriptively to characterize social outcomes, without implying that these outcomes are the result of political enforcement such as segregation or apartheid, or reli-gious sanction as in South Asia.

4. Bean and Tienda (1986) is the most comprehensive analysis of generational differ-ences among Latinos; Ortiz (1996) provides evidence that successive cohorts of U.S.-born Latinos in the Los Angeles region may be doing worse, not better.

tinue to do the state's dirty work. The crucial question is what kind of jobs their children, the emerging second generation, will manage to attain. Will they gain the education necessary to move into the good jobs of tomorrow? Or will they be channeled into dead-end jobs only marginally more attractive than those taken by new immigrants? Or will the result be somewhere in between?

Ethnic Change in California

Driven largely by immigration since 1965, California is now the most multi-ethnic state in the country. Non-Hispanic whites ("Anglos") now constitute only about half the population. African Americans continue to decline as a proportion of the state's population, with Asian Americans, at 12 percent of the total, now outnumbering them nearly two to one. Constituting nearly one-third of the state's population, Mexican Americans and other Latinos will be the single largest group early in the next century. California is undergoing a demographic transformation second only to the Yankee invasion 150 years ago, and unique in the recent history of the United States.

The profundity of these changes becomes clear by comparing today's ethnic profile with California in the past. California has been multi-ethnic since the arrival of the Spanish, but for the past century and a half the state has been dominated demographically as well as politically by "Anglo" whites. Up to the middle of this century, California's labor force (like its population) was nearly 90 percent white. Asians were never more than 10 percent of the population, and that share declined to 2 percent in 1950. African Americans constituted no more than 2 percent of the population until World War II brought the great migration from the South; their presence in California peaked at 7 percent in the postwar period and is now slowly declining. Despite the Mexican / Spanish origins of the state, it was only after the turmoil of the Mexican Revolution that the state's Latino population began to grow above the 3 percent level, to 10 percent in 1960.[5]

As figures 1.1 and 1.2 show, all that began to change in the 1960s. By 1960 California had reached its low point in foreign-born population (though it always remained above the national average). Figure 1.1 shows the dramatic turnaround: the percentage of foreign-born has increased

5. We have drawn or estimated these figures from U.S. Census of Population: General Social and Economic Characteristics, for 1950, 1960, 1970, 1980, and 1990; Persons of Spanish Surname 1960, Persons of Spanish Surname 1970, Persons of Spanish Origin 1970.

dramatically since 1970, and the rate of increase shows no sign of abating. The radical nature of this shift is reinforced by comparing the sharp rise in California's immigrant presence with the much more moderate change in the entire country. By the year 2000 over one-quarter of California's population will be foreign-born, compared to 9 percent for the nation as a whole.[6] And even that 3:1 ratio understates the relative impact of immigration in California for two reasons. First, a larger proportion of California's immigrants are recent arrivals, not senior citizens, and, relatedly, these young immigrants have produced a second generation of children who are still largely of school age. Indeed, this alone explains many of the current tensions around immigration in California.

Of course the newcomers are not just immigrants but nonwhite immigrants, which further contributes to potential tensions. The other pair of lines in figure 1.1 chart the growth of the aggregate nonwhite population in California and the nation. In 1950 California was nearly as white as the nation as a whole; today its proportion of nonwhites is twice the national average.

Figure 1.2 charts the growth of the four principal racial / ethnic groups in California from 1970 to 2000. All ethnic segments have grown in absolute numbers, but while the African American and white populations have grown slowly, the Latino and Asian populations have tripled in size in the past thirty years. The Asian growth rate has been faster, but it is Latinos who will displace whites as the state's single largest ethnic group, sometime around 2030 (California Department of Finance 1996). Indeed, the Latino presence is already comparable to that of whites in the state's public schools, each constituting about 40 percent of the enrollment overall. Latinos and Asians constitute ever-increasing proportions as one moves down grade levels (Linguistic Minority Research Institute 1996). Latinos and Asians are not just the two fastest-growing groups, they are also the youngest, guaranteeing that natural increase as well as immigration will be an important factor in the changing ethnic balance.

Figure 1.3 highlights the importance of natural increase, the demographer's euphemism for babies that will need health care, schools, and other institutions. In fact, the single largest component of population growth from 1990 to 1995 was natural increase of the Latino population, *not* immigration. This is a young population, and even if their birth rates were not above average (they are, though not as much as alarmists think),

6. National Year 2000 projections come from the Census Bureau web site; California projections come from the state Department of Finance, supplemented by estimations from the 1997 Current Population Survey, which yield similar results.

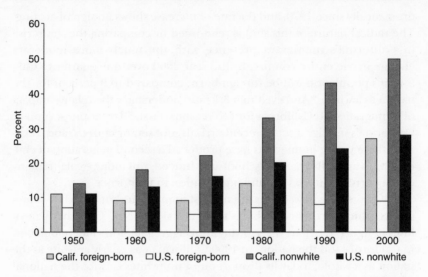

Sources: U.S. Census of Population: *General Social and Economic Characteristics,* 1950, 1960, 1970, 1980, and 1990; *Persons of Spanish Surname* 1960, *Persons of Spanish Surname 1970, Persons of Spanish Origin 1970.* California 2000 projections from California Department of Finance, *California Demographics* (Winter 1998). U.S. 2000 projections from Census Bureau web site.

Figure 1.1. Percentage foreign-born and nonwhite in California and U.S. populations, 1950–2000.

their low mortality rates due to the small portion of elderly and high birth rates due to the large proportion of women in child-bearing years would be enough to explain this spectacular rate of natural increase, which accounts for over half of all the population increase in the state from 1990 to 1995.

Figure 1.3 provides information about immigration itself that may surprise some readers. According to state estimates, Asian immigration outpaced Latino immigration about two to one in the first half of this decade. These data may underestimate Latino immigration, however, largely because they take insufficient account of undocumented immigration. But even if Latino immigration is double the state estimate, Latino natural increase would still be more than twice as important, and still the single largest source of population growth in California.

Of course this natural increase is not unrelated to immigration: young immigrant families and, increasingly, the maturing second generation (the children of immigrants) are disproportionately represented among

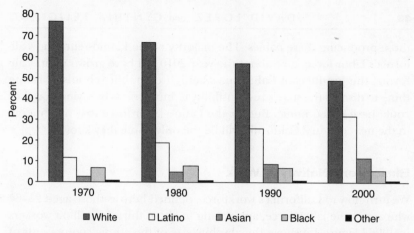

Sources: 1970–1990 U.S. Census of Population, Integrated Public Use Sample (IPUMS-95), Version 1.0. Year 2000 estimates based on 1997 Current Population Survey and estimates from California Department of Finance, *California Demographics* (Winter 1998).

Figure 1.2. Ethnicity of California population, 1970–2000.

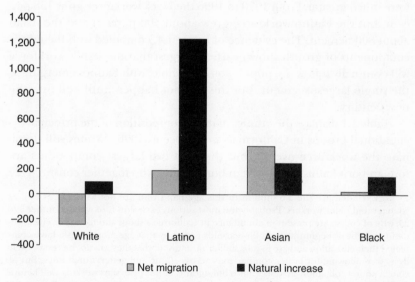

Source: Revised estimate by California Department of Finance, *California Demographics* (Winter 1998).

Figure 1.3. Components of California population growth by ethnicity, 1990 to 1995 (in thousands).

those producing these babies. The majority of the Latinos entering California's labor force after about the year 2010 will have grown up in California, the products of California's benighted public schools. It is one thing to dismiss the state's responsibility to immigrants by saying that they could have stayed home. But for the Latino labor force that will emerge in the next century, California will be the only home they know.

Ethnicity and Nativity at Work

We turn now to California's workforce, defined here as those aged 25–64 who are in the labor force, amounting to about thirteen million workers in 1996.[7] Figure 1.4 shows the absolute size of the ethnic components of California's work force from 1970 to 2000, and is quite important in several respects. It reveals that all four major ethnic components grew, though at different rates. The state's entire workforce more than doubled, from 5,955,000 in 1970 to an estimated 13,100,000 in 1996. Over the same period the white labor force kept pace up to 1990, after which time it has been essentially static. Even the African American workforce grew faster than the white, but rates of increase for Latinos and Asians were much greater. From 1970 to 1996 the black workforce grew 158 percent, but the Latino workforce grew about 500 percent and the Asian about 800 percent. The evidence of figure 1.4, combined with the ethnic components of growth shown earlier, suggest that the state's workforce will eventually follow the population as a whole, with Latinos emerging as the single largest segment. But this will not happen until well into the next century.

Table 1.1 displays the ethnic / nativity composition of the principal occupational groups in California's workforce in 1996.[8] Whites still dominate the workforce overall, but the next two largest components are foreign-born Latinos and foreign-born Asians, who together constitute 27

7. Excluded are the 3.5 million in this age band who are not working, as well as younger and older workers. Probably the most serious exclusion is of workers under age 25, who of course are present in abundance in California's shops and factories. The argument in favor of beginning with 25-year-olds is that by that age most people have completed their education and are in jobs similar in status to what they will do the rest of their lives, thus allowing for better comparisons across ethnic and generational lines. But of course poorer folk, most notably Latino immigrants in this case, start working well before age 25, and the Latino population is also on average younger. Just as census figures disproportionately undercount poor Latinos, we also know that excluding young workers disproportionately undercounts poor Latinos. Our estimates of the Latino presence in various jobs and industries, then, are conservative.

8. We have not distinguished between native and foreign-born whites or African Americans, since immigrants constitute only 8 and 6 percent respectively.

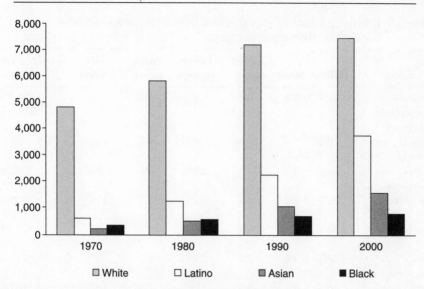

Sources: 1970–1990 U.S. Census of Population, Integrated Public Use Sample (IPUMS-95), Version 1.0. Year 2000 estimates based on 1997 Current Population Survey and estimates from California Department of Finance, *California Demographics* (Winter 1998).

Figure 1.4. Size and ethnicity of California workforce, 1970–2000 (in thousands).

percent of the workforce (if white and black immigrants were added in, the total would be 33 percent foreign-born). Over two-thirds of the Latino workforce is foreign-born, as is over 80 percent of the Asian workforce. Indeed, immigration from Asia and Latin America in the past thirty years has overwhelmed the older Latino and Asian second and third generations that, as recently as 1970, constituted half the Asian adults and 60 percent of Latino adults in California.

The occupational distribution of Latino and, to a lesser extent, Asian immigrants contrasts sharply with that of the (largely native) white group, as table 1.1 shows. Whites constituted 56 percent of all workers in 1996, but their representation in different occupational levels varied considerably. They made up 71 percent of all professional, managerial, and technical workers, but only 30 percent of all laborers. In marked contrast, immigrant Latinos constituted 17 percent of all employed Californians but 42 percent of the factory workers (operatives), 49 percent of the laborers, and only 5 percent of the professional and technical employees. The occupational distributions are less polarized for all the other groups:

Table 1.1. Ethnic and nativity composition of workforce aged 25–64, California, 1996 (percentage).

	White	Black	Latino native	Latino foreign	Asian native	Asian foreign	Total number (% of total)
Professional / technical workers	71%	5%	6%	5%	3%	10%	4,763,700 (36%)
Clerical / sales workers	59%	8%	10%	9%	3%	10%	3,285,600 (25%)
Crafts workers	54%	5%	10%	20%	2%	8%	1,574,200 (12%)
Operatives	32%	4%	10%	42%	1%	11%	1,242,800 (9%)
Laborers	30%	5%	9%	49%	1%	5%	869,300 (7%)
Service workers	38%	7%	8%	36%	1%	9%	1,385,400 (11%)
Total	56%	6%	8%	17%	2%	10%	13,120,000 (100%)

Source: 1995–1997 Current Population Survey.

African Americans constitute 4–8 percent of each major occupation, native Latinos 6–10 percent of each, immigrant Asians 8–11 percent of every occupation except for laborer (5 percent), and native-born Asians 2–3 percent of white-collar and skilled workers, though only one percent of the semi- and unskilled workforce.[9]

The two most ethnically distinct major occupational categories, then, are at the top (whites 71 percent of the professional and technical workers) and bottom (Latino immigrants 49 percent of laborers). Within these broad categories, of course, are specific occupations (Hollywood producer, grape picker) that are even more ethnic-specific. But instead of pursuing such occupational specifics, in table 1.2 we shift the focus to the ethnic groups themselves and their broad occupational and income profiles.[10] Looking first at whites, blacks, and native-born Latinos, we find the

9. Space limitations prohibit us from presenting gender breakdowns. For the most part the usual gender disparities cut across lines of ethnicity and nativity. That is, in most specific groups women are less likely to be skilled workers or laborers and correspondingly more likely to be clerical or service workers. The most striking gender disparities come not in occupational level but in income.

10. Table 1.2 is derived from 1990 Census data rather than from the 1995–97 Current Population Survey data on which Table 1.1 is based, in order to increase sample sizes for the smaller ethnicity and occupation categories.

familiar white / nonwhite disparity: nearly half of all white workers are found in managerial, professional, and technical positions, compared to less than a third of African Americans or native Latinos. Conversely, the latter two are about twice as likely to be factory or service workers. White / nonwhite income gaps are also substantial: whites earn about 25 percent more overall and maintain a substantial advantage at each occupational level except for service, where black workers earn slightly more. This anomaly is probably due to the tendency of blacks to be in the public sector, where service work is paid substantially better than in the private sector.

The occupational profile for U.S.-born Asian Americans is similar to that for whites, and is in fact somewhat elevated: Asian Americans have the highest proportion of professional, managerial, and technical workers and the lowest proportion of factory and service workers. In terms of income, they are similar to whites by occupational level and overall.

Turning to the two immigrant groups, we see two very distinct profiles. Latino immigrants provide the greatest contrast to whites and native Asian Americans: only 13 percent are in the top occupational category, and they are three to five times more likely than whites or native Asians to

Table 1.2. Occupation and earnings of workforce aged 25–64 by ethnicity and nativity, California, 1990.

	White	Black	Latino native	Latino foreign	Asian native	Asian foreign
Professional / managerial / technical	47%	32%	28%	13%	52%	40%
(Mean earnings, in thousands of dollars)	($36.1)	($29.0)	($27.6)	($22.9)	($35.1)	($31.3)
Clerical / sales	25%	30%	27%	12%	26%	24%
	($23.6)	($21.1)	($20.1)	($15.9)	($23.6)	($18.4)
Craft	12%	10%	14%	14%	8%	8%
	($28.6)	($26.9)	($27.1)	($18.2)	($30.4)	($22.1)
Operatives	6%	10%	13%	25%	5%	12%
	($23.4)	($22.1)	($21.3)	($13.7)	($21.3)	($15.5)
Laborers	3%	4%	6%	16%	3%	2%
	($20.5)	($17.9)	($18.4)	($11.6)	($19.2)	($13.9)
Service	7%	15%	11%	20%	5%	13%
	($13.9)	($14.3)	($12.4)	($97.6)	($16.0)	($12.5)
Total	100%	100%	100%	100%	100%	100%
	($29.2)	($23.2)	($22.4)	($14.6)	($29.4)	($22.6)

Source: 1990 U.S. Census of Population, Public Use Sample, Version 1.0.

be factory workers, laborers, or service workers. Overall, 48 percent of whites and native Asians are professional, managerial, or technical workers, and only 15 percent are laborers, factory workers, or service workers; the occupational profile for immigrant Latinos is just the reverse with 61 percent found at the three lowest occupational levels, compared to only 13 percent at the top. Furthermore, immigrant Latinos have the greatest income disparities at each occupational level and, of course, overall. The overall disparity (they earn about half what whites and native Asians do) is hardly surprising, but the magnitude of the disparity at each occupational level is worth calling attention to; at every level Latinos earn only about two-thirds what whites do, and also substantially less than any other group.

The reasons for these disparities are not difficult to discern: most Latino immigrants arrive with low levels of education, poor English skills, and little or no financial capital. They average only eight years of schooling and only 14 percent have any education above high school (Current Population Survey 1996). Averages do obscure individual differences: among immigrant Latinos are to be found millionaire surgeons and, more to the point, a substantial minority that have earned middle-class or "affluent working-class" status through dint of hard work and thrift. But the fact remains that two-thirds of all immigrant Latino workers are in low-paying, low-status "dirty-work" jobs.

Asian immigrants provide a more mixed picture, in some ways resembling whites and native Asian Americans, and in other ways resembling Latino immigrants. Forty percent are in professional, managerial, or technical occupations, more than African Americans or native Latinos. Like the latter, they are more likely than whites to be found in factory or service work and are markedly underrepresented among laborers.

This mixed occupational picture reflects the fact that recent Asian immigrants are probably the most diverse group in the history of immigration to the United States. About two-thirds come from middle-class backgrounds and arrive with high levels of education and good English skills. The other third have more humble backgrounds, such as the second wave of Southeast Asian refugees who were largely peasants, fisherfolk and small-town workers. Overall, Asian immigrants average thirteen years of schooling, close to the U.S. national average, and 62 percent have had some college education. In ways unique in U.S. immigration history, the well-equipped two-thirds move directly into professional, technical, and commercial occupations at or above the U.S. average.[11]

---

11. Schoeni, McCarthy, and Vernez (1996) examine the segments of the immigrant workforce in more detail, and attempt to assess their future prospects.

But the Asian immigrant experience today is by no means a uniform picture of smooth and rapid economic assimilation. High averages mask the struggles of the poorly educated minority, and some Asian immigrants, especially those with relatively modest English skills, settle for careers well below average for their level of education, Korean shopkeepers being the best-known example (Cheng and Yang 1996). And, as table 1.2 shows, at every occupational level their earnings are below whites' and native Asians', though always above immigrant Latinos'. This is true even at the lower rungs of the occupational ladder, suggesting that even the less well-prepared Asian immigrants are doing substantially better than their Latino counterparts. Yet, though blacks and native-born Latinos are somewhat more highly represented in manual occupations than Asian immigrants, the wages of the latter are substantially lower, suggesting that they, like immigrant Latinos, are found in lower-paying jobs and industries.

Table 1.3 provides an overview of the industries in which each group is found. By far the greatest immigrant concentration is in agriculture, where fully 62 percent of all those employed (not just laborers) are foreign-born Latinos, nearly four times their proportion of the total state workforce. They are also slightly overrepresented in construction, though that comparatively well-paying industry remains predominantly white. Whites also continue to predominate in the best-paying and most white-collar of industries, FIRE (finance, insurance, and real estate), where immigrant Latinos are the only group that is substantially underrepresented. In manufacturing, by contrast, the two most overrepresented groups are immigrant Latinos and Asians. In personal service, immigrant

Table 1.3. Major California industries by ethnicity and nativity, 1996.

	White	Black	Latino native	Latino foreign	Asian native	Asian foreign	Total number
Agriculture	28%	1%	6%	62%	—	3%	435,000
Construction	62%	4%	9%	20%	—	4%	817,900
FIRE	63%	7%	8%	7%	2%	12%	835,100
Manufacturing	45%	5%	8%	25%	1%	15%	2,280,300
Personal service	48%	5%	7%	27%	1%	11%	435,000
Trade	54%	4%	9%	20%	2%	11%	2,230,600
Transport	52%	10%	12%	12%	4%	10%	569,600
Other	56%	8%	8%	15%	2%	10%	5,064,300
Total	56%	6%	8%	17%	2%	10%	13,168,000

Source: 1995–1997 Current Population Survey.

Latinos are the only group that is overrepresented.[12] Both trade and transport have ethnic profiles approaching the overall average.

Comparing tables 1.2 and 1.3, we see that ethnic disparities are more substantial by occupational level than by industry. Agriculture is the only major industry that has become predominantly Latino. Not coincidentally, agriculture is also the only major industry where laborers are the single largest occupational category.

We noted earlier that Los Angeles and San Francisco have been affected by immigration in very different ways. Table 1.4 profiles the Latino and Asian immigrant and native white workforces in these two metropolitan areas, with comparisons to the state as a whole. Perhaps the single most important contrast is in relative size: Latino immigrants are 19 percent of the Los Angeles workforce, but only 6 percent in the Bay Area. Asian representation in the two workforces is much closer: 8 and 11 percent respectively. But the more important comparison is within each region: Latino immigrants are the single largest category of nonwhite workers in Los Angeles, and they are radically behind whites and Asians in educational, occupational, and income attainment. In San Francisco, Asian immigrants are the single largest category of nonwhite workers and, though they are not at parity with whites, in most important respects they approach them. (The one exception is the minority of immigrant Asians with little or no schooling. Though only one-tenth of the total, those with this educational level are virtually nonexistent among any ethnic group that has grown up in the United States.)

The most consequential differences between Los Angeles and San Francisco show up in the occupational distributions of each ethnic group. In Los Angeles, factory work ("operatives" in the table), service, and laborer are all identifiably Latino occupations, whereas in San Francisco the occupation with the greatest Latino representation is laborer, at 26 percent, and even here Latinos are substantially outnumbered by whites, who constitute 43 percent. These basic demographic differences go a long way toward explaining the less conflictual nature of racial / ethnic relations and politics in the Bay Area. In San Francisco the largest and most visible nonwhite immigrant group is at rough economic parity with whites; in Los Angeles the gap between whites and immigrant Latinos is a significant *dis*parity.

The next three tables map out the industrial distribution and ethnic composition of the three broad manual occupational levels in 1990:

12. Law enforcement and some other comparatively well-paying service industry subcategories are excluded from personal service.

Table 1.4. Immigrant Latino and Asian and native white workforces aged 25–64
in Los Angeles, San Francisco Bay area, and state of California, 1990.

	Latino immigrants			Asian immigrants			White natives		
	L.A.	**S.F.**	**Calif.**	**L.A.**	**S.F.**	**Calif.**	**L.A.**	**S.F.**	**Calif.**
% of labor force	19%	6%	17%	8%	11%	10%	48%	61%	58%
% < 9 years school	48%	37%	48%	10%	11%	10%	1%	1%	1%
% any college	17%	29%	14%	65%	63%	62%	68%	74%	67%
% white collar	23%	29%	25%	69%	62%	64%	74%	75%	72%
% operative / labor / service	59%	58%	61%	22%	29%	27%	15%	15%	16%
% of operatives	42%	13%	42%	7%	17%	11%	28%	44%	36%
% of laborers	48%	26%	49%	4%	7%	5%	27%	43%	34%
% of service workers	33%	17%	36%	8%	16%	9%	35%	43%	40%
% of household workers	72%	37%	54%	5%	12%	6%	11%	30%	27%
Average male earnings (thousands of U. S. dollars)	17.7	21.5	—	32.0	30.8	—	44.9	44.5	—

Source: 1990 U.S. Census of Population, Public Use Sample, Version 1.0.

operatives, laborers, and service workers. Each table includes the pro-por-
tion of the occupation that is immigrant Latino or Asian, the proportion
reporting that they entered the United States after 1985, and an
"equity index" for each group of immigrant workers, which is their average earnings divided by the average earnings of all workers in the same
occupation.

Table 1.5 profiles California's immigrant operatives. The core of this
broad occupational category is semiskilled manufacturing workers,
though half of all operatives are outside this sector, spread across a myriad of trade, transport, and other industries. Within manufacturing,
foreign-born Latinos constitute 41 percent of all operatives and immigrant Asians 14 percent. Thus these two nonwhite immigrant groups constitute fully 55 percent of all the manufacturing operatives in the state in
1990, a proportion that surely has continued to rise. In apparel manufacturing, nonwhite immigrants were 89 percent of all operatives, and in textiles, 78 percent. But if the apparel and textile industries in California are
totally dependent on immigrant labor, the reverse is not true: these industries employ only about 14 percent of all immigrant operatives.

Table 1.5. California's operatives by ethnicity, nativity, and industry, 1990.

	Number	Foreign-born Latinos		Foreign-born Asians		% newcomer[b] (Latinos only)
		Percentage	Equity index[a]	Percentage	Equity index	
Total	1,119,636	32%	.72	10%	.81	
Manufacturing	558,737	41%	.74	14%	.86	19%
Apparel	61,519	64%	.95	25%	.98	25%
Textiles	16,840	67%	.97	11%	1.03	20%
Machinery	124,237	30%	.83	27%	.89	16%
Food	53,181	39%	.72	6%	.78	14%

Source: 1990 U.S. Census of Population, Public Use Sample, Version 1.0.

[a] The equity index is the average earnings of the ethnic group divided by the overall earnings in the specified occupation and industry.

[b] Newcomers are foreign-born persons who report they entered the United States after 1985.

The equity indices show that Latino and, to a lesser extent, Asian immigrant wages lag behind others, even at this level of occupation / industry specification. In apparel and textiles, where the vast majority of the workers are Latino and Asian immigrants, the index means very little, but the substantial disparities in the machinery and food processing industries are more significant, all the more so because these fields have comparatively low proportions of newcomers. The highest proportion of newcomers, 25 percent, are found in apparel.[13]

Table 1.6 provides similar information for the state's laborers. Though a substantial portion of Asian immigrants do become factory workers, they are less likely than average and much less likely than Latino immigrants to work as laborers. This is especially true in agriculture, where labor is poorly paid, but it is also true in construction, where at least some laborers are well remunerated. As expected, the greatest immigrant Latino concentration is in agriculture (63 percent of all laborers). In construction, however, only about one-third of all laborers are Latino immigrants, reflecting the continuing dominance of this relatively well-unionized industry by whites. Ethnic inequalities in income are particularly great for construction laborers, probably because of unequal rates of unionization between whites and Latinos. Overall, immigrant

13. The true figure is almost certainly higher, since this is an industry with a large proportion of undocumented workers who either evade the census and survey takers, or who have reason to report they have been in the United States longer than they actually have been.

Table 1.6. California's laborers by ethnicity, nativity, and industry, 1990.

	Number	Foreign-born Latinos		Foreign-born Asians		% newcomer[b] (Latinos only)
		Percentage	Equity index[a]	Percentage	Equity index	
Total	531,418	41%	.73	4%	.87	—
Agriculture	189,578	63%	.89	3%	.81	21%
Construction	114,838	35%	.71	2%	.83	24%
Trade	86,692	23%	.76	6%	.87	20%
Manufacturing	51,137	38%	.76	6%	.92	19%

Source: 1990 U.S. Census of Population, Public Use Sample, Version 1.0.

[a] The equity index is the average earnings of the ethnic group divided by the overall average earnings in the specified occupation and industry.
[b] Newcomers are foreign-born persons who report they entered the United States after 1985.

Table 1.7. California's service workers by ethnicity, nativity, and industry, 1990.

	Number	Foreign-born Latinos		Foreign-born Asians		% newcomer[b] (Latinos only)
		Percentage	Equity index[a]	Percentage	Equity index	
Total	1,131,584	25%	.78	10%	1.0	9%
Household	79,630	54%	.91	6%	1.3	18%
Hotel	61,335	42%	.85	15%	1.1	13%
Laundry	82,490	9%	.90	11%	0.9	3%
Trade	292,897	30%	.89	15%	0.9	13%

Source: 1990 U.S. Census of Population, Public Use Sample, Version 1.0.

[a] The equity index is the average earnings of the ethnic group divided by the overall average earnings in the specified occupation and industry.
[b] Newcomers are foreign-born persons who report they entered the United States after 1985.

Latino laborers earn 73 percent of the average wage, about the same as among operatives. Of the four broad industries shown, Latino laborers in construction are somewhat more likely to be newcomers, but the rate of recent arrivals is 19 percent or more in each industry.

Table 1.7 describes the composition of service workers. These workers are spread throughout California's economy, with the greatest concentrations in trade and personal services (broken down into its three principal components: household services, hotel work, and laundry work). Overall, Asian immigrants are in service occupations roughly in proportion to their total representation in the labor force (10 percent); however, they

are underrepresented in private household work. In contrast, Latino immigrants constitute 25 percent of all service workers (they make up 17
percent of the total state workforce), holding over half of all household
service jobs and 42 percent of all hotel service jobs.

Of the three most stereotypical immigrant jobs—agricultural laborer,
garment factory worker, household worker—the latter is the most difficult to get at using the broad occupation/industry categories employed
in this chapter. Part of the reason is that household service, though growing again, is still a comparatively small occupation at the statewide level. It
may also be the most underreported occupation, since household workers are, by all accounts, the most undocumented workers in the state and
also probably the best hidden from census takers. Studies of Central
Americans in southern California document that Salvadorans and
Guatemalans are especially likely to be household workers, and of course
the vast majority are women (Lopez, Popkin, and Telles 1996, 296).

Income inequality is relatively modest within service occupations. But
it is worth pointing out that these are some of the lowest-paying jobs in
the state. The average wage for private household workers is only $7,297;
for Latinas it is $6,609. Asian immigrant service workers are paid at least
average or somewhat above average in these low-wage jobs.

Immigrant workers in service are among the least likely to be recent
arrivals to the United States, with overall rates about half that for laborers
and factory workers. The service job that is most associated with immigrants, private household work, has a newcomer rate approaching that
for labor or factory work, and considerably higher than that for other service jobs. But household workers constitute only 7 percent of all service
jobs. For other service work, it may be that the combination of language
skills and contacts needed to find jobs ensure that they remain the
province of better-settled immigrant workers.

A Glimpse at the Future: The Emerging Second Generation

The previous section was devoted to a cross-sectional overview of the situation of immigrant workers in California. But of course the overwhelm-
ing fact about California's workforce is change, not stasis. The future
course of immigration to California is impossible to predict, but it will
probably continue pretty much as before: poorly educated and non-
English-speaking immigrants from Mexico and Central America will continue to be available for the least desirable jobs throughout the economy,
and diverse but generally much better-educated Asian immigrants will
enter the job market up and down the occupational pyramid. Put an-

other way, Latin American immigration will continue to contribute to the appearance of a castelike social system. In contrast, Asian immigration, to the extent that it continues to be socioeconomically diverse, actually has the potential to *reduce* the association between class and ethnicity.

Whatever the future may hold with regard to immigration, in the next thirty years the children of immigrants will enter the labor force in numbers equal to or above the number of immigrants in the past thirty years. Where will they fit in? The answer is only beginning to emerge, and is fraught with complexities beyond the scope of this discussion; but we can offer a preliminary guess.[14] California's high school students of today will constitute half or more of its young workers a decade from now, the only other significant source being immigrants from Latin America and Asia (a reasonable assumption given the low rates of in-migration from other states in recent decades). Studies have shown that the relative performance of young people in school provides a good guide to where they will end up in the occupational / class structure in the future, both across ethnic groups and within them (Blau and Duncan 1967). Information about ethnic stratification among the state's schoolchildren, then, provides important hints about the future ethnic stratification of its workforce.

School data are rarely reported by generation, but there is a remarkable correspondence between ethnicity and generation among high-school-age youth in California today: over 90 percent of Asians are second or "1.5" generation (born abroad but schooled in the United States), as are over 80 percent of Latinos, whereas the corresponding figure for whites is under 20 percent and for blacks under 10 percent. To a considerable degree, then, high school students divided by ethnicity are also divided by generation.

How are California's ethnic groups doing in school? The more usual question today is, how are the schools doing? From most perspectives the answer is, poorly. But hidden behind the subpar average performances are significant ethnic differences, which are only partially captured by ethnic variations in high school graduation rates and average years of schooling. For decades Latinos have had low high school graduation rates, and these rates have not varied much by generation. The most recent data available, from the 1996 Current Population Survey, tell much the same story. By one common measure, the percent aged 16–21 who are either high school graduates or still in school, whites, Asians, and African Americans are bunched together at about 90 percent, with no sig-

14. See Portes and Zhou (1993) for a comprehensive discussion of the factors affecting the assimilation of immigrant children in the United States today.

nificant variation by generation. Latinos are 10–12 points below this level, again with no significant generational differences.[15]

As high school graduation is virtually universal (and perhaps more debased in value than in the past) and because most good jobs demand more in the way of qualifications, it is a poor indicator of group differences. Years of schooling is only a little better as an indicator, for most groups bunch up around 12–14 years on average, and in any case this measure can be applied only to age groups who have completed their education. In California there is, however, an excellent measure of the likelihood of entering the middle and upper-middle classes, for groups if not for individuals: eligibility for the University of California (UC).[16] In theory the top 12.5 percent of high school graduates are eligible for UC, though in fact about 20 percent are, by a combination of grades and test scores.[17] Less than half actually attend a UC campus, but it is a safe bet that most of this "talented two-tenths" do go on to college; they probably constitute the majority of those students who attend and graduate expeditiously from the state's second public university system as well the majority of private college enrollment.

Table 1.8 gives the high school graduation rates and UC-eligible rates by ethnicity, as well as the ethnic composition of the high school graduating class and the pool of those potentially eligible for the University of California. The total eligible figures are the key here: they suggest that whites will be three times more likely to be in the state's future elite than Latinos or African Americans, and Asians will be six times more likely. Put another way, 44 percent of Asian graduates are headed for the state's elite, compared to 8 percent of Latino graduates. These figures are re-

15. The very low rates of high school graduation sometimes noted for Latinos stems from lumping immigrants with natives; when only those raised in the United States are compared, the Latino rate is substantially higher, though still below average.

16. Of course there are other standards. Test scores are an obvious one, but until recently comprehensive and comparable scores for students across the state were not available. With the recent institution of the widely used "Stanford Nine" as the state's test of achievement for grades 2–11, that is changing. Explicit ethnic breakdowns are not yet available, but preliminary estimates made by the senior author suggest that ethnic differentials will be quite considerable, with Latino and black students averaging in the twentieth to thirty-fifth percentile, whites between the fortieth and fifty-fifth, and Asians between the fiftieth and seventieth percentile on the various grade and subject-matter tests.

17. Currently only about 11 percent meet all the technical criteria for entry, which include taking an SAT subject exam, something not required by many other colleges and universities. Ethnic disparities are similar among students technically eligible, and among those who actually attend the University of California. We use the broader category of all who are potentially eligible because we believe it better represents the state's academic elite.

Table 1.8. Educational achievement among California youth by ethnicity, 1995.

	All high school graduates (as % of all aged 16–21)	% of all high school graduates	% potential UC-eligible	% of all UC-eligible
White	92%	43%	26%	50%
Asian	89%	13%	44%	28%
Latino	82%	38%	8%	14%
Black	90%	6%	7%	2%
		100%		100%

Sources: High school graduation rate (students aged 16–21 graduated and/or still in school) from 1995–1997 Current Population Survey; UC eligibility data from California Post-secondary Education Commission (CPEC).

markably similar to the proportion of each group of immigrants who have professional, managerial, and technical jobs (see table 1.2). They suggest that inequality in the second generation will be massive, equivalent to the disparities between the two major sets of adult immigrants. The final set of figures represents the composition of the state's academic elite (top 20 percent): half are white, 28 percent Asian, 14 percent Latino, and only 2 percent black. These figures are a rough guide to the ethnic composition of the top quarter of the state's future occupational hierarchy.

Many factors could intervene to moderate these harsh contrasts: the correlation between high school grades and eventual status is not perfect. Furthermore, the Latino second generation will certainly experience social mobility in contrast to their parents, from the bottom to the middle rungs. But to the degree that upward mobility into the top half of the occupational structure requires successful competition with whites and Asians, it is not in the cards for most of the Latino second generation. Their future will depend not so much on individual achievement but rather on the quality of life for those in the middle of the state's class structure.

We can only make educated guesses about the future of the young people represented in table 1.8. Table 1.9 looks at a cohort about ten years older, those aged 25–34 who are in the workforce and largely finished with their formal education. It suggests that ethnic disparities in this generation may not be so great as those suggested by comparing immigrant Latinos with others, or by comparing today's Latino (and black)

Table 1.9. Educational and occupational status of native-born
California workers aged 25–34 by ethnicity, 1996.

	% some college	% college graduates	% white-collar	% craft	% unskilled
White	67%	32%	67%	14%	19%
Asian	73%	48%	75%	12%	13%
Latino	53%	16%	57%	16%	27%
Black	57%	16%	62%	13%	25%

Source: 1995–1997 Current Population Survey.

high school graduates with other ethnic groups. By the demanding standard of college graduation, the ethnic disparities are considerable: nearly
half of all young native Asian workers are college graduates, as are one-
third of whites. But only 16 percent of native Latino (or black) young
workers have a college education. The disparities diminish when the standard is having any post-secondary education. Latinos are 14 percentage
points behind whites and 20 points behind Asians in the proportion with
some college education. These data correspond closely with the percentage who are in white-collar occupations. The converse is that Latinos are
substantially more likely to have unskilled jobs, about twice as likely as
Asians.

In short, these educational data suggest that social disparities among
ethnic groups growing up in California today will be sharpest at the
upper levels, and possibly greater than the differences observable today
between whites and Asians on the one hand and Latinos and African
Americans on the other. At the lower end of the spectrum, perhaps one-
quarter of U.S.-raised Latinos (and African Americans) will end up as unskilled workers, 50–75 percent more than will be the case for Asians and
whites. U.S.-raised Latinos will form an increasing proportion of those
with jobs in the middle, the lower-status white-collar jobs and crafts. Or, to
summarize in less optimistic terms, competition with better qualified
whites and Asians will continue to keep them out of the top tier, and competition with more desperate Latino immigrants will keep them off
the bottom; one can only hope that the jobs will be there for them in
between.

Conclusion

Immigrants arrive in the United States with a broad array of backgrounds
and talents, and they find or create jobs that range across the entire oc-

cupational spectrum. But they do not simply blend into the native workforce: about half do, but the other half are without the educational, linguistic, social, and financial resources needed to move into jobs with a future. Not all of the latter are from Mexico and Central America, but the
vast majority are, just as the majority of the more fortunate immigrants
are from Asia.

The focus of this chapter has been on immigrant workers who fill the
semi- and unskilled jobs in California's booming economy, and our goal
has been the simple one of describing where immigrant workers are most
likely to be found. We have not dealt directly with the contentious question of their contribution to this boom, but it is virtually certain that these
low-wage workers have contributed to the well-being of other Californians, caring for their children and their lawns, cooking their food,
sewing their jogging suits, and operating the machines that stamp out a
myriad of inexpensive consumer goods. Nor have we considered the
question of intragenerational mobility among immigrant workers,
though the low wages and occupational status that persistently characterize Latino immigrants suggest that social mobility is modest for these immigrants during their lifetimes.

We have taken a first pass at a third question, which we consider to be
especially significant: the educational and occupational prospects of the
vast "new second generation," the children of today's immigrant workers.
About one-third, including most Asians and a minority of Latinos, seem
likely to end up at least as well off as native-born whites. But regarding the
other two-thirds, largely low-achieving students from struggling and overwhelmingly Latino immigrant homes, there is cause for concern. The
previous Latino second generation hardly excelled at school, but entered
a workforce that provided good, often unionized, jobs to many. But
changes in the economy, plus the vastly greater size of the new second
generation, make it difficult to predict that they will end up even as well
off as today's Chicano working class. If even a significant minority of the
new second generation do in fact join today's small urban "underclass,"
the social consequences may well be cataclysmic. Our conclusions on this
point must be tentative, as most of the new second generation are still too
young to be in the workforce, but evidence from school years and early
entry into the job market provide little basis for optimism.

Whatever the fate of the second generation, we can be certain that immigrants will continue to come, eager to take up the jobs others disdain
at wages that are miserable by U.S. standards but also five times the prevailing wage in Mexico. Industries such as apparel, food, other services,
most low-tech manufacturing, and, most important of all, agriculture, will

continue to be dependent on immigrant workers, and specifically on the continued arrival of fresh new recruits from across the border. Middle-class immigrants will integrate more or less smoothly into the top half of the information economy, joining the largely white and Asian middle class. The low-achieving second generation will be sandwiched somewhere in between. As for low-skilled immigrants, eager for any wages at all, they will continue to do the dirty work in all sectors of the economy, from the fields to the high-tech factories of Silicon Valley. We can only hope that at least some of them will be working under the protection of unions.

2

Immigrant Workers and American Labor: Challenge... or Disaster?

Roger Waldinger and Claudia Der-Martirosian

Somnolent for much of the past twenty-five years, American labor approaches century's end with new vigor. And not a moment too early, as the problems are legion. Unionization rates are down and still falling. Downward pressure on wages has not yet abated—even though the U.S. economy is enjoying a boom of unusual duration. The labor force is growing at galloping rates—making it hard for labor to simply tread water, let alone move ahead. And much of the job proliferation takes place in those sectors where unions have historically been weak, a situation aggravated by the fact that many of the new labor force entrants have uncertain, often transient connections to the organizations that employ them.

True, unions have learned a few quite potent new tricks, which they have used to some effect. But neither the arsenal of labor's weapons nor the political environment is such as to force employers to abandon the bad habits they acquired during the years of labor's decline. So the vicious cycle continues, with the steadily diminishing union presence at once weakening labor's appeal to potential members and increasing employers' motivation to resist organizing efforts.

Daunting as the situation may seem, the demographic transformation of America confronts unions with yet another challenge—the renewal of mass immigration. The 1930s and 1940s are known as the heyday of American labor; viewed from another perspective, they also encompass a period of highly restricted, indeed virtually negligible immigration. As such, labor's years of triumph represent a twentieth-century anomaly. Im-

Thanks to the University of California's Mexus Program for support for the research on which this chapter is based.

49

migration largely flowed unimpeded during the century's first two and a half decades, the World War I years excepted. And though the barriers put in place in 1924 were never entirely removed, the post–World War II turnaround is unmistakable, constant, and, in recent years, immense. If not record-breaking, immigration levels during the 1990s will fall short only of the total recorded during the first decade of this century; the 1980–2000 totals will significantly exceed the influx experienced during 1900–1920. Of course, correlation does not imply causality, as any social scientist knows all too well. Still, the historical record does suggest an uncomfortable relationship between America's high-water years of immigration and a flagging labor movement. And one only need look at the experience of the United Farm Workers, their ranks decimated just when immigrant labor surged through California's fields, to glimpse what immigration may have in store for organized labor.

If the picture is not hopelessly bleak, it certainly presents a somber aspect. The new "new immigration" of the late twentieth century is not as uniformly proletarian as the "new immigration" of old, but the numbers of new entrants moving in at the very bottom is impressive indeed (see Lopez and Feliciano, this volume). Convergence at the low end of the labor market both increases downward pressure on wages for less-skilled labor and adds to the looseness of the labor supply—neither of which developments gives labor any additional leverage. Many of the new immigrants are recent arrivals, altogether too uncertain of their status, standing, and orientation—will they settle down or return home?—to seriously consider unionization. Moreover, a substantial portion of the immigrant population—as many as one out of every four immigrants arriving each year—has an additional fear factor, associated with a condition rarely known earlier in the century, namely, a status prohibiting work in the United States. These "illegal" or "undocumented" immigrants—call them what you will—know all too well that the Immigration and Naturalization Service provides employers with an additional union-busting tool, yet another reason to desist from organizing activities.[1] Furthermore, the immigrants tend not to move into those industries where the labor presence remains entrenched—most notably, the public sector, where a varying combination of citizenship, educational, and testing requirements exclude many foreign-born workers. Instead, the newcomers head for notoriously union-resistant industries such as apparel or restaurants, where the addition of a seemingly limitless supply of labor makes organizing all the more difficult.

1. However, undocumented status may not prove an insuperable obstacle to unionization; see Delgado 1993.

But immigration does not necessarily spell bad news. In the past, many union leaders emerged from immigrant ranks; the history of American labor also includes countless extraordinary eruptions of immigrant militancy. And it is not simply hopeless nostalgia that suggests that the past may be prologue. Assimilation is a time-honored concept in the study of American immigration and now would not be the first time that "Americanization" involves a process whereby immigrants decide that they want—and deserve—the good things promised by American life.[2] If the newcomers have also acquired "a diploma in exploitation," to quote a rank-and-file immigrant janitor union leader (see Waldinger et al. 1998), and have come to resent the maltreatment and stigmatization experienced at the hands of employers and society alike, then immigrant workers may decide that unions provide them with a powerful instrument of collective voice.

From a historical point of view, one might also contend that it is labor, not the immigrants, that deserves the bad reputation. Few organizations could have rivaled the old AFL in its impassioned restrictionism—good reason for the immigrants of yore to be skeptical, if not skittish, about appeals to solidarity. This time around, however, organized labor does not seem likely to make the same mistake. Indeed, the AFL-CIO is one of the few mainstream organizations to have emerged as decidedly pro-immigrant, a stance marked not just by rhetoric but by action. As evidence, consider the efforts to organize America's newest workers, many of which are catalogued and analyzed in this volume.

This chapter offers an overview of the relationship between immigrant status and unionization, both nationally and in California, the capital of today's immigrant America. We analyze the factors affecting the likelihood that a worker will have a "union job," which we define as someone who is a union member or working in a unionized establishment. The occasion is the availability of a new data source, resulting from the recent adoption of questions about place of birth and parentage by the monthly Current Population Survey (CPS), an instrument which also collects information about union membership and employment in establishments covered by union contracts. Though the CPS does offer a rich source of information, we should issue some cautions on its limitations before proceeding any further. Most important, the data shed light on the factors associated with union membership among immigrants and native-born workers, a matter quite distinct from the factors that would influence immigrants and natives to *join* unions at differential rates. The

2. As in the earlier CIO period studied by Cohen (1990).

CPS provides a repository of information on demographic characteristics; however, it contains neither attitudinal data that would measure preferences for union membership nor relevant behavioral data concerning voting behavior in elections for union representation. One can argue, as some researchers have, that membership status can be equated with the "demand for union services," and thus serves as a reasonable proxy for the attitudinal and behavior indicators of interest (Duncan and Stafford 1980). Survey research does provide some support for this point of view, as union members appear to be significantly more likely than their nonunion counterparts to vote union in a hypothetical election for union representation (Leigh 1986). In the current context of declining union membership, moreover, where there are more persons wanting union jobs than union jobs available, those with such jobs would seem highly likely to prefer whatever benefits unionization generates. Though this asymmetry between the supply and demand for union jobs also implies a considerable interest in unionization among the nonunionized workforce (as survey evidence indicates), here we examine patterns of union membership among persons holding "union jobs" by ethnicity and nativity.

Second, the CPS inquires broadly about labor unions and employee associations, not differentiating between the two; the membership information that it obtains is of a highly general sort and cannot be used to generate estimates of the membership of particular unions.

Third, the CPS takes a cross-section of the labor force, a complication for those arguments about unionization that involve change over time. As we've already suggested, a variant of the assimilation hypothesis would suggest that propensities to unionize increase over time, a hypothesis operationalized by comparing successive immigrant cohorts. But the econometric literature on immigration shows that cohorts may not share common characteristics, in which case generalizations from the cross-section will not hold true. These caveats aside, the CPS provides a unique window into the patterns of union membership among America's new immigrant workforce.

Background

This chapter stands at the confluence of two distinct literatures, one on immigration, the other on unionization, each of which is only peripherally aware of the other's existence. Labor matters play an important role in the historiography of American immigration (see Bodnar 1985; Barrett 1992), but even the historians have not yet generated a unified framework, integrating the insights from the study of immigration and the study of unionization. The contemporary literature is still more wanting. True, there are a small number of insightful case studies examining organizing among immigrant workers, of which the best known is Delgado's 1993 book; but these contributions tend to be nested more firmly within the immigration than the union literature. Labor economists have been moved to pursue an occasional inquiry; though this work evinces some methodological sophistication (for example, DeFreitas 1993), it provides a limited engagement with the broader intellectual issues at stake. In this section, we seek to distill lessons from both the immigration and the industrial relations literatures in an effort to specify the likely factors affecting unionization among today's immigrant workers.

Immigrants

This chapter implicitly asks a simple question: Are immigrants more or less likely than other workers to have union jobs, other background factors controlled? The question has the appeal of simplicity; regrettably it is also simplistic, at least as concerns contemporary immigration to the United States. Earlier in the century, during the great wave of migration from southern and eastern Europe, the category "immigrant" captured a reasonably homogeneous experience. Of course, not all groups were the same; the Jews arriving from the Austro-Hungarian and Russian Empires differed in social characteristics and circumstances of migration from the Italians, the Slavs, and the Hungarians. But the Jews apart, and theirs was only a partial exception, most immigrants came with little skill; they moved into the bottom of the labor market, where they experienced a good deal of churning; often movement to the United States represented a temporary displacement on the route to return migration to the home country, if not the home community; and most immigrants were men, the advent of their wives and families representing a second-stage development signaling settlement.

The foreign-born population that has emerged in the three and a half decades since the Hart-Celler Act marked the renewal of immigration is strikingly different.[3] Today's newcomers unquestionably include a sizable mass deeply reminiscent—in characteristics, circumstances of migration, and societal reaction—to the labor migrations of the 1880–1920 period. Indeed, immigrants from Mexico simultaneously comprise the least skilled and the largest single national origins group among today's new-

3. Portes and Rumbaut (1996) outline a typology of contemporary immigration in much greater detail; our discussion here draws on their influential formulation.

comers: as of the mid-1990s, 27 percent of all foreign-born persons residing in the United States were born in Mexico; persons with an elementary education or less comprised the single largest group of adults in this contingent. Like the Italians or the Poles, the Mexicans are involved in a pattern of circular migration, in which many, perhaps most, depart with the intention of returning home. Though the longevity of Mexican migration and its deeply implanted networks ensure that high proportions drop out of the circular streams and settle in the United States for good, the process of putting down roots remains a protracted affair. That extended transition is likely to exercise a powerful effect both on the social processes that connect workers to union jobs and on the preferences for union membership, for reasons discussed in greater detail below.

There are other migrations, in addition to the Mexican movement to *el norte*, that are disproportionately dominated by proletarians who move in response to labor needs in the United States. Nonetheless, diversity in circumstances of migration as well as in socioeconomic characteristics represent the salient characteristics of today's newcomers. Ever since World War II, the U.S.-bound migration flows have contained an increasing number of refugees. The relative prominence of refugees reflects, in part, immigration's new role in U.S. foreign policy: until the end of the Cold War the doors were generally opened for refugees fleeing Communist regimes, while typically closed for all others, as in the Haitian or Salvadoran cases. Sociologically, the refugee population includes many besides those who officially qualify for refugee status, and one might expect the entire group to develop a propensity for both union jobs and union membership. As immigrants in a no-return situation, refugees typically have been quick to aspire to the standards enjoyed by the native population, a powerful reason why frustration in the search for upward mobility should produce a search for union jobs as well as pro-union sentiment. But their political history may push refugees in the opposite direction: as real or self-perceived victims of Communist regimes, many may be ideologically opposed to unions, despite strong instrumental considerations to do otherwise. Thanks to generous programs of government assistance, as well as the presence of former elites and home-country entrepreneurs, many refugee communities have developed ethnic economies of sizable employment potential, yet another reason why refugees may neither gravitate toward nor prefer union jobs.

Though the refugee flow is impressive in both relative and absolute terms, what most clearly distinguishes today's situation from the past is the large proportion of highly educated persons among the immigrant

population. Highly-skilled immigrants have played a modest but significant role in immigration to the United States ever since the enactment of
the Hart-Celler Act in 1965. Notwithstanding charges that America's immigrants are of "declining quality," the 1990 Census found that a college
degree was as common among immigrants as among natives (one out of
five). And among particular immigrant groups, the highly skilled are
often present at levels well above the U.S. average, with the college graduate share ranging from 27 percent among Russians to 65 percent among
Indians.

A significant proportion of those immigrants who arrive with high
skills discover that their premigration training yields no payoff in the
United States. Those who undergo such "blocked mobility" seek to get
ahead in different ways, often through entrepreneurship, which also
takes them out of the supply of persons seeking union jobs. Not every
group of highly skilled immigrants shows the same propensity for self-
employment; the Filipinos, for example, are highly educated but are particularly unlikely to work for themselves. More typical patterns, however,
are the high self-employment rates among Koreans, Indians, Chinese,
and Iranians, to cite the most notable cases.

Whether as business owners or salaried professionals and managers, a
good proportion of the recent arrivals begin not at the bottom but in the
middle class or above (see Lopez and Feliciano, this volume). In contemporary Los Angeles, for example, certain coveted professional occupations have become immigrant concentrations: more than 35 percent of
the pharmacists in the region are foreign-born, as are more than 25 percent of the dentists and over 20 percent of engineers, computer special-
ists, and physicians. As migration selectivity diminishes over time, most of
the important U.S.-bound flows include persons from all parts of the occupational spectrum. Even so, significant interethnic differences in occupational composition persist, such that the proportion of highly educated
persons or those working in upper white-collar professions distinguishes
many of the flows from Asia from those that come from Mexico, Central
America, or the Caribbean. The prevalence of professional, managerial,
and entrepreneurial activities among immigrants implies that many can
move ahead without the benefits that union jobs provide; that the size of
this more highly skilled population varies considerably among the major
immigrant streams reduces the likelihood that immigrant status as such
will have a singular, unvarying effect on employment in a union job.

Work and its Rewards

The relationship between the rewards of work and unionization preferences is well known. As Freeman and Medoff note, "The results of studies
are unequivocal across very different samples. One finds that increased
desire for unionization (expressed in union activity or votes for union) is,
indeed, a likely outcome of worker dissatisfaction" (1984, 146). While
one hardly expects it to be otherwise, knowing that more dissatisfied
workers are more likely to prefer unions also begs the question, which
must include both the causal nexus between satisfaction and union preference, on the one hand, and the factors that influence job satisfaction,
on the other. In general, dissatisfaction with the bread-and-butter aspects
of work provides the strongest push for workers to want union representation, especially among blue-collar workers. Though of lesser importance, job content also affects union preferences; not surprisingly, workers whose jobs possess more desirable features turn out to be less likely to
voice support for unionism.

These generalizations should cast immigrants as leading candidates
for unionization while also generating a strong preference for union
jobs, especially in light of unions' mitigating effects on undesirable job
features. Immigrants, especially the least skilled, are more likely than natives to occupy jobs whose characteristics—low pay, unhealthy or dangerous working conditions, limited chances for promotion, and minimal job
security—tend to be associated with higher levels of dissatisfaction. However, the conditions that generate dissatisfaction are surely evaluated in
relative terms. While today's "bad jobs" might rank favorably when compared with the "bad jobs" of fifty years ago, what matters is how they contrast with today's average jobs. As Bakke put it in a classic article (albeit
one composed in outdated vocabulary):

> The worker reacts favorably to union membership in proportion to the
> strength of his belief that this step will reduce his frustrations and anxi-
> eties and will further his opportunities relevant to the achievement of his
> standards of successful living (1967 [1945], 85).

But if immigrants do not use the same yardstick as natives, then the
factors making for frustration are likely to be quite different. For many
immigrants, the relevant standard is defined by significantly inferior conditions back home, not those that prevail in the United States. From that
perspective, employment in a sewing factory or as a janitor cleaning office buildings not only ranks higher in the status hierarchy in which the
immigrant grew up, but provides material rewards the likes of which the

newcomer never knew before. While the comparative frame changes over time, as exposure to the United States and its consumption standards pushes the immigrant's normative expectations higher, other factors—most notably, continued contact with and return travel to the home society—keep the older normative pattern in place.

Not every group is likely to experience change in normative expectations at the same rate. Those most committed to long-term settlement in the United States are most likely to experience rapid convergence with U.S.-based norms. But this is precisely why the most proletarian migrants may be least likely to experience their conditions as dissatisfying. Unlike their more skilled counterparts, the labor migrants begin as target earners, concerned with short-term rather than long-term rewards and assessing the adequacy of those rewards relative to some consumption objective located back home. Many of these initially temporary immigrants eventually drop out of the circular migration stream, their standards shifting as they settle down.[4] Even so, the phasing out of the back-and-forth flow is often an extended process, and the majority of those with at least one migratory experience probably never drop out—which means that at any point in time a large proportion of the most proletarianized immigrants see themselves as more likely to return home than to settle down.

"Demographic" Characteristics

So unhappy workers are likely to want unions. Some groups of workers—African Americans most definitely, women quite possibly—are both unhappier *and* more union-prone than the rest. The pro-union inclinations of African American workers is in fact one of the few matters on which almost all researchers who have studied the matter can agree; they are significantly more likely to want union representation and to vote for union representation, when given the choice, than whites. Furthermore, that relationship holds after controlling for background characteristics, including the much higher likelihood that African Americans will fill jobs at the lower end of the wage distribution, a characteristic strongly conducive to a union propensity regardless of race or ethnicity.

But the industrial relations literature is a good deal less certain as to how these intergroup differences in unionization propensities should be interpreted. As Farber and Saks suggest (1980), it may simply come down to differences in "taste": group differences in preference for unions may be exogenously determined. Alternatively, groups may make systematically distinctive evaluations of individual needs, on the one hand, and of

4. For elaborations of this theme, see Piore 1979 and Massey et al. 1987.

the rewards provided by employers and unions on the other. In particular, intergroup perceptions of the likelihood of employment discrimination and the potential for redress offered by unions could significantly affect both union propensities and preferences for union jobs. Indeed, African Americans discover that the wage standardizing and grievance procedures found in unionized establishments significantly reduce discrimination (Ashenfelter 1972). For that reason, it seems reasonable to conclude that "the 'nonwhite effect' appears to be a 'real' demographic effect in the sense that research has not yet developed attitudinal measures which would better account for differential unionism preferences" (Fiorito, Gallagher, and Greer 1986, 279).

This formulation implicitly assumes that such traits as race and ethnicity are real, existing characteristics of the individual, such that one's own and others' understanding of membership status are clear, consistent, and symmetrical. But this description fits awkwardly with the situation of immigrant workers, for whom membership in an ethnic group is not imported, but rather a phenomenon that emerges out of the migration experience itself. Immigrants do not arrive as "ethnics" but rather *become* ethnics. On the one hand, categorization as "other"—by dominants, competitors, and members of one's putative group—alters self-understanding; and on the other hand, shared experience with similarly categorized others imparts a sense of solidarity and an awareness of common interest. Most important, stigmatization and exclusion produce a reactive ethnicity, in which membership in a group is defined by virtue of opposition to dominants.

Assimilation

The concept of assimilation provides yet another key for understanding how immigrants may both secure union jobs and also come to change their views regarding the advantages of unionization. Of course, there are few more contested concepts in the social sciences than assimilation, and now is not the place and time to enter into that debate. The conventional definition will do just fine for the purposes of this chapter: assimilation involves the process whereby immigrants become increasingly like natives on a number of dimensions, moving up the economic ladder as they gain in skills and language ability, while also absorbing the values, orientations, and preferences held by the native-born population. In this sense assimilation might be expected both to generate the skills that will allow immigrants to obtain relatively scarce union jobs and also foster the preferences that would motivate immigrants to either seek out those jobs or unionize their unorganized employer, at rates more or less comparable to counterparts in the native population.[5]

Whether this hypothesis bears true will partly depend on how immigrants evaluate the costs and benefits of union membership. Since unions tend to reduce wage differences, the econometric literature emphasizes the importance of workers' place in the wage hierarchy, with those below the median wage more likely to benefit from the union wage effect and therefore more likely to seek union jobs, and those above the median wage influenced in exactly the opposite way (Abowd and Farber 1982). At the very least, the heterogeneity of today's immigrant population ensures that the economic appeal of union membership will vary greatly. To the extent that a substantial portion of today's newcomers move immediately or quickly into the middle class, their assimilation trajectories are unlikely to lead them toward union jobs or make those jobs attractive.

Not every immigrant group, moreover, will assimilate the expectations and orientations of the native population in identical rate or fashion, regardless of how proletarian its background. Workers from groups in which refugees predominate are likely to experience a quicker commitment to life in the host society, accelerating the rate at which they aspire to the average standards of compensation and therefore come to appreciate the redistributional union wage effect. By contrast, workers emanating from groups with a history of circular or temporary migration will be more likely to retain a dual frame of reference, which in turn reduces the impetus to seek out union jobs.

Not only are immigrants thus likely to assimilate economic expectations and orientations at varying rates, the social nature of the processes of migration and incorporation makes for divergent paths up from the bottom. As Portes and Rumbaut argue, the fate of new arrivals largely depends "on the kind of community created by their co-nationals" (1996, 84). Labor migrants enjoy easy access to jobs at the bottom of the labor market, thanks to a dense web of social networks linking veterans and newcomers. However, those same connections funnel labor migrants into a narrow set of occupations and industries from which exit is difficult, in large measure because dependence on ethnic networks chokes off the flow of new information, constraining diffusion and the search for new opportunities. Similar influences affect members of more entrepreneur-

5. For a prominent recent example of a largely unself-conscious application of assimilation, see the National Research Council's report, *The New Americans* (Smith and Edmonston 1996). For the controversies surrounding the use and nature of the concept, see the essays in the special issue of the *International Migration Review* 31: 4 (1997).

ial streams while pushing them in a different direction: in this case, the business success of co-ethnics gives rise to a distinctive motivational structure, breeding a community-wide orientation toward small business and encouraging the acquisition of skills within a stable, commonly accepted framework. Regardless of the precise modality, the social structure of the immigrant community has an enduring effect on the trajectories that immigrants follow, reducing the likelihood that otherwise comparable immigrants will move into union jobs at a similar pace.

Summary

Thus the process by which immigrants develop a "demand for union services," to borrow the economists' language, is likely to take a variety of forms, proceeding along not one but several timetables. For all immigrants, time is likely to be the most decisive consideration, as both interest in the benefits obtained through unionization and the ability to obtain union jobs increase with time spent in the United States. In this respect, time points to the importance of assimilation: because standards change with settlement, the longer immigrants live in the United States the more likely their frame of reference will shift from the conditions prevailing in the country of origin to those prevailing in their new home.

However, time does not yield a uniform effect. Workers emanating from groups with a history of circular or temporary migration may be more likely to assimilate in a delayed fashion. Workers from groups dominated by refugee flows are likely to experience a quicker commitment to life in the host society, which in turn will accelerate the impact of time.[6]

Furthermore, time generates new self-understandings, and not simply because immigrants come to view themselves in terms consistent with the categories of the U.S. system of race and ethnic relations. As immigrants become ethnics, their perception of fairness in the employment system evolves, as does their view of the need for redress through unions. Reactive ethnicity is likely to exercise a powerful effect on Mexican immigrants: though preferences for unionization will be depressed, relative to other immigrants, at early stages of the migration, they should shift more sharply upward in the later stages of settlement. On the other hand, the social structure of Mexican migration is likely to impede access to existing union jobs, even relative to other immigrants of similar socioeconomic background.

The socioeconomic diversity of the immigrant population further complicates the impact of time. For the large middle-class contingent

---

6. Unfortunately, our sample size precludes an adequate test of this latter hypothesis.

among today's immigrants, occupational position will either preclude unionization—as among those who work as managers—or reduce its attractiveness or feasibility—as among the many immigrants who are employed in higher or even low white-collar positions. The importance of socioeconomic diversity suggests that controls for demographic characteristics and for industry or occupation will reduce the effects of immigrant status and time.

Data and Variables

This section analyzes data drawn from a four-year (1994–97) combined Current Population Survey (CPS) for the month of March.[7] The CPS inquires into union membership among only a relatively small portion of eligible respondents, and we have restricted the sample further to encompass only those aged 20–65 and who were also employed as wage and salary workers. The analysis, therefore, excludes the self-employed. The analysis is based on a sample of almost 32,000 persons, 2,998 of whom are foreign-born. The limited size of the foreign-born sample makes meaningful national-origin disaggregations for most immigrants problematic. Consequently we have merged data from several questions to recode the sample into five mutually exclusive "ethno-racial" groups: whites, blacks, Mexicans, other Hispanics, and others, the latter a largely Asian grouping. We also use controls for nativity and year of immigration to distinguish native from foreign-born members of these groupings. As additional controls, we use data on geographical location, gender, education, age, and industry of employment.[8]

7. The Current Population Survey is a monthly survey of a national probability sample of approximately sixty thousand households. In light of the limited size of the two populations of interest to us—immigrants on the one hand and union members on the other—we have sought to increase the size of these target populations by merging the March CPS samples from 1994 through 1997. However, the nature of the CPS precludes utilization of each year's full CPS sample. The CPS retains respondents during a two-year period, interviewing individuals for four consecutive months, dropping them from the sample for the next eight months, and then re-interviewing them for another four consecutive months, after which time they are dropped from the sample completely. Consequently, half of the persons interviewed in any given month reappear in the following year's sample in the same month. To avoid duplicate cases, we have retained nonoverlapping halves of the 1994, 1995, and 1996 samples, and included the entire 1997 sample. This procedure almost triples the size of the sample.

8. We have recoded industry of employment into six mutually exclusive categories, separating the public sector from all private sector industries, and recoding private sector industries into five categories: construction / manufacturing; agriculture, mining, and forestry; transportation, communications, and utilities; wholesale / retail trade; and finance, insurance, real estate and other services.

Characteristics

The immigrants in our sample differ from natives along a series of dimensions, as table 2.1 shows. First of all, natives are more likely to hold union jobs: just over 18 percent of native-born workers are unionized, as opposed to just over 15 percent for the foreign-born. Differences in age and labor force experience are negligible, in part because our sample is limited to workers aged 20–65. Immigrants are more heavily male than natives, which makes the difference in unionization rates even more striking, as generally male workers in the U.S. are more unionized than female workers.

Still more impressive are native / immigrant differences in ethnic characteristics. The native-born population in our sample remains overwhelmingly white. By contrast, whites comprise less than a quarter of the foreign-born; Hispanics, divided here between Mexicans and other Hispanics, account for the largest group of immigrants, followed by "Asians / Others."

By historical standards, relatively high skill levels distinguish today's immigrant population; but a smaller proportion of immigrants have gone beyond the high school degree than is true among the native-born. A much greater difference is found at the lower end of the spectrum: immigrants are disproportionately concentrated among persons who have not obtained the high school degree— a very small group among the native-born.

Though found in all major industrial sectors, immigrants evince a different sectoral distribution than natives. Construction and manufacturing constitute a sector of immigrant overconcentration; the public sector, not surprisingly, has relatively low levels of foreign-born employment.

We also note the relatively recent origins of the immigrant workforce, of whom just under 60 percent arrived in the United States after 1980. Even this figure probably underestimates new arrivals' share of the immigrant population, since our merged (1994–97) sample is such that it does not fully capture immigration throughout the 1990s.

Geography offers a final axis of differentiation. The geographic distribution of immigrants and natives is almost perfectly asymmetrical, the six states containing 65 percent of the foreign-born being home to less than 30 percent of all natives. California, with 26 percent of the foreign-born workers, contains only 6 percent of all native-born adults of working age.

Table 2.1. Characteristics by nativity, wage and salary workers aged
     20–65.

	Natives (n = 27,703)	Immigrants (n = 2,998)
Holding union jobs	18.1%	15.1%
Mean age	40.3	39.8
Mean labor market experience	20.9	21.6
Male	50.0%	56.0%
Education		
Less than high school	7.6%	28.0%
High school diploma	33.7%	22.7%
More than high school	58.7%	49.4%
State		
California	5.8%	25.9%
New York	5.5%	12.8%
New Jersey	3.6%	8.0%
Illinois	4.1%	4.8%
Florida	4.1%	8.1%
Texas	4.7%	5.5%
Other states	72.3%	34.8%
Race		
White	83.2%	24.3%
Black	9.8%	6.3%
Mexican	2.7%	23.2%
Other Hispanic	1.8%	19.1%
Asian / other	2.6%	27.2%
Industry		
Agriculture / mining / forestry	1.7%	3.6%
Construction / manufacturing	21.7%	26.9%
Trans. / comm. / utilities	6.4%	4.3%
Wholesale / retail trade	18.5%	18.5%
Fin. / ins. / real est. / other services	32.9%	36.2%
Public admin. / public sector	18.9%	10.5%
Period of Immigration		
Before 1980		42.4%
1980–1989		36.1%
1990–1997		21.6%
U.S. Citizen		36.1%

But it is not simply that immigrant and native workers live in different regions of the country; there are geographic variations within the immigrant population as well. Those many immigrants who move to California differ significantly from their counterparts who settle elsewhere, as table 2.2 shows. Disparities in native-immigrant unionization rates stand at the top of the list: natives are unionized at almost twice the rate of immigrants in California, whereas elsewhere the difference is on the order of less than 20 percent. Educational characteristics also make California distinct; its native-born workers are far better educated than those elsewhere, but its immigrants are more likely to be concentrated among the very least schooled, making for an extraordinary large educational gap between natives and immigrants. More than half of California's immigrants are Hispanic, almost three-quarters of whom are Mexican; elsewhere, Hispanics comprise less than 40 percent of the foreign-born workforce. And California's immigrants are longer settled than those residing elsewhere in the United States, a characteristic reflecting California's importance as a prime immigrant destination ever since the late 1960s.

Thus California stands out from the rest of the nation with respect to the social characteristics of its immigrants, and with respect to the size and nature of differences between immigrants and natives. Not surprisingly, those differences are associated with distinctive patterns in immigrant/native unionization rates, as tables 2.3 and 2.4 show.

Overall, California still ranks as a state with relatively high unionization rates. Native-born workers are just a little less likely to have union jobs than their counterparts in New York or New Jersey, but far more so than in such immigrant states as Texas or Florida. Immigrant Californians are far less unionized than their New Jersey or New York counterparts, but compare favorably with foreign-born workers in Texas or Florida.

Nonetheless, a sizable foreign-native gap in unionization rates distinguishes Californians within almost every social category, residents of San Francisco excepted. Whether men or women, better educated or less educated, Mexicans or Asians, manufacturing workers or workers in trade, immigrant Californians are far less likely to hold union jobs than their native-born counterparts. Immigrants in the other forty-nine states are also less likely to hold union jobs than comparable native-born workers, but the gap is modest, especially by comparison to California. Moreover, unionization rates among recent immigrants to California are highly depressed.

Table 2.2. Characteristics by nativity, wage and salary workers aged 20–65, California vs. other 49 states.

	California		Other 49 states	
	Natives (n = 1,614)	**Immigrants** (n = 777)	**Natives** (n = 26,089)	**Immigrants** (n = 2,221)
Holding union jobs	24.7%	13.4%	17.7%	15.8%
Mean age	39.8	38.3	40.4	40.3
Mean labor market experience	19.9	20.6	21.0	21.9
Male	51.0%	59.2%	49.9%	54.8%
Education				
Less than high school	5.1%	33.1%	7.7%	26.2%
High school diploma	24.9%	21.1%	34.3%	23.2%
More than high school	70.4%	45.8%	58.0%	50.6%
Location				
Los Angeles	51.4%	68.7%		
San Francisco	20.9%	16.6%		
Other metropolitan	25.2%	13.5%		
Non-metro	2.5%	1.2%		
Race				
White	71.7%	13.6%	83.9%	27.9%
Black	7.5%	1.9%	10.0%	7.8%
Mexican	13.6%	39.8%	2.0%	17.4%
Other Hispanic	2.6%	14.4%	1.7%	20.7%
Asian / other	4.7%	30.2%	2.5%	26.1%
Industry				
Agriculture / mining / forestry	0.9%	3.9%	1.8%	3.5%
Construction / manufacturing	17.9%	30.2%	21.9%	25.7%
Trans. / comm. / utilities	7.5%	4.0%	6.3%	4.4%
Wholesale / retail trade	18.5%	18.4%	18.5%	18.5%
Fin. / ins. / real est. / other services	35.4%	33.3%	32.8%	37.2%
Public admin. / public sector	19.8%	10.2%	18.8%	10.6%
Period of immigration				
Before 1980		41.6%		42.6%
1980–1989		42.5%		33.9%
1990–1997		16.0%		23.5%
U.S. citizen		30.0%		38.3%

Table 2.3. Proportion of wage and salary workers aged 20–65 holding union jobs, United States (percentage).

	Natives **(n = 27,703)**	**Immigrants** **(n = 2,998)**
Gender		
Male	21.0%	15.7%
Female	15.2%	14.4%
Education		
Less than high school	14.8%	14.7%
High school diploma	19.1%	17.4%
More than high school	24.9%	16.9%
State		
California	24.7%	11.7%
New York	29.5%	26.4%
New Jersey	23.9%	25.2%
Illinois	21.5%	15.9%
Florida	12.3%	5.7%
Texas	9.1%	7.8%
Other states	16.6%	12.8%
Race		
White	17.2%	16.2%
Black	28.1%	23.4%
Mexican	24.7%	10.3%
Other Hispanic	23.6%	16.2%
Asian / other	25.1%	14.4%
Industry:		
Agriculture / mining / forestry	9.6%	1.9%
Construction / manufacturing	20.0%	15.1%
Trans. / comm. / utilities	32.1%	24.8%
Wholesale / retail trade	6.5%	6.3%
Fin. / ins. / real est. / other services	5.9%	11.4%
Public admin. / public sector	44.7%	44.1%
Period of immigration		
Before 1980		25.0%
1980–1989		12.9%
1990–1997		9.4%
U.S. Citizen		
Yes		20.50%
No		12.10%

Table 2.4. Proportion of wage and salary workers aged 20–65 holding union jobs, California vs. other 49 states (percentage).

	California		Other 49 states	
	Natives (n = 1,614)	**Immigrants** (n = 777)	**Natives** (n = 26,089)	**Immigrants** (n = 2,221)
Gender				
Male	28.4%	14.6%	20.6%	16.2%
Female	20.9%	11.7%	14.8%	15.3%
Education				
Less than high school	16.9%	9.7%	14.7%	16.8%
High school diploma	25.8%	11.6%	18.8%	19.2%
More than high school	24.9%	16.9%	17.5%	13.6%
Location				
Los Angeles	26.4%	11.4%		
San Francisco	24.9%	20.9%		
Other metropolitan	22.4%	14.3%		
Non-metro	12.5%	11.1%		
Race				
White	24.0%	17.9%	16.80%	15.90%
Black	28.1%	26.7%	24.50%	23.10%
Mexican	25.6%	12.3%	13.90%	8.80%
Other Hispanic	19.1%	15.2%	24.00%	18.70%
Asian / other	30.7%	11.1%	20.40%	15.70%
Industry:				
Agriculture / mining / forestry	13.3%	0.0%	9.5%	2.6%
Construction / manufacturing	18.0%	8.9%	20.1%	17.7%
Trans. / comm. / utilities	35.5%	19.4%	31.9%	26.5%
Wholesale / retail trade	13.4%	5.6%	6.1%	6.6%
Fin. / ins. / real est. / other services	10.0%	10.0%	5.6%	11.9%
Public admin. / public sector	64.1%	54.4%	43.4%	40.7%
Period of immigration				
Before 1980		21.4%		19.5%
1980–1989		8.8%		14.6%
1990–1997		4.8%		10.5%
U.S. Citizen				
Yes		24.90%		19.3%
No		8.50%		13.6%

Multivariate Analysis

Multivariate analysis can provide a more rigorous assessment of the factors associated with the probability of holding a union job. We seek to determine the likelihood of being a union member; as membership is a dichotomous category, we use logistic regression to predict the probability of membership status.[9] Because the coefficients produced by logistic regression are difficult to interpret, we exponentiate them to generate odds ratios. An odds ratio less than one indicates a negative relationship between a given independent variable and the probability of being unionized; an odds ratio greater than one points to a positive relationship. To enhance readability and facilitate intuitive understanding, our discussion below refers to graphical representations of the odds ratios. Detailed results appear in the chapter appendices. We will first examine patterns for the entire United States, and then review the findings for California.

We begin by looking at the effects of time, asking whether immigrant/native differences in unionization diminish as length of settlement in the United States increases. As figure 2.1 shows, immigrants in the more recent cohorts are indeed significantly less likely to be unionized than native workers; among immigrants of the longest tenure, however, foreign birth proves to be positively associated with union membership. The overall pattern persists after controlling for ethnicity, with other Hispanics, blacks, and others significantly more likely to be union members than whites, and Mexicans significantly less likely to be union members. Because there are strong effects linking ethnicity and union membership, controls for ethnicity slightly mute the impact of time among the most established of the foreign-born. Applying controls for demographic characteristics eliminates the union propensity among the longest-settled immigrants, while leaving the effects of migration in either the 1980s or 1990s virtually unchanged. Insertion of the industry dummies alters the association between immigrant status and union membership, though the effect is inconsistent: older immigrants are now

9. When analyzing categorical dependent variables, linear regression is not an appropriate method. Linear regression assumes continuous dependent variables. In analyzing our dichotomous dependent variable (union membership), we used logistic (or logit) regression. Logistic regression predicts the probability that an event occurs. Unlike linear regression, logit (or logistic) regression refers to models with a logit as the left-hand-side variable. A logit is the log of odds that an event occurs. Thus the estimated (logit) coefficients are reported in terms of log odds. The interpretation of log odds is rather difficult. Instead of log odds, odds allow a more intuitive interpretation, especially with dichotomous predictors. For dummy predictors, the odds ratio equals the antilogarithm of the logit coefficient. In this chapter, we present odds ratios for all predictors.

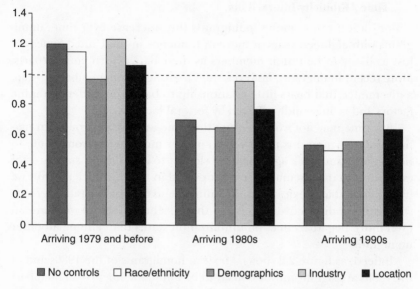

Figure 2.1. Odds of holding union job, United States: effect of immigrant cohort before and after controls.

significantly more likely than natives to hold union jobs; immigrants of the 1980s no longer differ from native counterparts; and though immigrants of the 1990s remain less likely than natives to hold union jobs, the effect is no longer as strong. Still, the most recent immigrants are only about half as likely as natives to be union members, other relevant background factors being controlled (see appendix A).

Location

Immigrants tend to converge on just a handful of states; ironically, those same immigrant-receiving states differ significantly in the industrial relations environment, as we've already noted. Compared to Californians, workers in New York are about 50 percent more likely and those in Florida over 50 percent less likely to hold union jobs. More important, adding variables for location to the controls applied earlier alters the effects and significance associated with migration cohorts: newcomers of the 1980s or the 1990s again become significantly less likely to be union members; older migrants are now no more likely than natives to hold union jobs.

Time / Ethnicity Interactions

Unionization rates among immigrants thus increase over time; immigrants with eighteen years or more of residence in the United States are just as likely to be union members as their native-born counterparts. More recent immigrants, however, show a strong union membership gap, a divergence that bears little relationship to background demographic factors and is only mildly affected by sectoral location.

But time may not work in quite the same way for all groups. In particular, labor migrants involved in circular movements from home to host society and back again may be slowest to adjust their standards of evaluation to the circumstances that prevail in the host society. Thus we hypothesize that Mexicans, as the quintessential labor migration group, will display a distinctive pattern, in that recency of arrival will have an even more negative effect on unionization status than among all other immigrants.

Indeed, as figure 2.2 shows, Mexican immigrants of the 1980s and of the 1990s are significantly less likely to be union members than members of all other immigrant groups. While the divergence is greatest among the immigrants of the 1990s, the cohort effect appears quite robust; ap-

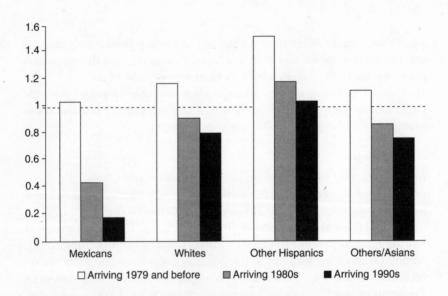

Figure 2.2. Odds of holding union job, United States: immigrant cohorts by ethnicity (background factors controlled).

plication of demographic and industrial controls shows that recent Mexican immigrants are less likely to be union members than their demographic counterparts working in the same industries.

The California Factor

Multivariate analysis confirms the initial comparison between the United States and California: immigrants in California are less likely to hold union jobs, as figure 2.3 shows. But unlike the pattern in the United States as a whole, immigrant Californians are significantly less likely to hold union jobs than native-born workers regardless of cohort, with the unionization gap especially wide among more recent arrivals. Sequential controls for ethnicity, demographics, sector, and location slightly diminish the difference between natives and immigrants in each cohort, but without altering the essential pattern: for immigrant Californians, a union job remains, if not out of reach, then awfully hard to find (see appendix B).

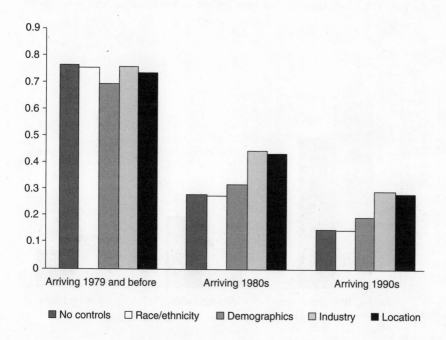

Figure 2.3. Odds of holding union job, California: effect of immigrant cohort before and after controls.

Propensity or Social Process?

Thus our analysis shows that immigrants are less likely than natives to hold union jobs for reasons that have relatively little to do with the social factors that otherwise distinguish immigrants from natives. But if background characteristics don't account for the disparity, what does? In the current environment, group differences in unionization rates are likely to be closely related to group differences in access to union jobs; as we've suggested, the process of immigrant incorporation systematically reduces the probability of moving into those sectors or organizations where union jobs are most likely to be found. On the other hand, circumstances of migration and settlement generate distinctive economic expectations and job preferences that can affect access to the types of positions that tend to be covered by union contracts. So can one reduce intergroup differences in unionization rates to employment patterns? Or do inter-group propensities for unionization play any role in the process?

Our data preclude any definitive assessment of immigrant propensities to unionization, but they do allow for an indirect test of the hypothesis that the circumstances of immigrant incorporation and settlement

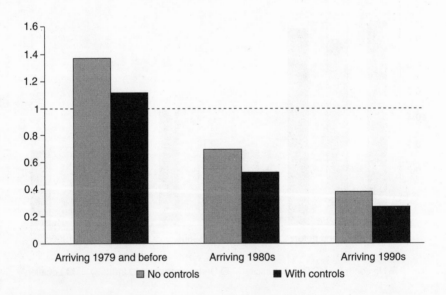

Figure 2.4. Odds of union membership, United States: effect of immigrant cohort before and after controls.

may *reduce* the preference for unionization. Though getting a union job may be a matter of employment patterns, persons who hold such jobs choose whether to become union members or not. Of those persons in our sample who hold union jobs, as we've defined them in this chapter, 10.5 percent are not union members. As figure 2.4 shows, although immigrants who arrived before 1980 are more likely than their native-born counterparts to be union members, if covered by a union contract, those immigrants of the 1980s and 1990s who hold union jobs are significantly *less likely* to be union members than native-born unionized workers, a disparity that holds after controlling for education.

Conclusion

In this essay, we plumb a new data source to assess the factors associated with unionization among America's new immigrant workers. The effort yields a sobering conclusion: however much benefit they might derive from unionization, immigrant workers have difficulty finding union jobs. To be sure, the picture is not uniformly negative. Over time, unionization rates rise among immigrants, so that among the more settled of the arrivals, unionization rates are somewhat higher than among their native-born counterparts. However, the more recent cohorts are distinctly less likely to be union members than their native-born counterparts, a disparity that persists after controlling for a broad range of background factors. Furthermore, the difference between natives and immigrants is even greater among the largest, and most uniformly proletarian of contemporary immigrant groups, namely the Mexicans, among whom recent arrivals are especially unlikely to be union members. Union jobs are most elusive in California, home to one out of every four immigrant workers, where even the most settled immigrant workers are unlikely to hold a union job.

Our analysis is pitched in the language of variables, but it's always important to recall the distribution of populations among the values on those variables. From this perspective, our findings regarding unionization rates among the more recent cohorts would be of considerably reduced import had immigration to America subsided; were most immigrants of established vintage, recentness of arrival would have little net effect on the overall native / immigrant unionization gap. Similarly, if more immigrants lived in New York than California, recency would have a much milder overall effect, and immigrant unionization rates would soon surpass those of the native-born. However, the reality is rather different.

The great majority of immigrant workers have moved to the United States since 1980, with two-and-a-half times as many in California as in New York. Working-class immigrants have other characteristics—such as low levels of education and concentrations in industries of low union densities—which further reduce access to union jobs.

This paper can shed light only on the factors associated with access to existing union jobs, and that is a matter of little import to the future of organized labor. Immigrant workers may well find it difficult to connect with those jobs located in the shrinking union sector, but the factors influencing their prospective behavior may prove more crucial. Indeed, the central finding of this chapter is consistent with other research documenting the troubles that immigrants encounter in their search for progress in America. Today's newcomers thus have ample reason for turning to unions to voice their discontent; they are also quite capable of doing so, as the other chapters in this volume show.

Nonetheless, the factors that make union jobs elusive may weaken the appeal of unionization itself. Immigrant modes of incorporation generate a logic of their own; such logic will not always breed a preference for unionization, job problems notwithstanding. Likewise, continuing home-country ties generate a dual frame of reference, which in turn blunts the impact of those frustrations encountered in the United States. And as we noted above, the limited evidence available does suggest that recent immigrants are less likely than comparable natives to choose union membership, when offered the possibility.

Thus immigration is unlikely to add a silver lining to the dark clouds facing American labor. Granted, labor has been misled in recent times; its new leadership—should it last—provides some reason for hope. Yet the obstacles it confronts are so deep-seated that even a greatly improved leadership equipped with superior strategy may not suffice. As we've argued, the characteristics of the new immigrant workforce—its size, composition, and most important its recent arrival—strongly suggest that immigration adds to, rather than subtracts from, the many difficulties facing organized labor. While we admire the optimism that impels union organizers in the face of these odds, the argument and analysis in this chapter warrant pessimism, which seems very much the order of the day.

Appendix A

Logistic Regression Results Predicting Holding Union Jobs, United States, 1994–97 (**odds ratios for figure 2.1 in bold**)

Model A	Odds ratio	Std. error	z	P>|z|	[95% conf.	interval]
bef 1980	**1.201839**	0.0794123	2.782	0.005	1.055851	1.368012
1980–89	**0.7007825**	0.0661929	–3.764	0	0.5823478	0.8433037
1990–97	**0.5344614**	0.0728039	–4.599	0	0.409229	0.6980175
Model B						
bef 1980	**1.115299**	0.0824009	1.477	0.14	0.9649452	1.289081
1980–89	**0.6441107**	0.0659292	–4.298	0	0.5270285	0.7872033
1990–97	**0.4994239**	0.0709873	–4.885	0	0.3779905	0.6598691
blacks	1.599969	0.0753601	9.978	0	1.458878	1.754704
mexicans	0.8522537	0.0758867	–1.795	0.073	0.7157738	1.014757
other hispanics	1.475955	0.1317466	4.361	0	1.239062	1.758138
other	1.16258	0.0948038	1.847	0.065	0.9908562	1.364065
Model C						
bef 1980	**0.9692626**	0.0733386	–0.413	0.68	0.8356721	1.124209
1980–89	**0.6497235**	0.0674068	–4.156	0	0.5301747	0.7962293
1990–97	**0.5621713**	0.0809544	–4	0	0.4239289	0.7454942
blacks	1.777984	0.0859411	1.906	0	1.617275	1.954662
mexicans	1.051407	0.0967923	0.545	0.586	0.8778278	1.259309
other hispanics	1.742445	0.1593462	6.072	0	1.456521	2.084497
other	1.262371	0.1046999	2.809	0.005	1.072974	1.4852
age	1.066229	0.012217	5.597	0	1.042551	1.090445
female	0.6570613	0.0206463	–13.366	0	0.6178162	0.6987993
work experience	1.027302	0.0134818	2.052	0.04	1.001215	1.054068

	Odds ratio	Std. error	z	P>|z|	[95% conf. interval]	
exper squared	0.9986955	0.0001151	−11.323	0	0.9984698	0.9989212
less than HS	0.8538642	0.0622357	−2.168	0.03	0.7401968	0.9849869
more than HS	0.8569842	0.0406179	−3.256	0.001	0.7809603	0.9404088

Model D

	Odds ratio	Std. error	z	P>|z|	[95% conf. interval]	
bef 1980	**1.230827**	0.1000538	2.555	0.011	1.049549	1.443414
1980–89	**0.9605481**	0.1047883	−0.369	0.712	0.775639	1.189539
1990–97	**0.7440377**	0.1113939	−1.975	0.048	0.5548262	0.9977756
blacks	1.564817	0.0825558	8.487	0	1.411095	1.735285
mexicans	0.8654121	0.0846433	−1.478	0.139	0.7144462	1.048278
other hispanics	1.515685	0.1493756	4.22	0	1.249454	1.838644
other	1.020046	0.0902508	0.224	0.823	0.857646	1.213198
age	1.001278	0.0125183	0.102	0.919	0.9770408	1.026116
female	0.6951388	0.024655	−10.253	0	0.6484573	0.7451809
work experience	1.07014	0.0152119	4.769	0	1.040737	1.100374
exper squared	0.9989847	0.0001227	−8.268	0	0.9987442	0.9992253
less than HS	0.7576113	0.0594396	−3.538	0	0.649627	0.8835453
more than HS	0.8335047	0.0425263	−3.569	0	0.7541867	0.9211646
agr / min / fores	0.1108646	0.017489	−13.942	0	0.0813795	0.1510328
const / mfg	0.2782648	0.0126843	−28.062	0	0.2544821	0.30427
TCU	0.520164	0.0312589	−10.876	0	0.4623682	0.5851843
trade	0.0885022	0.0056713	−37.839	0	0.0780564	0.1003459
FIRE / services	0.0904891	0.0045899	−47.365	0	0.0819258	0.0999475

Model E

	Odds ratio	Std. error	z	P>|z|	[95% conf. interval]	
bef 1980	**1.06378**	0.0886573	0.742	0.458	0.9034648	1.252543
1980–89	**0.76843**	0.0859561	−2.355	0.019	0.6171482	0.9567955
1990–97	**0.6422665**	0.0969293	−2.934	0.003	0.4778086	0.8633294
blacks	1.592599	0.0850411	8.715	0	1.434348	1.768311
mexicans	1.012552	0.104884	0.12	0.904	0.8265068	1.240475
other hispanics	1.39744	0.1412378	3.311	0.001	1.146313	1.703583
other	1.013749	0.0910982	0.152	0.879	0.8500396	1.208987
age	0.993819	0.0125426	−0.491	0.623	0.9695376	1.018709
female	0.6935151	0.0248086	−10.231	0	0.6465567	0.7438841
work experience	1.07867	0.0154765	5.278	0	1.048759	1.109434
exper squared	0.9989659	0.0001239	−8.339	0	0.998723	0.9992089
less than HS	0.7495692	0.0594657	−3.633	0	0.6416279	0.8756696
more than HS	0.8409902	0.0433575	−3.359	0.001	0.7601634	0.9304112
agr / min / fores	0.1168272	0.0184988	−13.56	0	0.0856568	0.1593403
const / mfg	0.2711065	0.0125008	−28.307	0	0.2476799	0.2967489
TCU	0.5037195	0.0307303	−11.24	0	0.4469508	0.5676985
trade	0.0857332	0.0055388	−38.024	0	0.0755366	0.0973062

	Odds ratio	Std. error	z	P>|z|	[95% conf. interval]	
FIRE / services	0.0851743	0.0043843	−47.85	0	0.0770004	0.0942157
NY	1.459146	0.1354191	4.071	0	1.216469	1.750235
NJ	1.14397	0.1187679	1.296	0.195	0.9333455	1.402126
IL	0.8705907	0.0911953	−1.323	0.186	0.7090057	1.069002
FL	0.3791937	0.0446571	−8.234	0	0.3010345	0.4776457
TX	0.6213894	0.0471358	−6.272	0	0.5355444	0.7209949
other states	0.2715013	0.0324886	−10.896	0	0.214741	0.3432646

Appendix B

Logistic Regression Results Predicting Holding Union Jobs, California, 1994–97 (**odds ratios for figure 2.3 in bold**)

Model A	Odds ratio	Std. error	z	P>|z|	[95% conf.	interval]
bef 1980	**0.7644336**	0.1109301	−1.851	0.064	0.5751994	1.015924
1980–89	**0.2808074**	0.0569236	−6.265	0	0.1887374	0.4177909
1990–97	**0.1503715**	0.0635172	−4.485	0	0.0657077	0.3441239

Model B						
bef 1980	**0.7549722**	0.1257016	−1.688	0.091	0.5447627	1.046296
1980–89	**0.2756519**	0.0610945	−5.814	0	0.1785268	0.4256164
1990–97	**0.1477767**	0.0636305	−4.441	0	0.0635464	0.3436538
blacks	1.308275	0.2667965	1.318	0.188	0.8772306	1.951123
mexicans	1.039622	0.1522656	0.265	0.791	0.7802008	1.385302
other hispanics	1.083548	0.2698437	0.322	0.747	0.6650698	1.765342
other	1.047406	0.203712	0.238	0.812	0.7154235	1.53344

Model C						
bef 1980	**0.6955648**	0.122331	−2.064	0.039	0.4927587	0.9818403
1980–89	**0.3173513**	0.0720513	−5.055	0	0.2033686	0.4952185
1990–97	**0.1984953**	0.0866765	−3.703	0	0.0843447	0.4671351
blacks	1.39704	0.2911591	1.604	0.109	0.9285573	2.101885
mexicans	1.452269	0.2332618	2.323	0.02	1.060054	1.989602
other hispanics	1.306141	0.3319918	1.051	0.293	0.7936582	2.149544
other	1.025638	0.2062967	0.126	0.9	0.6914863	1.521265
age	1.029152	0.0357719	0.827	0.408	0.9613751	1.101707
female	0.6566181	0.0691256	−3.996	0	0.5341982	0.8070925

	Odds ratio	Std. error	z	P>|z|	[95% conf.	interval]
work experience	1.037087	0.0418562	0.902	0.367	0.9582112	1.122456
experience						
squared	0.9992317	0.0003928	−1.955	0.051	0.9984622	1.000002
less than HS	0.5526986	0.1464757	−2.237	0.025	0.3287788	0.9291225
more than HS	1.053317	0.1665284	0.329	0.742	0.7726542	1.43593

Model D

	Odds ratio	Std. error	z	P>|z|	[95% conf.	interval]
bef 1980	**0.7615226**	0.1501429	−1.382	0.167	0.5174383	1.120745
1980–89	**0.4478394**	0.1086695	−3.311	0.001	0.2783402	0.7205577
1990–97	**0.2964742**	0.1344857	−2.68	0.007	0.1218618	0.7212841
blacks	1.21872	0.2987035	0.807	0.42	0.7538379	1.97029
mexicans	1.401794	0.2519948	1.879	0.06	0.9855242	1.99389
other hispanics	1.043667	0.2927806	0.152	0.879	0.6022458	1.808631
other	0.8697137	0.196842	−0.617	0.537	0.5581156	1.355278
age	0.9617607	0.0380726	−0.985	0.325	0.8899612	1.039353
female	0.5162449	0.0646946	−5.276	0	0.4038175	0.6599733
work experience	1.088059	0.0496427	1.85	0.064	0.9949845	1.18984
exper squared	0.9995898	0.0004368	−0.939	0.348	0.9987341	1.000446
less than HS	0.4725562	0.14026	−2.526	0.012	0.2641236	0.8454729
more than HS	0.9745917	0.1724209	−0.145	0.884	0.6890195	1.378523
agr / min / fores	0.0254489	0.0190634	−4.901	0	0.005862	0.1104824
const / mfg	0.0902857	0.0161818	−13.417	0	0.0635417	0.1282858
TCU	0.2406038	0.0514047	−6.668	0	0.1582866	0.3657301
trade	0.0719906	0.0142057	−13.334	0	0.0489003	0.105984
FIRE / services	0.0720755	0.011554	−16.407	0	0.052642	60.0986821

Model E

	Odds ratio	Std. error	z	P>|z|	[95% conf.	interval]
bef 1980	**0.7376172**	0.1464471	−1.533	0.125	0.4998421	1.088502
1980–89	**0.4367066**	0.1068892	−3.385	0.001	0.2703012	0.7055561
1990–97	**0.2862236**	0.1298044	−2.758	0.006	0.1176738	0.6961955
blacks	1.150279	0.2824509	0.57	0.569	0.7108707	1.861297
mexicans	1.411128	0.2568898	1.892	0.059	0.9876628	2.016155
other hispanics	1.03212	0.2907066	0.112	0.911	0.5942658	1.792583
other	0.8177714	0.1873813	−0.878	0.38	0.5219039	1.281366
age	0.9524951	0.0379817	−1.221	0.222	0.8808871	1.029924
female	0.5209592	0.0654156	−5.193	0	0.4073057	0.6663264
work experience	1.098306	0.0503242	2.046	0.041	1.003972	1.201504
exper squared	0.9995841	0.0004365	−0.953	0.341	0.998729	1.00044
less than HS	0.4577067	0.1365863	−2.619	0.009	0.2550213	0.821482
more than HS	0.9693333	0.1723118	−0.175	0.861	0.6841649	1.373363
agr / min / fores	0.0282969	0.021266	−4.744	0	0.0064869	0.1234367
const / mfg	0.086731	0.0156443	−13.555	0	0.0609027	0.1235128

	Odds ratio	Std. error	z	P>|z|	[95% conf. interval]	
TCU	0.2242095	0.0484532	-6.919	0	0.1467924	0.3424557
trade	0.0698902	0.0138633	-13.414	0	0.0473777	0.1031001
FIRE / services	0.0682211	0.0110895	-16.518	0	0.0496083	0.0938174
SF	1.25093	0.1928156	1.453	0.146	0.9247634	1.692136
other Metro	0.7667482	0.117202	-1.738	0.082	0.5682528	1.03458
non-Metro	0.4831946	0.2426792	-1.448	0.148	0.1805575	1.29309

3

"Organize or Die": Labor's New Tactics and Immigrant Workers

Rachel Sherman and Kim Voss

After years of falling union density, many in the American labor movement have begun to heed the admonition, "organize or die." The AFL-CIO and some of its affiliated unions have started to put real resources and effort into organizing the unorganized, including immigrants. The approach they advocate is more aggressive, more confrontational, and more strategic than that used by most unions in the postwar period. Using an arsenal of innovative strategies, unions in a range of industries have waged high-profile organizing campaigns.

Recent research suggests that these novel tactics succeed, despite fierce employer opposition and an unfavorable organizing climate. Bronfenbrenner and Juravich (1994), for example, found that union tactics accounted for more variation in the outcomes of NLRB representation elections than any other factor. More important, as another recent study indicates, unions that innovate in general and especially in terms of organizing are more successful in recruiting members than unions that do not (Fiorito, Jarley, and Delaney 1995). In particular, the use of an "aggressive rank and file intensive campaign" (including rank-and-file participation, highlighting issues such as dignity and justice, and devoting resources to organizing campaigns and organizer training) was associated with win rates significantly higher than those of campaigns that did not employ these tactics (Bronfenbrenner and Juravich 1998).

The authors' names are in alphabetical order; each contributed equally to this collaboration. We gratefully acknowledge the financial support of the Institute of Industrial Relations at the University of California, Berkeley, as well as the helpful comments of Ruth Milkman and Sanford Jacoby.

However, despite the effectiveness of these innovations, few unions are actually using many of them. In 1994, only 15 percent of the unions surveyed by Bronfenbrenner and Juravich used five or more of the new intensive tactics. Indeed, they report little change in the way most unions run organizing campaigns (1998).

In this chapter we take up the issue of tactical innovation within the labor movement and its relationship to immigrant unionization. Using in-depth interviews with local union organizers and staff in northern California, as well as secondary information on particular tactics and campaigns, we look closely at the process by which new tactics are implemented in local and International unions. We argue that significant organizational innovation is required to implement new tactics, and that the impetus for such innovation typically arises from a combination of three factors: crisis within the local union, support from the International union, and the presence of innovative staff from outside the labor movement in the local.

Crisis within the local union is often accompanied by a shift in employment patterns, as nonunionized immigrants replace native-born union workers. Indeed, all the unions we studied had the potential to organize immigrant workers. The jurisdiction of the Hotel and Restaurant Employees (HERE) includes numerous immigrant workers (see Wells, this volume); some of the Service Employees International Union (SEIU) target industries, such as building services and health care, also employ high numbers of immigrants; and the jurisdiction of the United Food and Commercial Workers (UFCW) includes many workplaces with immigrant workers, such as food processing firms and ethnic grocery stores. Moreover, successfully organizing immigrant workers, though different in some particulars from organizing nonimmigrant workers, is in principle the same process that leads to the successful organization of nonimmigrant workers, requiring local unions to approach workers with an understanding of their particular culture, interests, and work situation. Unions that have done a good job of organizing immigrant workers have also done well at organizing native-born workers, because of their successful organizational restructuring and adherence to a flexible model of organizing. The immigrant status of workers is certainly something organizers must keep in mind when conducting campaigns, but it is just one of several important factors, including the type of job the workers do, their race/ethnicity, and their age.

This chapter begins with a description of the innovative tactics that unions are using. We then present data on local unions in northern California, asking why some have innovated fully while others have not, and we expose the relation of tactical to organizational innovation. Here we also discuss differences among the locals' efforts to organize immigrants. Finally, we identify factors that help to explain both tactical and organizational innovation and discuss their implications for immigrant organizing.

Because it is local leaders and staff who decide to innovate and implement new tactics, variation occurs at the local level. Yet in-depth comparative analysis of particular locals is rare; most research takes as the unit of analysis either organizing campaigns (Bronfenbrenner 1993) or the International union (for an example of this as related to tactical innovation, see Delaney, Jarley, and Fiorito 1996). We took local unions as our unit of analysis. Our research strategy was to study both locals that have adopted labor's new tactical repertoire and those that have not, so we could discover through comparison what differentiates more and less innovative locals.

We began by consulting with labor leaders and labor scholars in northern California to find out which International unions active in the region had locals that were doing significant amounts of organizing, as only currently organizing locals might be using new tactics. Our informants identified three such unions: SEIU, HERE, and UFCW. We then focused on fourteen local affiliates of these International unions, first making sure that each International had both more and less innovative locals.

This approach of selecting our cases by initially identifying the relevant International unions had the advantage of allowing us to compare locals both within and among Internationals, so that we could better distinguish the features common to innovative locals. Our design also reduced some potentially confounding variation: because all our Internationals organize in the same sector of the economy and in the same region of the country, sectoral and regional variation cannot account for the differences we observed between more and less innovative locals.[1]

---

1. We conducted interviews of approximately two hours with union staffers and organizers in almost all the major northern California locals affiliated with SEIU, HERE, and UFCW, a total of fourteen locals. We conducted twenty-nine interviews in all, twenty-three of them with organizers and staff members. We also interviewed five people affiliated with other labor movement institutions (the South Bay Labor Council, the AFL-CIO Organizing Department, the AFL-CIO Organizing Institute, a building trades union, and a San Francisco labor law firm). The interviewees were chosen primarily because of their role within the organization, and also because of their tenure within the local. The first round of interviews was done in early 1997; we then carried out follow-up telephone interviews with most of our original interviewees in the locals during late 1997 and early 1998.

We also obtained extensive National Labor Relations Board (NLRB) data on organizing campaigns conducted by the locals we studied in the period 1985–95. In addition, we

Recent Tactical Innovations in the American Labor Movement

Some of the tactics unions have traditionally used to recruit new workers include organizing "hot shops" (firms where workers are enthusiastic about unionizing because of an immediate workplace grievance); focusing primarily on economic issues, especially wages and benefits; conducting top-down campaigns from union headquarters, with minimal participation by bargaining-unit members; reaching out to workers through gate leafleting, letters, and other kinds of nonpersonal contact; and dropping campaigns that did not develop quickly enough (Green and Tilly 1987; Perry 1987; Bronfenbrenner 1993). Recognition has usually been gained through the process established by the NLRB.

These tactics grew increasingly ineffective over time, as employers began aggressively to manipulate the NLRB election process and to hire anti-union consulting firms on a regular basis. Major economic transformations such as the decline in manufacturing employment also helped to undermine the potency of labor's traditional tactics. For the unions we studied, the rise of "big box" retail stores and the increasingly corporate ownership of hotels and medical services were also crucial changes in the environment.

Unions are now using a variety of tactics that emphasize worker participation, confrontation, pressure from arenas other than the worksite itself, and strategic planning (see *Labor Research Review* 17, 18, 20, and 21; Bronfenbrenner and Juravich 1994, 1998; Grabelsky and Hurd 1994; Brecher and Costello 1990; Johnston 1994; AFL-CIO 1985; Green and Tilly 1987). Here we describe four new types of tactics used in organizing campaigns: intensive worker organizing, corporate campaigns, strategic targeting, and obtaining union recognition without an NLRB election. Though not all of these tactics are new in absolute terms—many have historical precedents in 1930s labor organizing or in other social movements—they are new relative to most of the union organizing campaigns of the last forty years.

The first tactic is what Bronfenbrenner and Juravich call a "rank and file intensive strategy." This includes: creating worker committees; conducting house visits, in which organizers have significant face-to-face contact with workers; focusing on issues such as justice and dignity, rather than solely on economics; and promoting solidarity actions on the job, such as wearing union buttons or organizing groups of workers to "delegate" the boss (Bronfenbrenner and Juravich 1994). This approach en-

---

reviewed the local and labor press, as well as International and local union publications, for information on organizing drives and contract campaigns.

courages worker militancy as well as leadership development and worker empowerment. The committee structure is especially important: it should reflect the organization of the workplace and the demographic make-up of the workforce. The focus on direct contact and worker participation is a major contrast to the organizing model of the postwar era.

Another innovation is the corporate campaign (see *Labor Research Review* 1993; Perry 1987; Howley 1990), which includes tactics focused on expanding the arena of conflict beyond the point of production or service provision, where traditional campaigns have been centered. In corporate campaigns, unions do sophisticated research and financial analysis in order to find ways to attack the employer's image, profits, and ability to conduct business as usual; organizers describe this as "finding the Achilles' heel" of the company. For example, stockholders or potential lenders might be informed of financial problems with the company, or the union might publicize a company's regulatory violations related to consumer health and safety. In the arena of food service, for example, a "cockroach leaflet" gives stomach-turning information culled from USDA records. Unions may also attack secondary targets such as businesses that share members of the board of directors with the primary target, or subsidiary businesses of the main target. This tactic is especially effective when related companies have a higher public profile and are therefore more vulnerable to negative publicity. Sometimes unions also focus on officers or managers of the company, picketing their homes or targeting them in other jobs or public positions they hold.

Third, unions use strategic targeting to decide which businesses to organize. Rather than merely organize opportunistically at "hot shops," unions target particular employers because of their strategic importance in the industry, which is determined on the basis of size, location, or other characteristics such as their competition with unionized businesses. As one organizer told us, "We're actually trying not to do hot shops because a hot shop is hot today and cold tomorrow, and also it may not make sense. We're trying to organize an industry, not one shop" (Mark, HERE Local B).[2]

A fourth innovative tactic is to circumvent the NLRB electoral process, which our informants universally described as biased against unions. In the period before an election, employers often take advantage of their access to the workers to convince them to vote against the union, using a variety of coercive and/or persuasive measures. These range from hold-

2. To protect the confidentiality of our informants we have identified them by pseudonyms, and the locals are identified by letters rather than numbers. In a few cases, quotations are attributed to anonymous interviewees to further ensure confidentiality.

ing "captive audience meetings" (in which workers are shown videos of strikes and riots, or bags of groceries and automobiles that represent what their union dues could buy in a year) to raising wages and otherwise attempting to address workers' grievances. Furthermore, employers can file challenges to the bargaining unit, the workers' classifications, and other technical details, which can draw out an already lengthy process for months or years. Finally, NLRB penalties for unfair labor practices are very mild.

Given these weaknesses of the NLRB process, some unions attempt to obtain voluntary recognition from employers based solely on getting 50 percent plus one of the cards signed. This process is often accompanied by a neutrality agreement, in which the employer agrees not to wage an anti-union campaign. The agreement is usually secured by using whatever external leverage the union has with the company to pressure the employer, although sometimes worker pressure is also involved. As part of the non-NLRB strategy, some unions have held elections supervised by community groups or respected citizens. In using this tactic, unions not only avoid a process they consider stacked against them but gain leverage because employers are uncomfortable with an approach that they cannot manipulate as effectively (see Howley 1990).

Though card checks have long been a feature of the labor movement, and neutrality agreements have been used for many years by some unions, the combination of the two is new. Furthermore, the use of card checks in conjunction with other new tactics is "a strategy linked to action, and not just a deal with an employer. That it would be accompanied by worker actions, community actions, a whole corporate pressure campaign to push a company into neutrality, that's new" (Pamela, HERE IU). In addition, avoidance of the NLRB is often accompanied by other attempts to use labor law strategically. While organizers view the NLRB with skepticism, they will use the process to their advantage when they can, to cost the employer time and money and to generate negative publicity.

Unions are also currently using some traditional tactics in novel ways. For example, though they have always tried to garner the support of politicians, unions are now making new demands of public officials such as pressuring them for neutrality agreements in city-funded development projects. Another revitalized tactic is the boycott, which, although it has a long history in the labor movement, now appears in a more aggressive incarnation: rather than simply adding the firm's name to a boycott list, the union uses intensive industry research to find ways to pressure clients to respect the boycott. Direct actions also have a long history in the labor movement, but today unions are using civil disobedience more often, frequently with a major symbolic component designed to attract media attention. Finally, unions are creating coalitions with community groups around a variety of issues from health care to discrimination.

These tactics cover a broad range, from worker mobilization to corporate pressure to political and community appeals. Organizers stress the need to use multiple tactics simultaneously. As one organizer said:

> I always tell new organizers, when you look at a program and look at strategy, imagine a wall full of buttons, and you push until suddenly you're successful. And you don't know which ones to push. And the ones you push this time and that bring you success, are not the same ones that you push next time to bring you success. Different things cause people to react differently. (Scott, UFCW Local Z)

Another organizer explained that "the way to think about it is, how many guns can you point at someone and blow them away" (Michelle, HERE Local B). The idea is to pressure the target from as many directions as possible, and it may be impossible to discern which particular tactic is the final straw.

Our interviews and the limited literature on the subject show that though many unions use some innovative tactics, very few have adopted the entire collection of tactics described here. Only a few International unions have fully endorsed the new approach to organizing, and even their locals may continue to rely on old tactics or eschew new organizing altogether. Why, then, do some unions innovate while others do not, especially in the current, hostile climate?

Tactical Innovation and Organizational Change

Tactical innovation has gone hand in hand with innovative changes in local union organization: the locals that used the highest number of innovative tactics had also undergone significant internal organizational changes, without which it would have been impossible to adopt the new tactics.

We identified three types of locals. The first group, the full innovators, have all done significant organizing involving labor's new tactical repertoire and have innovated the most organizationally. The partial innovators, in contrast, have used only a few of the new tactics, and have changed little as organizations. A third group, the mandated innovators, are all currently engaged in comprehensive organizing campaigns, but they are just beginning to adopt the new repertoire and to reconstruct their organizations. In addition, their tactical and organizational innovations have come largely in response to pressures and encouragement from the International union.

Full Innovators

Five of the fourteen locals are full innovators: HERE locals A and B, and SEIU locals F, G, and H. Each has organized using strategic targeting, worker mobilization, non-NLRB recognition, civil disobedience, public pressure, and community alliances. The recent histories of these locals demonstrate that running major innovative campaigns is impossible without profound organizational change. When asked about new unionization tactics, our interviewees spontaneously discussed organizational as well as tactical innovation. All the locals in this group reported having established organizing departments with full-time directors, full-time researchers, and sizable staffs of full-time organizers. All recruited bilingual organizers who mirrored the racial and ethnic background of the workers being organized. And all of them instituted new programs to train current union members to do some of the tasks involved in organizing, as well as to handle some of their own problems on the shop floor.

The full innovators devote between 15 and 30 percent of their budgets to organizing, up from 2 or 3 percent before they adopted the new repertoire. To pay for organizers and researchers, these locals have either reduced the number of field representatives who handle members' grievances or required them to do substantial organizing as well. Whereas once the ratio of organizing staff to servicing staff was extremely lopsided in favor of servicing, today the ratio varies from a low of 1:2 to a high of 2:1. As a result, current members are receiving proportionately less servicing than they did in the past.

These resource shifts require major changes in the roles that members play in the union. Innovative organizing tactics rely on new levels of commitment, participation, and organization on the part of members, both to support organizing and to handle some of their own worksite problems. Members have been asked to endorse aggressive organizing programs in these locals, and they usually run the local's Executive Board, which allocates funds to organizing. They are also encouraged to do more of the hard work of organizing, including going on house calls, engaging in civil disobedience, identifying potential organizing targets, and conducting research.

These new demands have often been a major challenge because of members' fears about a possible decline in servicing. However, the fully innovating locals have tried to educate members about the importance of organizing to their own contracts and standard of living:

> [We] spent a lot of time with the executive board, we spend so much time with the membership.... [At] the annual leadership conference this year, the whole thing was on why we have to change, and a whole industry analysis of what's going on....And by that I mean they look at this, and they can come to no other conclusion. Where we don't build and organize new workers, we're all going down the tubes. So that's the biggest thing, is members seeing that it's in their best interest, direct interest, that we better organize.... So it's done by really being very logical, and thoughtful, and spending time figuring out how to present it so it's easy for folks to make a connection. (Steve, SEIU Local G)

In some cases, members have defined their self-interest as new organizing, and given it priority over traditional concerns such as increasing their own wages or benefits or augmenting their strike fund. In 1996, for example, HERE Local A members voted overwhelmingly (approximately 1,600 to 200) to put the two dollars each member paid every month for a strike fund into an organizing fund instead, despite the fact that they had recently experienced a major strike. All the full-innovator locals have also begun to train members to handle more grievances by themselves, by enlisting the aid of a shop steward rather than a field representative. Such reorganizing of tasks is key in being able to shift resources to organizing.

This change requires directly challenging the old mentality of servicing, in which membership dues are paid in exchange for a union staff that process grievances and take care of members' problems for them (like "an insurance agent," as one organizer put it). One organizer who had worked with both full and partial innovators said:

> [P]art of it is just the orientation that the members have. They have this culture that "we pay our dues, the local union hires representation staff, and therefore they take care of my needs. And therefore they file grievances for me." It's...a third-party mentality. It's "the union office will deal with worksite problems for me," as opposed to "we're the union here and we oughta be able to work out our problems directly with the supervisor." (Rosa, SEIU Local H)

Members can be very resistant to these changes, especially to pressures to become more active in the union. Diana, a staff member of the AFL-CIO Organizing Institute, summarized the problem: "The real challenge to an organizing local isn't about money or staff—it's about the members taking responsibility for their union again, and being like the front lines of the fight....And I think that's probably the biggest challenge...because we've lulled members in this country into thinking that the union is a service to them, not a force for change." One organizer described it this way:

> There's also a lot of resistance and a lot of pressure from the membership to do things the old way. They don't want to get involved, in large part, they don't want to have to take responsibility, they'd much rather have someone that comes in and takes care of their problems for them. And if...that's how they're used to having things done, if someone new comes in and says "no, you have to do it, you pay your dues, yeah, but *you* have to stand up to the boss, that's not my job," their initial reaction is, "Geez, service has just gone down the hill, now we have a union rep that has no backbone or that's a wimp or that won't stand up for us or take care of my problems, what do I pay my dues for?" So it's not just sort of laziness or complacency or conservatism on the part of the union staff, there is a real resistance that you have to fight through. (Mike, HERE Local B)

Staff resistance is another major obstacle to implementing organizational change. Field representatives, particularly those who have worked for many years for the union, fear losing power, or even losing their jobs, and having to do something they don't know how to do. Such change also means working harder and being more confrontational. One organizer said about staff members with whom she had worked:

> For most field reps, it scares them 'cause it means they have to give up a little power....I've had comments from local staff [who] say, "Well, if we train our shop stewards to be able to process grievances, what are we gonna do?"...[I]t means working differently. It also means...longer hours 'cause to build up an internal structure at a worksite, that's a lot of one on ones. You've really gotta know what your unit is like and know who the leaders are. And it's also doing a fight. Taking on the boss, where you may have kind of a decent relationship with the boss, right? So I think it's a real challenge. (Rosa, SEIU Local H)

The full innovators have often dealt with these problems by hiring staff from outside the rank and file, who often have little or no experience in the labor movement.

Of the three groups we are examining here, full-innovator locals have been most attentive to the needs of immigrant workers. They have organizing staffs that not only speak the language of the largest immigrant groups but are also of the same ethnic background. Many of these organizers were involved in community organizing among immigrants and people of color before joining the labor movement. Thus they have not only a deep understanding of immigrant concerns but also key network connections.

These elements translate into a greater attention to immigrant issues in organizing campaigns. Bilingual organizers are able to seek out immigrant workers and address their issues specifically. In addition, union meetings and publications, including organizing flyers, are conducted in or translated into the language of members and potential members. Themes of weekly pickets in one hotel organizing campaign included Cinco de Mayo and Day of the Dead, and involved cultural props such as a mariachi band. Picketers routinely chanted in Spanish.

Full-innovator locals are also sensitive to the increased sophistication of employer attacks on immigrant workers during organizing campaigns. Several of our interviewees told of employers hiring different immigrant groups in an effort to pit one group against another, as in the case of janitorial firms that are now hiring eastern European immigrants. Another interviewee told of a firm that now specializes in multilingual union busting. Another extremely common strategy is the manipulation of immigrants' possible undocumented status: employers threaten to review I-9 forms, to call the Immigration and Naturalization Service (INS), or to fire workers for presenting invalid social security numbers or other irregularities. Many of these tactics violate antidiscrimination laws, but the vulnerability of undocumented immigrants often prevents them from fighting back.

Full innovators deliberately frame their campaigns as responding to the needs of immigrant workers. For example, when in the course of the Justice for Janitors campaign in San Jose 110 (out of 170) Latino workers were dismissed as a result of INS scrutiny of employment records, the local in charge of the campaign organized demonstrations protesting the dismissals as racist and anti-Latino. This kind of framing has two advantages. First, it builds on ethnic ties to promote solidarity within the immigrant group. Second, it attracts support from groups that might not support a campaign framed only in terms of labor rights. One of our interviewees described the companies being targeted in San Jose: "The high-tech community...doesn't care at all if they're perceived as being anti-union but really cares if they're seen as being...racist [and] anti-Latino" (Julie, SEIU Local F). Other interviewees pointed out that many progressive politicians and community groups care more about racial and immigrant discrimination than about anti-unionism.

The immigrant organizing campaigns of the full innovators demonstrate the tactical flexibility and perseverance characteristic of their campaigns generally, which integrate immigrant-oriented tactics into the repertoire outlined earlier. For example, during one bitter hotel organizing drive, one of the full-innovator locals used almost every new tactic, including worker rallies, direct actions that led to arrests, a boycott, and a corporate campaign that involved shareholder pressure, in conjunction with immigrant-oriented strategies. At the time of the interview, another full-innovator local had been locked in battle since 1994 with an intransigent anti-union hotel; the union framed the campaign in terms of immigrant rights, particularly after the employer fired fifteen immigrant workers for having invalid social security numbers in 1996. Though short-term success appeared elusive, the local continued to devote many resources to the campaign, including placing substantial political pressure on the city council and organizing frequent direct actions to undermine the business. Why? To cost the company "a hell of a lot of money" and put it out of business so that other employers won't try similar tactics.

In sum, fully innovating locals are more likely than others to try to organize immigrant workers and to develop multidimensional campaigns for doing so. Yet these locals are not engaged in drives to organize immigrants per se. Rather, they target particular shops primarily for strategic reasons and then try to respond to those specific workers' issues and situations. One organizer explained:

> Maybe we're a little bit opportunist about it. But I know that when I'm talking to Latinos I say "It's the Latinos, it's Latino hotel workers," because those are all the Latinos they know. They all hang out, all their friends are janitors, landscapers, hotel and restaurant workers...or clean private homes. So there is a work-based thing that's subsumed under that. If I'm talking to a white banquet server, I say "They're robbing the banquet people at the [hotel], you talk to me about how they reduced your corkage fee, well, let's break down what the pool tip is." It's another hotel worker, it's another union member. If it works that it's a woman, if it's, I feel, someone who's got some big feminist consciousness about it, then I use that. I mean I kind of use whatever works. (Linda, HERE Local B)

Partial Innovators

Six of the fourteen locals are partial innovators. They include HERE locals C, D, and E, and UFCW locals X, Y, and Z. All these locals report an increased emphasis on organizing new workers over the past few years. All have launched more organizing campaigns than they had previously, and all have experimented tactically. However, none of the locals in this group has initiated and carried out a comprehensive organizing campaign.[3] Instead, they have adopted a few of the new tactics and combined these with more traditional strategies.

Partial-innovator locals tend to engage in "hot-shop" campaigns rather than strategically target their organizing. As one organizer said, "We basically take on anything" (Milo, SEIU Local X). Some of the interviewees recognized this lack of targeting as a problem, but only one has begun to formulate the kind of strategic plan for organizing that has enabled the full innovators to resist the temptation to pursue hot shops.

The partial innovators have also made many fewer organizational changes. They have smaller organizing departments than the full innovators, with ratios of organizers to field representatives ranging from a low of 1:6 to a high of slightly over 1:4.[4] With one exception, they do not hire researchers, and the majority have no organizing director.

Having shifted fewer staff from servicing to organizing, these locals have fewer resources for organizing. As we have seen, one of the organizational changes the full innovators made to free up resources was to institute a shop steward program that trained stewards to handle more grievances. Some of the partial innovators have begun to do more such training, but their programs are far less developed than those of the full innovators. In some cases, union officials pointed out, contract language does not allow stewards to perform union activities, such as handling grievances, on the job.

Union culture also affects the possibility of reallocating tasks. Some union staff see handling grievances and other jobs as the work of the business agents, not the members; sometimes leaders are not sufficiently committed to organizing to devote more resources to it. Leaders also see political risks in having shop stewards handle grievances. They may fear jeopardizing their own power by delegating responsibility and bringing in new blood:

> I had been sent to a number of conferences and... they said you should put
> [stewards' language] in the contract, so I got to bring it back and sell it to
> not only the members but to the president of the local.... In these small lo-

3. We use the word "initiated" advisedly. Two of the locals at the time of the research were participating in strategically targeted, comprehensive organizing campaigns, but in both cases the initiative for the campaigns came from the International union, and International organizers are overseeing the campaigns.

4. One local is not figured in this calculation because it had just recently decided to allocate a much larger proportion of its staff to organizing. It is not yet clear how this reallocation will change the local's use of tactics or organizational structure. Our guess is that before this reallocation, this local would have had an organizer-to-field-rep ratio at the high end of this range.

cals, you get elected to this job, and it's every three years, and after a while you don't feel like going back and tending bar anymore. Well, you start bringing in real sharp young people [as stewards]. And [the officers] say, "wait a minute, they might want my job." So I think that's one of the reasons it's kind of slow to change some of this stuff. (Peter, HERE Local C)

Some organizers in partially innovating locals would like the union to make the kind of resource shifts and other changes that full innovators have made, but the political and cultural resistance is too strong. "We plan to activate our stewards and get them to be doing more stuff, but I don't see them handling grievances. That is not our philosophy. I mean, it is mine...I've been pushing it for years, but the predominant feeling at least in California locals [of this union] is that business agents handle grievances, not the members" (Bob, UFCW Local Y). An organizer in another partial-innovator local expressed a similar sentiment: "Right now, I couldn't get this president to hire anybody from the outside. I mean even though he professes an interest in organizing, and he actually does have more of an interest in organizing than his predecessor, it's still not something to go into the red because of....Even though if I was president, we would be in the red to organize" (Anonymous).

Only one of the locals in this group has begun to formulate a program to train current members to take more responsibility for organizing new members. The majority of interviewees seemed to think member mobilization was a worthy goal but had made few concrete efforts to accomplish it. One organizer went so far as to say that although he has tried to mobilize his members to support other unions' campaigns, he would only try to mobilize members on his own organizing drives as a last resort.

Some of the partial-innovator locals are trying to organize immigrant workers, and a few have run successful campaigns. In general, though, organizational roadblocks have prevented them from adding ethnically diverse staff and from engaging in the kinds of strategic, multifaceted campaigns developed by the fully-innovating locals. Unions that have not changed their staffing patterns have not been able to hire organizers, or even business agents, who are capable of responding to the immigrant workforce. Typical of the partial-innovator locals, HERE Local C has an all-white staff, none of whom speaks the languages of the major immigrant groups. An older staff member we interviewed recognized this as a problem but said that it couldn't be changed unless "somebody dies, or quits, or something" (Peter, HERE Local C). Later he indicated that he would like to get some of the immigrant workers more involved in the union as stewards: "then if everything works out they will be the next generation of officers and *we'll* just turn it over to *them*" (emphasis added). Even when pressed, though, he had no vision of how this change might be accomplished, illustrating how organizational inertia is a substantial impediment to immigrant organizing. Such older staff members not only lack the skills to deal with immigrants but also can manifest unconscious racism, as in the case of one interviewee who described racial conflict in one workplace as "Spanish against Orientals, basically." One of our informants also mentioned more overt racism among business agents.

The partial innovators' occasional forays into organizing immigrants highlight both the learning they have done in this area as well as the organizational obstacles to sustained success. One UFCW local's membership is largely in the retail grocery business, but two years ago it organized a factory of sixty Latino workers who made biscotti cookies. The factory was a hot shop; one disgruntled worker had a cousin in the local who put him in touch with the union. The local successfully organized the factory through an NLRB election, using a Spanish-speaking member-organizer and Spanish-speaking representatives from other locals to communicate with the workers. And when one of the workers got in hot water because his social security number came up differently on his payroll form from his application form, the local immediately took him to an immigration attorney and paid the fee. The union also negotiated a clause addressing immigration rights in the first contract. (Soon after, however, the factory shut down local operations, in the face of which all the union could do was negotiate a severance package.)

That organizing drive changed the thinking of the local staffer we interviewed. Recognizing that many of the members of the local are undocumented, he began to wonder, "Why don't we have...immigration language...in every contract?" (Scott, UFCW Local Z). He also began to see the need for culturally sensitive organizing techniques, realizing that "Hispanics tend to do things as families. Therefore children come [and] you better have doughnuts and cokes, and a place for the kids to sit and color, and whatever." Reflecting on the campaign, the organizer added, "The thing about organizing, it challenges you...and then it challenges you to do more of whatever it was you stumbled upon." The next time this local faces immigrant workers, it should be better able to approach them appropriately. However, the experience with the biscotti factory had not at the time of the interview inspired the local to hire an organizer from the immigrant community. Nor had the local begun to target its organizing drives strategically. Such initiatives would require organizational changes that the local has thus far avoided.

Recent efforts by another partial-innovator local further illustrate the organizational obstacles that hinder successful immigrant organizing as well as the learning that can take place in immigrant campaigns. UFCW Local Y considers the retail grocery business its base constituency, and it currently represents 90 percent of the workers in this area. However, this figure is less than the 98 or 99 percent it once was, largely because several new stores have opened to serve the large Vietnamese population in the county. The decision to target this newer sector of the grocery industry was a strategic one, which also entailed the organization of immigrants. Toward this end, two years ago the local hired a Vietnamese woman who was a former English teacher. The local got a surprise, however, when it discovered that although the markets' clientele and some of their workers are Vietnamese, the majority of the workers are Chinese, as are the owners. At the time of the interview, the local had held and lost NLRB elections in two of the markets. They are currently looking for a Chinese organizer, but, having hired one organizer from outside the rank and file, this time around they want to find a union member to train as a temporary organizer.

This local has no research department, and one wonders whether they would have misidentified the ethnicity of the workforce and ownership of the markets if they had. On the other hand, hiring the Vietnamese organizer did lead the local to broaden its organizing outlook. At the time of the interview it was engaged in a campaign involving primarily immigrant workers that resulted from a Vietnamese worker's contacting the local after hearing the organizer's radio show. So the local is paying more attention to immigrant workers. The company in question, however, is not in a strategic industry for the local, but is basically a hot shop.

A third UFCW partial-innovator local has also been learning about immigrant workers in some of its recent campaigns. In one campaign, twenty-four of forty workers at a fish processing plant, mostly recent immigrants, were fired as part of an anti-union drive, and the local made contact with immigrants' rights organizations as it began to frame the campaign as one of immigrant rights. Yet this local was not strategically targeting employers; as the organizer said, "We go after anything." The fish processing plant was a hot shop, born of organizer leafleting in the area. Until this local begins to target particular segments of the industry it is unlikely to incorporate immigrant workers successfully.

In short, several of these locals have begun to realize the importance of immigrant workers either in their existing membership or in the pool of potentially organizable workers, and they have made some changes in how they think about organizing immigrants. But partially innovating locals have been less able than the fully innovating locals to make the kind of organizational and cultural changes necessary to devise successful immigrant organizing campaigns—just as they have been less successful in organizing native-born workers.

Mandated Innovators

We characterize three of the locals in our sample as mandated innovators; all three are locals of SEIU (Locals P, Q, and R). All of them have recently planned innovative organizing campaigns and have begun to institute organizational changes by hiring organizing directors and staff and creating member organizing programs. In contrast with the full innovators, these SEIU locals have made these changes in response to a recent mandate of the International union requiring locals to increase resources spent on organizing (to 10 percent in 1996, 15 percent in 1997, and 20 percent in 1998), establish organizing departments, create strategic organizing plans, and implement member organizing programs. One organizer said of her local, "There's never been a lot of money dedicated to organizing. And this past year, the International Union...has set some standards....And so we're taking a huge jump in terms of the amount of money that we're putting into organizing, and we're starting from scratch, pretty much" (Donna, SEIU Local P).

Although most of the workers represented by these locals are professional and semiprofessional public sector workers, some have recently branched out into organizing lower-paid immigrants. Following the lead of the International and the more advanced locals, these locals are beginning to attend to the cultural and language needs of immigrants, as well as to the potential abuses to which employers can subject them.

For example, Local R organized Latino immigrant workers at a cafe at a prestigious local university to add to the maintenance workers it already represented there. When the university demanded that the union include the high-turnover student workers, most of whom were white, in the bargaining unit, the union developed the innovative tactic of bringing the Latino workers and their families to the residences of the students to explain why the union was important to them. Thus the students, who otherwise might not have voted or voted against the union, came out in favor of the union and the local won the election.

Another example is the home health care campaign coordinated by the SEIU International and involving both mandated- and full-innovator locals. As they confront the monumental task of organizing thousands of dispersed, very low-wage, often immigrant workers in several Bay Area counties, organizers in all participating locals have used immigrant-sensitive tactics such as bilingual organizers and multilingual materials (including the election ballot). The organizing drive has provided an opportunity for the mandated innovators, less experienced with immigrant workers than the full innovators in the campaign, to learn about innovative strategies in general and immigrant organizing in particular.

In sum, the partial and mandated innovators have begun to adopt some of labor's new tactics and have made some organizational changes. But they have not yet been able to make the kind of organizational shifts the full innovators have, and consequently have not been able to adopt the full tactical repertoire. Why did the full innovators make the necessary organizational changes, while the partial and mandated innovators did not?

Differences between Full and Partial Innovators

We found that three factors *in conjunction* distinguish the full innovators from the others: the experience of a crisis and the interpretation of that crisis as serious enough to require change; support from the International union (IU); and the presence in the local of organizers with social movement experience outside labor. Any one of these factors alone was not enough to spur full innovation; only in combination do they explain the difference between full and partial innovators. In the case of the mandated innovators, the absence of these factors explains the lack of innovation prior to the IU mandate.

Crisis

The labor movement has been in decline for many years, and beginning in the 1980s most of the locals we studied lost members and negotiating power. These crises are often especially important in stimulating immigrant organizing because in some industries, such as building services, the decline of unionization has precipitated an increase in the proportion of immigrants working in the industry. By the same token, unions that have not experienced crises of membership, such as the UFCW's grocery sector or SEIU's public sector, tend to have fewer immigrant workers in their jurisdictions. Almost all our interviewees, whether in full- or partial-innovator locals, talked about this larger crisis in the labor movement as providing an impetus to organize. But for some this crisis was interpreted as an imperative to make more substantive organizational and tactical innovations, and for others it was not. Why?

First, the objective crisis may actually have been worse in the unions that innovated fully. As one HERE staff member noted:

> Y'know, we fell harder than some other unions, and we've been driven harder and faster into changing. I mean [another union has] twenty thousand members and we've got two thousand, so we think nothing of going out to [demonstrate at a hotel] every Friday night. We're pretty driven to do that. I don't know, if you were sitting on top of twenty thousand members maybe you'd feel okay...you just might not be driven to go picket. (Pamela, HERE IU)

Diana, staff member at the AFL-CIO Organizing Institute, had this view:

> I think everyone has had enough problems that they should have opened the doors [to change] long before now, but some unions have been able to maintain a budget, their treasuries, their staff, and whatever, and usually when they have to start laying people off or when jobs are threatened, *then* it does provoke some kind of a crisis, when the dues base [generating revenue] really drops.

Conversely, locals that were still having some success in negotiating contracts were less likely to innovate fully. For example, an organizer from a partial-innovator local admitted, "We have been somewhat of a— not a sleeping giant, but a giant that maybe dozed off a little bit, because we never have to worry about market share" (Scott, UFCW Local Z). Another organizer for a partial-innovator local that resulted from a merger of several locals attributes his own interest in organizing to his experience of decline in his original local: "I always saw the need for it, especially having been president of this local that took such a drastic cut in members so quickly" (Milo, UFCW Local X). This organizer was relatively isolated in his vision of the importance of organizing, however, as others in the merged local had not had the same experience.

Second, in conjunction with problems of declining membership numbers and contract quality, there were often internal crises in the locals that became full innovators. In HERE Locals A and B, problems within the local (in one, a disastrous strike, and in another, mismanagement) gave rise to new leadership that was more committed to organizing. Locals that were temporarily taken over by the International union or placed under "trusteeship," usually because of internal problems (including four full-innovator locals and one HERE partial-innovator local), also experienced organizational shake-ups that facilitated innovation. A former SEIU organizer described the freedom the International had to implement experimental strategies in the building services:

> [I]n some of the locals, especially when they started [Justice for Janitors], there [was] this willingness to experiment in an industry that they had lost and was an embarrassment to them, right, and so they had nothing to lose 'cause it was gone, and the contracts and the members were already so embittered in a lot of these places that whatever they did was gonna be an improvement, right? So in some places it's just gotten so bad, and that's the way it was in building service in the mid-eighties in some places, including here. (Diana)

An organizer from SEIU's building services local described the implications of this transition for greater integration of immigrant members:

> [Before the trusteeship], those were, at least from what I hear—I wasn't here then—but much more of kind of the old school locals, you know, just entrenched leadership that didn't represent the workforce, that couldn't speak Spanish, that was just kind of holding onto this dying thing. So there was that real housecleaning when [the new local president] came in...he came in first as a trustee and then was elected president. That laid the groundwork for doing this kind of organizing.... [He] is very strategic and has a clear understanding of this industry and what that takes, and he saw that this was the way to go. He had tried to make some of these changes earlier on and been unsuccessful. So he was really, I think, important in that and also having the International support for what was at that time a pretty small local....I don't think the campaign, the organizing could have happened, without both those things. (Julie, SEIU Local F)

Another SEIU organizer echoed these comments, adding that the stronger public sector and health care locals did not innovate until after the building services locals. Other organizers from SEIU and HERE confirmed the idea that trusteeship led to organizational change, both because it removed political obstacles to devoting major resources to organizing (Steve, SEIU Local G) and because the staff brought in to trustee the local from the IU was likely to be committed to organizing already (Charles, HERE Local D). This latter point brings us to another major factor in facilitating the adoption of the model: the influence of the International union.

International Union Influence

In three of the four full-innovator locals, the IU played a major role in facilitating tactical and organizational changes. These changes occurred in several ways, including IU placement of people with a commitment to organizing in locals under trusteeship; IU organizers and/or financial resources given to locals that were organizing; and an IU mandate to allocate resources to organizing.

Of the three International unions we looked at, SEIU is the most institutionally committed to organizing, and it has now mandated that all its locals develop an organizing program. The IU itself is now directing 45 percent of its resources to organizing and has been actively promoting a model of militant organizing longer than most other unions. For many years the International regularly sent its own organizers to locals to lead organizing drives, as well as to direct national campaigns, as was the case in Justice for Janitors. SEIU local G, a full innovator, participated in the IU-designed Dignity campaign in nursing homes across the country in 1994–96, and as we have mentioned, several Bay Area locals are involved in the current effort sponsored by the International SEIU to organize home health care workers in California. The International has also had a training program for organizers since the early 1980s. International union organizers are often sent in to help start organizing programs, and to show the locals that they can be successful:

> I worked for the International and I was one of those folks. [At one local], I worked with them to develop and organize; [at another local], I worked with them to get up an organizing program, get involved. So there was a big emphasis and we would go back and have our meetings and talk about which locals had our program, how to get them on the program, and what we could do to help. Part of it was just going in and doing campaigns and winning and saying it can be done, and part of it was engaging in the political conversations. (Josh, SEIU Local R)

HERE has not implemented nationwide campaigns in this way, nor has the IU mandated organizing to the same extent. However, HERE is directing increasing numbers of resources to locals that organize, and the IU did provide major support to intensive organizing in Las Vegas, with extraordinary success. In the HERE IU the strategic model seems to have been diffused largely through individual leaders. Interviewees describe a genealogy of organizing leaders beginning with Vincent Sirabella, who became president of the New Haven local beginning in 1957 and later organizing director for the International. In the 1970s in New Haven, he began to recruit staff from outside the union, and in 1985 he started a program of sending IU organizers to different cities (Shostak 1991, 60–61; Hurd 1986). The model was then diffused, through the 1984–85 Yale strike, to a new generation of leaders such as John Wilhelm, who had come into the union through Sirabella's recruiting program and went on to train many organizers who are now in locals, including Local B. The International as a whole is now beginning to endorse strategic organizing (symbolized by Wilhelm's recent ascension to the presidency of the union); it has always supported some organizing, but up to now it has been the locals connected to people in the more progressive sector of the International that have used a strategic approach.

The UFCW IU began to pay more attention to organizing in the wake of major loss of market share in the Midwest in the mid-1980s. In 1994 they instituted the Special Projects Union Representative (SPUR) program, in which the IU pays the expenses of member organizers temporarily taken off their regular jobs. One staff organizer said, "There's a big, big push coming down.... They have placed more of an emphasis on [organizing] in recent years, because we see our market share eroding" (Bob, Local Y). Furthermore, the former organizing director is now the IU president, which at least two interviewees saw as favorable to organizing. Yet the initiative seems to rest primarily with the locals: "They [the IU] do a lot of, 'if you show me you're gonna do something, I'll match you' " (Milo, UFCW Local X). And this program seems less comprehensive than SEIU's, nor do there appear to have been particular leaders who strongly influenced organizing (at least not in the Bay Area) as there were in HERE.

Overall, IU leadership has been critical in leading to full innovation as well as in disseminating the strategic model among locals that have not yet implemented it.[5] Much of the change in locals was supported, if not initiated, by the IUs; this process has not been one of bottom-up local in-

---

5. Interviewees from both full- and partial-innovator locals pointed out some drawbacks to IU involvement in organizing. First, it can engender conflict between the International and the local staff, whom some organizers characterize as feeling threatened by the arrival of IU organizers. Conflicts can also arise when IU organizers are sent into locals where there is no significant commitment to organizing or where the philosophy of organizing is different, and the outcome of these kinds of conflicts then affects the internal politics of the union. Furthermore, locals can become dependent on outside organizers and focus solely on servicing the membership. Some interviewees cited this problem as part of the reason HERE and especially SEIU have begun to encourage locals to develop organizing. However, the IU clearly has the ability to influence locals' choice to give priority to organizing and to influence the strategy they choose.

novation that later reached the top echelons of the bureaucracy. Rather, progressive sectors of the IU exerted influence over locals in crisis, leading to full innovation. Later the IU as a whole, at least in HERE and SEIU, began to endorse a strategic organizing approach. The question then arises of where these progressive sectors of the IUs came from, which brings us to the final factor that has influenced full innovation: individual innovators, in both locals and Internationals.

Individual Innovators, Outside Experience, and Cultural Change

The third major factor in full innovation is the presence of individual leaders who interpreted the crisis as a mandate to change, initiated the changes in union culture, and rearticulated the union's mission. Although notably absent from the literature on union innovation, these individuals, particularly those with activist experience outside the labor movement, were indispensable to the process of innovation because they were less caught up in traditional models of unionism and had experience with alternative models of mobilization.

In all the locals we identify as full innovators, organizers working both for the IU and for the local have participated in other kinds of social activism, which contributed to their more militant vision of how to build union power. Many of the older people interviewed (those over forty) and other major figures in their local unions had a background in community or welfare rights organizing, particularly with the Association of Community Organizations for Reform Now (ACORN) and the United Farm Workers (UFW).[6] One organizer said of the worker-centered approach to organizing that he and several colleagues implemented at HERE Local A:

> We didn't know any different. We all came out of the Farm Workers. [Another organizer] had had a lot of experience.... And actually he and I had met in 1975 working on the boycott. And [another organizer] and I met in 1976 working on the boycott. So we were all UFW—there's lots of old UFW mafia in the labor movement.... So the idea of, like, "if you're gonna win, you're gonna involve workers"...we never thought there was any other way to do it. (Paul, HERE Local A)

Many key leaders in the IUs also came out of other kinds of activism. John Wilhelm was involved in Students for a Democratic Society (SDS); Steven Lerner, the architect of the Justice for Janitors strategy, worked originally

---

6. Though the UFW is, of course, a labor organization, it has always used different strategies and tactics than the more institutionalized industrial and service unions.

for the UFW; Andy Stern, the current SEIU president, was active in the student movement of the 1960s. One labor lawyer we interviewed argued that the strategy of corporate analysis has roots in the antiwar movement. Asked what differentiated unions that had innovated fully from those that had not, one HERE organizer replied:

> I would say a big part of it is a lot of activists from the '60s got into—SEIU definitely. A lot of SEIU people are either '60s activists, there's a huge pile of 'em that come out of ACORN, there's a pile of them that come out of other [organizations]....So a lot of people that plugged into SEIU, I mean a lot of the people that Sweeney brought in—I mean maybe similar to John Lewis saying "let's bring in the Communists 'cause they know how to organize"—I think SEIU realized that let's bring in these activists who were involved in the civil rights movement, the antiwar movement...who were involved in some sort of, not necessarily sectarian organization, but in some sort of political organization, some sort of socialist organization, even, who are actively committed to building the union movement, and have some new ideas about how to do that, and will use the strategies developed in the civil rights movement, and the welfare rights organizations, the women's rights movement, all these different organizations, and get them plugged in and involved....And where unions have done that, there's been more militancy. (Mike, HERE Local B)

The upcoming generation of younger organizers (in their twenties and early thirties) have also had experience with ACORN or with student activism, particularly in Central American solidarity groups and anti-apartheid struggles on college campuses. Many of them are college-educated, and for some, campus activism has been crucial to their development. Thus there are two types of experience, related to age: that of organizing and political activism of the 1960s and 1970s, and that of the campus activism and identity politics in the 1980s and 1990s. Organizers in both groups have backgrounds in community organizing, and some identified this experience as the source of both their skills and their organizing philosophy.

Immigrant organizers, too, have often had community organizing or political experience in their home countries or in the United States. One organizer from a mandated-innovator local had done community organizing in the Philippines, for example; another HERE organizer had been active in political causes in Mexico before coming to study in the United States. A Vietnamese organizer with a full innovator had immigrated as a young refugee and became active in community activism in San Francisco before joining the union's staff.

Many of the full innovators, then, recruited staff from outside the rank and file, often as part of an effort to create an organizing staff that mirrors the demographics of the membership or targeted workers, particularly in terms of language and ethnic diversity. However, some fully-innovating locals are now concerned that they do not have enough organizers from the rank and file, particularly as they begin to emphasize the role of members in organizing, and are trying to hire more of them.

In contrast, the partial innovators have few organizers from outside the labor movement. HERE Local D has all rank-and-file organizers (all of whom also serve as business agents), as does Local C—with the exception of the IU organizers who are working on a particular campaign. UFCW locals have not hired many people with other activist experiences, either, although some UFCW organizers claim to see this as desirable, in part because of the IU's SPUR program (taking members off their jobs to work for the union). It may also be due to continuing resistance to hiring from the outside. One interviewee described how an organizer from outside the rank and file had been met with suspicion in the local: "And he came on board and just one of those things, he just was always doing so much more work than we paid him for, and he was really into it, and scared the shit out of the other people in the local. 'How come he's doin' all this stuff for free? There must be somethin' wrong with him! What's his agenda?' "

All the mandated locals, on the other hand, now have organizers from outside the labor movement, many of whom originally worked for the International. However, these organizers had been hired very recently at the time of the interviews.

Conclusion

The analysis reported here highlights the organizational embeddedness of labor's new tactical repertoire. In the locals we studied, a combination of three things had to occur for locals to become full innovators: they experienced a crisis and interpreted it as serious enough to necessitate change, they received support from the International union, and they had organizers with experience in other social movements.

Though crisis in local unions was often accompanied by an influx of immigrants into union jurisdictions, our research indicates that successful organizing of *all* types of workers depends on the union's ability both to take workers' specific needs into account and to design strategic organizing campaigns, which in turn requires significant organizational and tactical change. Ultimately, successful organizing of immigrant workers is not different in principle from organizing any workers. Unions must appeal to all workers on the basis of their particular needs, taking account of their different interests and life situations. Women and minority workers, like immigrants, may be discriminated against on the job; young, countercultural workers may require a culturally sensitive response from the union as much as immigrant workers do.

One difference among the unions we looked at was the degree of choice they had about whether to target industries in which many immigrants are employed. The HERE locals and the SEIU building services locals have no choice about organizing immigrants, who make up a large percentage of workers within the industry. SEIU health care locals and UFCW, on the other hand, can choose to focus on areas in which there are immigrant workers or not. Unions that choose to do strategic targeting of immigrants, or that are forced to, should hire organizers who are immigrants themselves or have the language skills needed to deal with immigrants. They must be sensitive to the dangers that confront immigrants, especially undocumented ones who choose to stand up to their employers, and take measures to protect them.

What are the implications of our findings for locals that have not yet innovated completely? How might locals go about organizing immigrants and other workers more strategically? Any predictions about future innovation are largely speculative, but the experiences of the full innovators are suggestive.

As far as local unions are concerned, the most important step is to make organizational changes within the local. They need to create full-time organizer positions and organizing departments, and to allocate resources to organizing. They need to find trained organizers who are able to analyze targets and come up with creative strategies, and who speak the language of the people they are trying to organize. One possibility is borrowing organizers from other locals or the International to help get organizing programs started and train new organizers. Also, hiring organizers with experience in other movements can bring in new strategies and tactics. Hiring or gaining access to researchers is also important for the local's ability to choose strategic targets and find a variety of ways to pressure those targets. Finally, getting members involved both in organizing new workers and in taking on more responsibility on the job is essential.

As we have seen, these shifts are not always easy to make, because they may mean eliminating field rep positions and/or training workers to take on more of their own representation, both of which can be politically difficult. This transition may be harder in locals that have not experienced the three factors that lead to full innovation (crisis, IU support, and outside innovators). The absence of crisis and the presence of traditional staff may make for greater resistance to change. Our interviews indicate that getting support from members for shifting the local's priorities from servicing to organizing, including dedicating funds to that end, is key. Thus staff and member education efforts are an integral part of a transition to organizing.

The AFL-CIO's recent call to organize is also likely to lead to the expansion of new tactics, although the organization has no power to force unions to change. The AFL-CIO's endorsement of the strategic model does suggest that cultural expectations within the labor movement are shifting, and that unions that do not innovate will be held in lower regard as innovation becomes more widespread. One organizer who faced resistance in his local said of the AFL-CIO shift:

> I think it's the greatest thing to happen in a long time. Because even though to some people it's penetrating very slowly, it's there. And it's a constant bug up their ass that this is something you know you should do, and if you don't remember we're gonna remind you. And if they don't remind him I'm gonna remind him. And I'm gonna constantly pound on you about the thirty percent [of resources that should be devoted to organizing]. And if you don't hear it from me, you're gonna hear it from Sweeney. (Milo, UFCW Local X)

The increase in the numbers of organizations pursuing a strategic model and restructuring themselves accordingly may also lead to greater legitimacy and therefore to greater dissemination of the model (Minkoff 1994).

In some cases, organizers in less innovative locals can learn from locals that have already made changes. Several of our interviewees remarked that earlier-innovating locals provided a model for them, and some organizers mentioned staying informed about other locals' campaigns in order to see how they might apply innovative models to their own organizing. Locals that have already made organizational changes may be able to mentor other locals in the same International that are making the shift to organizing.

Furthermore, new routes to gaining personnel will also probably encourage change. The training provided by the Organizing Institute, International unions, and other entities will presumably produce organizers and staff committed to the strategic model. As the demand for organizers and their prestige within the local increase, more people will become interested in entering the field.

There is a danger that unions will adopt the rhetoric of innovation without making concrete organizational and tactical changes, or without making them completely. As Bronfenbrenner and Juravich's research (1998) shows, some locals adopt a few tactics without using them comprehensively. Though locals may find it difficult to make all changes at once, it is important to think in terms of a model and to recognize the need for concrete organizational changes. Otherwise, locals run the risk that their new strategies will fail, and that innovators will become discouraged and stop organizing for good.

4

Immigration and Unionization in the San Francisco Hotel Industry

Miriam J. Wells

Through an in-depth study of the hotel and lodging industry in San Francisco and the union that represents the majority of its workers, Local 2 of the Hotel Employees and Restaurant Employees (HERE), this chapter explores the ways that immigrant incorporation has shaped the forms and outcomes of union mobilization.[1] The analysis focuses on three areas of impact—the processes of union organizing, the structures of union organizations, and the content of union contracts. Through it, I demonstrate that in certain contexts demographic change is fostering organizational change. In the case examined here and likely in comparable circumstances elsewhere, union practices and programs have been reshaped in order to reach and gain the support of immigrant workers.

1. The larger project on which this analysis is based explores the relations between unionization and globalization in the San Francisco hotel industry. This project has been funded by the National Science Foundation and the University of California, Davis. I am grateful to my interviewees for their generous sharing of experience and organizational records, to my research assistants Josh Aroner, Alyssa Kelly, and Laurel Edwards for their dedicated work, and to Karen Brodkin, Sanford Jacoby, and Ruth Milkman, who read and provided thoughtful critiques of the initial draft. The analysis here employs data from the 5 percent Public Use Microdata Sample gathered by the U.S. Bureau of the Census, and from the *Statistical Year Books* of the Immigration and Naturalization Service. It draws as well on sixty-three interviews of from one to four hours long conducted between October 1996 and May 1998 with hotel workers and managers, union staff, employers' association spokespersons, government officials, representatives of community and immigrant organizations, and the staff of several firms that do research on the hotel industry. Books and newspapers treating the hotel industry, globalization, ethnicity, and unionization were consulted, as were historical records housed in the San Francisco State University Labor Archives and Research Center, the San Francisco Public Library, and the Bancroft Library at the University of California, Berkeley.

The analysis proceeds by briefly describing Local 2; showing how the immigrant and ethnic/racial composition of San Francisco and of its hotel industry has changed in recent years; and examining the ways in which the immigrant composition of the workforce has affected the organizing approaches, organizational structure and practices, and contractual provisions of the union.

Union Mobilization in the San Francisco Hotel Industry

HERE Local 2 is a particularly interesting case, not only because its membership is exceptionally diverse, but also because it began conscious attempts to incorporate that diversity well ahead of the wider U.S. labor movement and because it has done so while maintaining a remarkable level of union density. As a result, its experience offers insight into the long-term processes and impacts of relatively successful immigrant inclusion.

Diversity in the San Francisco hotel workforce involves race, ethnicity, and nationality, as well as gender and occupation. Over the past thirty-five years, the industry's workforce has shifted from predominantly native-born and non-Hispanic white to overwhelmingly immigrant and minority. Moreover, in an effort to match the increased scale of hotel ownership and management with an aggregation of union influence, in 1975 the HERE International consolidated its five prior craft locals in the San Francisco hotel industry (cooks, bartenders, food servers, bellmen and room cleaners, and kitchen help) into Local 2, a single organization that represents them all. This merger drew all of the hotel crafts together within a single organization, and it brought to the organization's collective attention the historically unequal status and power of the different groups. In the same period the union underwent a transformation of organizational philosophy, one that challenged the bureaucratic, top-down, business-union principles which had dominated the HERE locals since before World War II and that encouraged more participatory, egalitarian principles emphasizing rank-and-file democracy and the surfacing of previously unheard voices.

These principles were purveyed especially by a set of activists who entered the industry in increasing numbers over the course of the 1970s as a base from which to organize. These included community leaders from San Francisco's Latino and Chinese communities, student activists from the wider Bay Area student movement, and organizers from the United Farm Workers. As a result of what union staff term this "left-radical presence," internal pressures to increase rank-and-file democracy intensified. They culminated in the 1978 ouster of Local 2 President Joseph Belardi, former president of the Cooks' Union and the effective head of San Francisco's hotel unions since the late 1940s. A new slate of leaders was elected with the express aim of involving women and immigrants and improving their status.[2] Together these changes deepened members' desire for a sharp break from the conciliatory, bureaucratic business unionism of the previous decades. On July 7, 1980, 94 percent of the members voted in favor of the industry's first strike since World War II. The union's key demands were an end to racial, ethnic, and gender discrimination in hiring and worker treatment; contract enforcement and the empowerment of shop stewards; an increase in wages, including particular pay hikes for "back-of-the-house" workers such as room cleaners and stewards; and work quotas and meals for room cleaners. The strike lasted five weeks and resulted in dramatic improvements in all of the key demand areas, including the highest wages for culinary workers in the country (Richmond 1981).

Not only does the scale of immigrant advent, or the duration and dynamism of attempted immigrant incorporation, make this case of special interest; so does the sustained vitality of Local 2 as an organization in the face of changes that have decimated many other local unions. Historically, the labor movement in San Francisco has been exceptionally strong and militant. From World War II into the mid-1980s its hotel and restaurant industries were overwhelmingly unionized (Cobble and Merrill 1994; Josephson 1956). Widely inclusive employer organizations represented large and small hotel owners and restaurant owners, and these regularly signed union contracts. Over the course of the 1980s, however, chains began to replace local owners and the largest hotel and restaurant employer organizations disbanded. In 1983 a disastrous strike gutted restaurant membership, and in 1984 a top-down agreement between the management of the newly opening Ramada Renaissance Hotel and several hotel unions, recognizing those unions as the exclusive bargaining representative of affected workers, was challenged in the courts and found unlawful.[3] This ruling eliminated the major means used previously

2. This commitment was reinforced by the influence of Vincent Sirabella, a representative of HERE International who was renowned for his dedication to organizing and who served as trustee and then close advisor to Local 2 from 1979 through the 1980s.
3. The contract violated the "Bernhard Altmann doctrine" established in 1961 in *International Ladies' Garment Workers' Union, AFL-CIO, v. National Labor Relations Board and Bernhard-Altmann, a Texas Corporation*, 81 Sup. Ct. 1603. In this ruling, the Supreme Court held that it was an unfair labor practice for an employer and a union to enter into an agreement recognizing the union as the exclusive bargaining representative of certain employees without a majority of them having authorized such representation. Although this practice had been unlawful since the 1961 ruling, it did not come under legal chal-

for preserving and expanding hotel union membership, and it forced the union to turn to bottom-up organizing. Increasingly, newly built and purchased hotels began to set up shop without union contracts, and the unionized proportion of the industry began to decline.

Faced with these circumstances, Local 2 responded with a concerted dedication of resources to organizing, consolidating its position as an early torchbearer of innovative unionism (see Sherman and Voss, this volume). In preparation for the August 1986 hotel contract negotiations, and with help from HERE International, newly elected Local 2 President Sherri Chiesa announced a "back-to-basics" campaign designed to build member involvement in every unionized hotel. This approach involved building union committees in every hotel craft and department. To facilitate this campaign, the local shifted the focus of hotel field representatives away from traditional grievance filing and bureaucratic follow-up toward forms of member servicing that build organization. To ensure that contracts continued to be enforced and member grievances heard, members were encouraged to take active roles in the initial stages of grievance identification and direct conflict resolution, thus freeing field representatives to operate as organizers. This approach generated a strong member showing and good contract results in 1986, and it has been elaborated and refined since. In 1989 Local 2 extended the approach to organize the workers in the city's major nonunion hotels: first the Parc 55 (formerly the Ramada Renaissance), where a contract was signed in 1993; subsequently the Marriott, where a collective bargaining agreement has been concluded but a contract is still in negotiation; and others. In January 1996, in recognition of the importance of organizing the unorganized and the tremendous dedication of time and resources required to do so, the membership voted overwhelmingly to change the bylaws in order to authorize moving $200,000 from the union's strike fund to create an organizing fund. It also directed the monthly two-dollar-per-member strike fund deduction to the organizing fund. This vote institutionalized a distribution of about one-third of the union's staff and financial resources to organizing—a commitment that is one of the largest in the country by a union of its size. At the present, Local 2 has collective bargaining agreements with fully 80 percent of the Class A hotels in the city, and its contracts set the standard for the local industry. Not only are

lenge in the San Francisco hotel industry until the mid 1980s, as the local hotel unions became increasingly militant and as hotel owners became larger and less rooted in the local context.

San Francisco hotel wages and benefits currently among the best in the country, but they have improved exponentially since the mid-1970s.

The Immigrant Transformation of San Francisco and Its Hotel Workforce

Over the past thirty years, San Francisco has shifted from a populace of primarily white native-born citizens to one that is primarily minority, noncitizen, and immigrant. Asian-Pacific Islanders and Hispanics have been the main contributors to this demographic transformation.[4] In the primacy of these two categories of recent immigrants, San Francisco is similar to other U.S. immigrant-receiving locales; but in their relative sizes and character, its immigrant population is distinctive. Like Los Angeles (see Waldinger and Bozorgmehr 1996), San Francisco experienced particular influxes of Southeast Asians in the aftermath of the Vietnam War in the late 1970s and early 1980s, and of Central Americans in the course of civil wars there in the 1980s and 1990s. Because immigrants tend to settle where their friends and relatives are located—a tendency enhanced by recent immigration laws that favor family reunification—groups with a long-standing presence in the area have expanded most. Particularly notable are the Chinese, who formed a thriving settlement in the city following the Gold Rush of the mid-nineteenth century; Filipinos, who began to settle there in the first decades of the twentieth century as they were first drawn into and then pushed out of California agriculture; and Salvadorans, who have had a substantial residential nucleus in San Francisco's Mission District since the 1930s.

Thus although fully 87 percent of San Franciscans were non-Hispanic whites in 1950, by 1990 this proportion had shrunk to 47 percent. Meanwhile, the Asian-Pacific Islander proportion quintupled from about 5 percent in 1950 to 29 percent in 1990, making San Francisco's Asian proportion almost three times that of Los Angeles. Almost two-thirds of San Francisco's Asians were Chinese in 1990 and almost one-fifth were Filipino. Meanwhile, the Hispanic proportion of the city's population more than tripled, from 3 percent in 1950 to about 13 percent in 1990. Unlike Los Angeles where over 90 percent of Hispanics are Mexican—and un-

4. "Asian-Pacific Islander" is the aggregate "Asian" category used by the U.S. Bureau of the Census; "Hispanic" is the term used for Spanish-speaking individuals. In this article, "Asian" and "API" will be used interchangeably with "Asian-Pacific Islander," and "Latino," the aggregate term preferred by immigrants from Latin America, will be used interchangeably with "Hispanic." The data presented here represent the Census's coverage of the City and County of San Francisco, which are coterminous.

like Miami and New York where many are from the Caribbean—San Francisco's Hispanics are about equally divided between Central Americans (38 percent) and Mexicans (40 percent), with relatively few Caribbeans.[5] The black proportion of San Franciscans has always been relatively small, although it increased up to 1980, then fell thereafter in accord with shifts in the local economy that moved many manufacturing jobs out of the city to the wider Bay Area (Potepan and Barbour 1996).

Even within the state that houses the largest proportion of the nation's foreign-born residents (see Lopez and Feliciano, this volume), San Francisco stands out for its vast immigrant presence. While only 5 percent of the city's residents were foreign-born in 1970 according to the U.S. Census, by 1990 34 percent were—a proportion comparable to that of Los Angeles (33 percent), and far greater than the national (8 percent) or even the state (22 percent) average. The immigrant influx is overwhelmingly composed of Asians and Hispanics, who accounted for 56 and 21 percent, respectively, of the city's foreign-born population in 1990. And whereas most whites and blacks in the city's population are native-born (84 percent and 96 percent, respectively, in 1990), Asian-Pacific Islanders and Hispanics are predominantly immigrant (69 and 57 percent respectively). San Francisco's hotel workforce has also been transfigured over the past thirty years, as immigrants have moved increasingly and unevenly into the industry's occupational hierarchy.

The Division of Labor in Hotels

San Francisco's recent immigrants are particularly concentrated in the service sector. Only about 18 percent of service workers in the city were immigrants in 1970, but by 1990 fully 55 percent were—the highest proportion of immigrants in any occupational sector. The hotel industry is notable within the service sector for the substantial size and fixed investment of each firm and the large number of workers and wide range of occupations engaged by each. Hotels have a pyramidal occupational structure, with a small proportion of managerial and administrative positions at the top and a large proportion of service positions at the bottom. "Front-of-the-house" jobs that involve regular interaction with guests (such as bellman, receptionist, and bartender) are ranked and paid more highly than are "back-of-the-house" jobs (dishwasher, room cleaner, and

5. Some scholars (Wallace 1986, 1989) and immigrant support groups believe that San Francisco's Central Americans may be more undocumented, and thus more undercounted, than the also heavily undocumented Mexican population. Thus the Central American proportion of San Francisco's Hispanics may be even greater than stated in the text.

janitor). Gender and color historically contribute to this ranking: white men generally occupy the most privileged positions and women of color the least. Different skills are also required in the front of the house, limiting mobility from the back to the front. Most important of these is the ability to communicate well in English; formal training, technical expertise, and middle-class demeanor are among the others. Within this pyramid, jobs are clustered by function. Housekeeping is the largest functional cluster with 27 percent of total employment in 1990; food service and food preparation are also substantial.

Functional clusters vary in their range of occupations and avenues for upward mobility. They also vary in the extent to which their labor processes require, encourage, and/or permit personal interaction and interdependency. These characteristics in turn shape the social relations among hotel workers. Thus a range of occupations are engaged in the kitchen—from dishwashers and food preparers to chefs, sous-chefs, and chefs' assistants. Some of these jobs require teamwork and establish relationships that could lead to promotion. For example, food preparers often work in groups or assembly lines to prepare food, and especially diligent preparers may be sponsored by chefs to become their assistants. Similarly, sous-chefs work closely with executive chefs, on whom their job retention and promotion are often dependent. In food service, waitpersons rely heavily on bussers, whose assistance may make the difference between receiving tips or not. As a result, many share their tips with bussers, and even sponsor them in their bids to become servers. Such occupations and functional divisions tend to involve complex linkages of friendship, trust, obligation, and dependency across occupational and ethnic group boundaries. In housekeeping, by contrast, the vast majority of employees are room cleaners who work alone to complete their tasks. Opportunities to socialize on the job are few and interoccupational mobility channels are limited. Thus workers in housekeeping are less likely to develop significant relationships or dependencies with individuals whom they did not previously know.

The Changing Hotel Workforce

San Francisco hotel workers have always been less white and more immigrant than the city's population as a whole, and this contrast has intensified over recent years. Overall, the white and black proportions of workers in the industry have shrunk, while the Asian-Pacific Islander and Hispanic proportions have exploded. Between 1970 and 1990 the proportion of non-Hispanic white hotel workers dropped from 60 to 34 percent and that of blacks from 16 to 6 percent. Meanwhile, the proportion

of Asians expanded from 12 to 36 percent and that of Hispanics from 12
to 23 percent.

Immigrants account for the bulk of this ethnic restructuring. The
proportion of immigrants in the hotel workforce increased from 22 percent in 1970 to fully 48 percent by 1990—14 percentage points more than
the immigrant share of San Francisco as a whole. As in the city, Asian-
Pacific Islanders and Hispanics are the most significant immigrant
groups. Between 1970 and 1990 the immigrant share of Asian hotel workers rose from 38 to 93 percent, and that of Hispanics rose from 59 percent to 84 percent. In contrast, black hotel workers received only a small
infusion of immigrants, and the immigrant share of whites was relatively
small and unchanging. Overall, 56 percent of the industry's immigrants
are Asian-Pacific Islanders and about 22 percent are Hispanic. Asians and
Hispanics are also significantly more immigrant-dominated in the industry than in the city, revealing the role of the industry as an entry point for
immigrants.

Table 4.1 provides a breakdown of the ethnic and racial composition
of the hotel industry relative to that of San Francisco as a whole. It shows
that the Chinese and Filipinos are the largest Asian nationality groups in
the industry and that Salvadorans are the largest Hispanic group. Overall,
the proportion of Central Americans in the industry is almost twice that
of Mexicans, while in the city the two groups are roughly equal. The table
also shows that the primarily native-born groups (whites and blacks) are
relatively more highly represented in the city, while the primarily immigrant groups (Asians and Hispanics) are more highly represented in the
industry. Moreover, nationality groups that in San Francisco contain a
larger proportion of more educated, affluent, and acculturated individuals, such as the Chinese and Japanese, are more highly represented in the
city than the industry, while groups with a higher proportion of recent
immigrants and overall lower economic and educational levels, such as
Southeast Asians, and especially Filipinos and Salvadorans, are more
highly represented in the industry.

Immigrants and Hotel Jobs

The U.S. Census data provide a detailed portrait of the changing distribution of ethnic and immigrant groups in hotel occupations. Immigrants increased in all job categories between 1970 and 1990, most particularly in
those carried out in the back of the house. Immigrants were already represented in back-of-the-house jobs in 1970, but by 1990 the proportion of
immigrants in such jobs had increased more than in other parts of the industry. Thus the immigrant share of cooks rose from 43 to 77 percent, that

Table 4.1. San Francisco hotel industry and city population by race and ethnicity, 1990.

	% of industry	% of city population
White (non-Hispanic)	**34.1**	**46.9**
Black	**6.1**	**10.7**
Asian-Pacific Islander	**35.6**	**28.5**
Chinese	14.7	17.5
Filipino	13.7	5.4
Japanese	0.3	1.5
Vietnamese	2.1	1.3
Cambodian / Laotian / Thai	0.9	0.5
Asian Indian	0.9	0.3
Korean	1.0	0.9
Indonesian	0.6	0.1
Other Asian-Pacific Islander	1.4	1.0
Hispanic	**22.9**	**13.3**
Mexican	6.6	5.2
Puerto Rican	0.5	0.6
Central American	12.7	5.0
Guatemalan	0.5	0.6
Salvadoran	9.0	2.7
Nicaraguan	2.0	1.4
Other Central American	1.2	0.3
South American	2.5	0.8
Other Hispanic	0.6	1.7
Other	**1.2**	**0.6**

of food preparers from 67 to 80 percent, and that of room cleaners from 15 to a striking 85 percent over this twenty-year period. Because room cleaners comprise about 27 percent of all hotel workers, they currently contribute the largest proportion of immigrant workers in the industry. However, immigrants are also more present in the front of the house than in the recent past. Whereas in 1970 only one-fourth of managers and receptionists, clerical workers, bartenders, and bellmen were foreign-born, by 1990 over one-third of managers and receptionists, almost one-half of bartenders, and about one-fourth of the rest were immigrants. Food servers and especially bussers (and also front-of-the house workers) were already largely immigrant in 1970 (46 and 29 percent respectively), but had become even more so by 1990 (50 and 83 percent respectively).

The Census data also document the changing ethnic composition of different job categories. Though a detailed job-by-job characterization of these changes is beyond the scope of the present chapter (see Wells

1999), some summary observations are relevant. First, the representation of ethnic and racial minorities increased in all job categories between 1970 and 1990, both because of the influx of immigrants and because of affirmative action and civil rights pressure on the industry. In certain occupations the ethnic increase involved a major reconfiguration of occupational demographics. Room cleaners are the most striking case in point. In 1970 almost half were black, another fifth were white, and the rest were Asians and Hispanics. By 1990 whites and blacks combined totaled only 14 percent of room cleaners, Asians comprised over half, and Hispanics over one-third.

Second, the Census indicates that, industry-wide, no hotel occupation is entirely dominated by a single ethnic group. Observation and interviews with union staff and workers confirm the unevenly diverse composition of hotel occupations. The major reason that the clustering of immigrant groups in particular occupations is uneven is that immigrants tend to hear about and apply for jobs where their friends and relatives work. In some cases, individuals planned to apply for work in a particular job category and hotel even before leaving their country of origin. As a result, although the Census documents a range of ethnic and racial groups in all occupations industry-wide, within a particular hotel only a few groups may be present. Some hotels have only Korean and Filipina room cleaners; others have Mexicans, Salvadorans, Vietnamese, and Chinese; a few have clusters of Eritreans, Ethiopians, and Bosnians. In all the instances that I observed, however, and about which I learned through my interviewees, there were at least two—and usually more—nationality groups within the job categories of particular hotels, so that individuals with cultural differences also shared economic interests. The occupation that comes closest to exhibiting a pattern of ethnic segmentation is that of steward (dishwasher), which is a heavily Latino occupation in San Francisco. In certain hotels stewards are entirely Latino, although still of mixed Central American, Mexican, and sometimes South American nationality.

The Impact of Immigrants on the Processes and Products of Unionization

These patterns of immigrant involvement have shaped the processes, structures, and contractual products of union organizing. Local 2 has not remained static in the course of immigrant incorporation. Rather, the methods through which it builds support among members and the contracts it has evolved to reflect and protect their concerns have been altered by the immigrant influx into the workforce. To demonstrate this point, we will examine immigrant impact in three realms: on workers' receptivity to unions, on the union's methods of making contact with and building support among workers, and on union structure, contracts, and benefits.

Immigrant Background and Receptivity to Unions

Immigration has drawn into the hotel workforce individuals who have varying prior experiences with and attitudes toward unions, generating systematic differences among immigrants in their receptivity to the union.

Asian workers vary in receptivity. Immigrant Chinese workers, especially those from the mainland, tend to be less initially receptive. Because of their experience in China, they think of unions as outside forces, arms of the government, rather than organizations formed by and for workers. Some were union members on the Chinese mainland; one was a business agent who spent frustrating years trying to get the union to deliver the protections and benefits to which members were entitled; others formed their unfavorable opinions of unions through the media and the experience of friends. Also the family focus of the Chinese immigrant community discourages organizational affiliation outside the family, and cultural mores encourage deference to authority. These values are alive and well in employer-employee relationships in San Francisco's Chinatown, where many Chinese hotel workers have relatives and worked previously. Among Southeast Asians, Hmong and Cambodian former peasants tend to be unfamiliar with unions and require considerable convincing, whereas Vietnamese from urban areas are more receptive. According to union organizers, Filipino immigrants are initially "low-key" but "tough once they're in." Individuals who were poor in the Philippines are particularly likely to have had favorable contact with unions there. Quite a few were union members or leaders; others engaged in collective action through their participation in demonstrations against President Ferdinand Marcos.

Latino immigrants are especially receptive and militant union members. Not only do they often come from countries with strong and legitimate labor movements, but many were union members or leaders there. Moreover, many Mexicans and especially Central Americans engaged in dangerous authority-challenging struggles in the chain of events that led to their emigration. Local 2 staff consider Central Americans particularly eager and loyal union members. As one organizer put it: "My perfect union drive would be with Salvadorans. I'd pick them over Mexicans any day, though Mexicans tend to be positive toward the union too. Salvadorans have been in revolution for the past fifteen years or so. They are in for the long haul. They are more solid and committed on some deeper level to the union. They know the need to fight and have a deeper faith that they will win."

Despite these different tendencies in initial receptivity to the union, and counter to stereotypes that immigrants are difficult to organize, Local 2's staff find that immigrants are, if anything, easier to organize than native-born workers. They attribute this fact to many immigrants' previous experience with oppositional politics, to the stronger union traditions in their countries of origins, and to the fact that many have less to lose and more to gain. Young white workers, they say, tend to think that unions are anachronistic and that their leaders are "old fat white guys." Older white workers tend to think that unions are good but weak, so they too are initially disinclined to take part. African Americans tend to be militantly pro-union—both well informed of their rights and quick to speak about violations—but they comprise a small portion of the current hotel workforce. The reluctance of whites is the dominant native influence.[6]

Immigrants' receptivity to the union may also be affected by the sorts of jobs they hold. The fact that most hold lower-level jobs may increase their willingness to take risks. One organizer articulated this connection as follows:

> It's not true that immigrants are hard to organize. They are *more* [her emphasis] supportive of unions than native workers. The fact is, most are situated in the lowest-paid, hardest, highest-turnover jobs. This means they can find another position easy. It also means that a union contract is their only protection. We point this out. They don't have the protection of citizenship or a job with seniority. I'd rather try to organize immigrant room cleaners any day than a food server who is a citizen, who gets tips and a good wage and is paying off a mortgage. That sort of person is not so willing to risk.

The desirability of unionized hotel jobs, however, fosters immigrants' commitment to those jobs, which also can encourage involvement. The hotel industry provides many with their first job in the United States, and unionized hotel work is, for many, a plum. For example, as of August 1998 room cleaners at Class A unionized San Francisco hotels are paid

---

6. Union staff are convinced that the dwindling representation of African Americans in the industry reflects employers' recognition that they are "fighters" and thus the conscious choice not to hire them, paralleling the practices of employers elsewhere (see Neckerman and Kirschenman 1991; Waldinger 1997).

$12.09 an hour for an eight-hour day, including a half-hour paid lunch period. Between 85 and 90 percent qualify for full health and welfare benefits.[7] Tipped employees such as bartenders, bellmen, and food servers earn substantially more. Thus one union staff member observed:

> These jobs are very desirable. And if an immigrant gets a food server job, he sticks with it because he has it made. It's a good job for him and he is a loyal worker. He is also likely to be a loyal union member. He is committed to the job and wants to make it work. If a U.S. citizen gets that same job, he is less committed. He has more opportunities and is likely to move on.

Staff also remark that hotel managers are mistaken about the tractability of immigrants. Staff believe that managers hire immigrants in part because they expect them to be fearful and easy to manipulate. This expectation (which the present project lacks sufficient data to corroborate) fails to take account of who the immigrants actually are—not only the fact that many are predisposed in favor of unions, but also that some are well educated and come from the middle class.[8] These characteristics generate a sense of entitlement among immigrant workers that encourages them to speak out.

In the end, union staff find that immigrants' differences in receptivity flavor the processes of union organizing but do not determine the outcomes of immigrant involvement. Organizers use their understanding of varying backgrounds to alert themselves to the concerns and misperceptions that immigrant workers might have and to sensitize themselves as to who might need encouragement. This process helps organizers overcome reservations and avoid practices and positions that might sour some immigrants on the union.[9] In the course of union campaigns, organizers find that individual immigrants often depart significantly from the tendencies of the group, but that given the right circumstances individu-

7. Qualification for benefits is one of the major differences between union and nonunion hotels in San Francisco. At union hotels, workers qualify for full benefits with as few as fifteen hours of work a week, which most get. By contrast, they need to work 30.5 hours to qualify at one of the large nonunion hotels which is currently being organized. According to a recent survey done by the union, 85 to 90 percent of workers at union hotels get full benefits, as opposed to only 60 to 70 percent of workers at comparable nonunion hotels.

8. The Census shows that the educational level of San Francisco hotel workers has risen substantially over the past thirty years. In 1970 only 18.5 of them had twelve or more years of education, but by 1990 fully 46.5 percent did.

9. For example, they avoid the use of "Maoist" language to frame collective interests because mainland Chinese immigrants could find it distasteful.

als of all backgrounds become active members. The determining factors in building union support, they find, are the skill of the organizer and the experience of work. One organizer articulated this perspective as follows:

> Yes, groups do differ in receptivity to the union, but what really counts is the organizer's skill and what's going on at work. How good are organizers at identifying groups, at seeing who the leaders are, at drawing people out about what concerns them, at getting them to dream about what it would be like if things could change? In the end it all boils down to their experience at work: who they are pissed at, what they want. These things come up for all workers, whatever their backgrounds. These are the things we help them discover they have in common.

Reflecting the organization's left-leaning political stance, Local 2's staff are outspoken about the primacy of class over ethnicity as a principle of group formation. This conviction was repeated in almost every staff interview. It included such framings as the following: "My perspective is centuries old. There are not a lot of differences on the job. You still have capital, labor, and the concern for respect. These don't change because of racial or ethnic background."

Ethnic Divisions and Organizing Approaches

Immigration has drawn into the hotel workforce individuals with diverse national and cultural backgrounds and varying networks of prior acquaintanceship and affiliation. This diversity has shaped the social relations among workers and thus the processes of union mobilization. As Local 2 began its efforts to draw in immigrant workers in the late 1970s, and especially as these efforts became more systematic and thoroughgoing after the mid-1980s, it developed methods of organizing that were consciously geared to this end. First, and perhaps most important, it has hired hotel field representatives and organizers who are fluent in the four major languages of the workforce: Cantonese, Tagalog, Spanish, and English. It uses peer and outside translators to communicate with workers who speak other languages. It also tries to hire organizers and staff who reflect the demographic characteristics of the workforce, although its leaders readily acknowledge that it has not yet achieved full representativeness. Thus the individuals who have served as Local 2's hotel field representatives (the staff who head up organizing within already unionized hotels) over the past year include three Latinos, one Latina, one Filipino, one Chinese man, three white men, and two white women. The individuals who are explicitly assigned to organizing the unorganized include two white men, one Filipina, one Latina, one Chinese man, and two (at some points four) white women.[10]

Organizers attempt to develop rank-and-file committees within every hotel craft and department. They begin by identifying the natural leaders within each—the individuals whom others respect. Early on, Local 2 organizers recognized that natural leadership and relations of trust among workers were structured differently in different segments of the occupational structure, and they have shaped their organizing approaches accordingly. In housekeeping, which as we have noted engages mostly immigrant women and whose labor processes and mobility structures do not encourage links among individuals not previously connected, social relations tend to be confined within the national-origin (or, in the case of Latinos, pan-ethnic) group. Leadership and trust in this department are structured along ethnic lines. Latinos often form a single social grouping, because of both their common language and their greater background similarities and shared residential environments (Wells 1999). As a result, union organizers base their organizing approaches in housekeeping on the substratum of the ethnic group. They speak immigrants' native languages, identify leaders within each ethnic group, and use these individuals to communicate between the union and their constituencies. Eventually they bring the ethnic leaders together in a single committee and develop a set of demands and concerns that represent the entire occupation.

Organizing processes in food service, where workers speak English and have more interconnections across occupations and ethnic groups, are quite different. There, leadership development and union committees are not ethnically based. The natural factions among workers cut across ethnicity; leaders may be native-born or immigrant, male or female, and of any ethnic or racial background. Organizers in food service operate only in English, and their building of union committees takes little or no account of ethnicity. Among dishwashers, by contrast, ethnic background does play a role, but in a different and less marked manner than among room cleaners. Although dishwashers, like room cleaners, are predominantly recent immigrants, their linguistic commonality may be more important than their nationality in establishing natural factions

10. Local 2's assignment of individuals to positions is somewhat fluid, responsive to the demands of organizing drives and the availability of resources. Thus individuals who are hotel field representatives at one point in the year may be assigned to high-priority nonunion organizing drives such as that currently being waged at the Marriott, as resources permit.

and leadership. This is because some stewarding departments are entirely Latino, though usually of more than one nationality. In such departments Spanish is the lingua franca on the job, non-Latino workers often speak Spanish, there is usually only one natural leader and factional group, and organizers operate solely in Spanish. In other hotels, stewards include a substantial number of Chinese and a scattering of Filipinos and other nationalities, necessitating multilingual organizers and creating two or more factional groups.

Not only are organizing approaches geared to the ways that ethnicity structures the social relations within different hotel occupations and departments, but they are also shaped by the composition of Local 2's membership. Local 2's leaders contrast its challenge in this regard with that of HERE Local 11 in Los Angeles, whose use of Mexican cultural symbolism in its appeals is highly representative and effective. Local 2's Latinos, by contrast, are significantly heterogeneous. Central Americans outnumber Mexicans, and no single group dominates. Moreover, Asians outnumber Latinos, and this category lacks cultural and social unity. As a result, Local 2 cannot base its appeal in the experience or symbolism of any single group. Instead it mobilizes workers around the unifying experience of work. It deploys ethnic symbolism eclectically as a means of signaling respect for and inclusion of the various groups. For example, the organization celebrates holidays such as Cinco de Mayo and Chinese New Year; it develops chants in the major languages and serves ethnic foods on picket lines. In one memorable case union organizers smuggled fortune cookies pronouncing that "health, happiness, and medical benefits come through a union contract" into an ethnic potluck held by management for workers.

The immigrant composition of the workforce has also drawn Local 2 into more extensive involvement with the wider community. The union has long recognized that it cannot effectively defend immigrant workers on its own. Since the late 1970s it has sought the help of immigrants' communities to identify workers' broader problems and concerns, to build credibility, and to augment the union's leverage within the city's broader political economy. As a result, Local 2 regularly maintains contact with a wide range of immigrant community organizations, including churches, neighborhood associations, organizations dealing with health and affordable housing, legal and immigrant defense organizations, and several broad community coalitions. These liaisons have broadened Local 2's alliance structure as well as the range of community issues about which it speaks out. These now range from rent control and affordable housing to U.S. immigration laws and foreign policy.

Immigrant Involvement and Union Structure, Practices, and Contracts

In comparison with other union locals, Local 2 faced earlier and more vigorous pressure to incorporate immigrant minorities, spearheaded by the community, student, and farm labor activists that entered the industry in the 1970s and 1980s. Thus, paralleling its use of language-matched organizers, in the late 1970s the local began to print its materials in the four major languages of the workforce, guided by a principle articulated as "the equality of languages." Translators for each language were present at all union meetings to solicit the concerns of immigrants. Immigrants were drawn as extensively as possible into the rank-and-file committee structure within hotels, so that this structure now reflects the varied patterns of social relations established within different hotel departments. Immigrants have also been hired as organizers and staff, and included on all slates of candidates for union office since the late 1970s. Immigrants have been represented in the leadership since the mid-1980s, which required a policy change within the HERE International. Until the election of Local 2 President Sherri Chiesa in 1985, members of HERE locals had to be citizens to hold union office, as was common in U.S. unions at the time. This posed a serious difficulty for Local 2, whose members were by then primarily immigrant, and which was just then launching a major effort to mobilize its membership. Hence, President Chiesa brought to the first convention of the International following her inauguration a resolution proposing that this provision be eliminated. Despite considerable opposition, the measure was passed. At present, the president of Local 2 is a white male, the vice president is a Salvadoran immigrant male, and the secretary-treasurer is a Vietnamese immigrant female.

Over time, immigrant concerns have also altered union contracts. Six such changes are worthy of note. First, immigrant workers' continued ties to relatives abroad have motivated the institution of an extended leave policy. This policy, first articulated in 1980,[11] came directly out of a large group of grievances filed primarily by Filipino workers who were denied leave to visit sick family members, attend funerals, or otherwise tend to relatives in the Philippines—or who had been terminated when they failed to return "on time" after such visits. Mexican workers, staff report, experienced such problems more rarely because Mexico is closer and air transport there is relatively easy and inexpensive. This issue and the contract provision dealing with it provoked a "huge battle," according to

11. See 1980 contract, General Rules, Section 14: Leave of Absence.

staff, because they intrude into the area of work rule restrictions, constraining employers' ability to run their businesses as they like. This struggle is reflected in elaborate contract language, which includes a stipulation inserted by employers that they are entitled to make a case-by-case determination of the legitimacy of employees' claims.

Second, in the 1980–83 contract, wording was inserted guaranteeing that "no employee...shall suffer any loss of seniority, compensation, or benefits due to any change in the employee's name or social security number."[12] This provision protects immigrant workers who used false names and social security numbers before they received their legal immigration status, and then went in to change this information after they became legal.[13] Union staff report that these stipulations, and the union's focus on maintaining job security despite the insecurity of immigration status, have significantly reduced harassment of immigrants.

Third, in the 1986–89 contract, the union took more direct action by adding immigration assistance to the legal benefit plan. This benefit arose expressly from the recognition by staff and workers that the passage of the 1986 Immigration Reform and Control Act (IRCA) would create "havoc" among the members in their scramble to secure amnesty or otherwise legitimate their immigration status. In the late 1980s alone, this benefit helped over fifteen hundred Local 2 members gain amnesty under IRCA. According to Local 2's records, the immigration portion of the legal benefits package is the most-utilized portion of all benefits.

Fourth, also in the 1986–89 contract, language was added stating that "in cases where it is appropriate to a particular job and where it is advantageous to the Hotel to have a position staffed by a multilingual employee, the Hotel recognizes this as an asset."[14] This provision, which is highly valued by workers, emerged from grievances in certain hotels after supervisors insisted that only English be spoken on the job and disciplined workers who spoke their native languages. Workers experienced

12. See Section 10: Change of Status.
13. In the 1983–86 contract, hotel employers secured a change to this section stipulating that falsification of such information given at the time of employment could be grounds for discipline, up to discharge—wording that became especially important to them after the Immigration Reform and Control Act of 1986 established fines for employers who knowingly hired undocumented workers. The union secured a companion modification in 1983 stipulating that if an employee had a problem with his or her residency status in the United States, the employer would first meet with the union to discuss the "job related impact on said employee."
14. See Section 8: No Discrimination.

such actions as gratuitous and belittling, as well as dishonest, since, given the substantial share of foreign-born guests, employers benefited from their multilinguality. The union responded by grieving the supervisors' behavior and initiating the change in the contract. This wording not only prevents hotels from requiring that only English be spoken, but it does so with affirmative language that signals respect for immigrant workers' linguistic abilities.

Fifth, over the years, Local 2 has increasingly used the Education Fund portion of its Health and Welfare and Pension benefits package to develop immigrant workers' English language skills. Training in English as a Second Language was initially "employer-driven," but it is something the union, workers, and management all value. Hotel owners support it because it helps them give better service. They want as many of their workers as possible, even those whose jobs do not formally require facility in English, to be able to interact graciously with guests. For example, guests often ask room cleaners directions, and their ability to speak English would improve the service given, even though it is not required to carry out their formal job descriptions. Workers and the union support English language training because it improves workers' job skills, widens their employment options, and helps them express their concerns to employers and the union. Moreover, it assists them in becoming citizens—a benefit that has become increasingly important since the recent changes in welfare and immigration laws.[15] This use of the Education Fund began as a pilot project for a limited group of hotels; it can now be used by any hotel employer for classes involving any union member.

Finally, in 1994 Local 2 augmented its Health and Welfare and Pension benefits package with a Child Care/Elder Care Program. This program includes two facets directly responsive to immigrants. Its child care provision provides coverage for "informal child care" to accommodate the practice, especially common among immigrant workers, of having a relative rather than a formal child care provider take care of children. The program also includes an elder care provision that covers sick and disabled elders, to accommodate the fact that immigrant members, in the words of one union leader, "have a larger sense of family"; they are much more likely than native-born members to live in extended family households with elders for whom they are responsible.

15. Local 2 does not directly involve itself in citizenship preparation to the extent of some other union locals with largely immigrant memberships. Although it has from time to time organized citizenship preparation classes, for the most part it leaves such initiatives to the considerable number of other organizations in the Bay Area that do so.

Conclusion

As this chapter illustrates, the flow of immigrants into particular locali-
ties, industries, and occupations can transform the processes, structures,
and contractual products of union organizing. Such transformations are
particularly likely in innovative unions such as Local 2, which have shed
the traditions of white male domination and bureaucratic, top-down
unionism. Here, a shift in organizational philosophy which legitimated
the participation and concerns of women and minorities, and a serious
threat to union vitality—occasioned by the changing structure of the industry and the devastating 1983 restaurant strike—motivated concerted
attention to mobilizing immigrants. The recent rededication of the AFL-
CIO to rank-and-file organizing, and its explicit identification of immigrants as important subjects of such mobilization, may well generate
comparable transformations elsewhere. Certainly HERE Local 11 in Los
Angeles—whose membership is also overwhelmingly immigrant and
which underwent a similar, though more recent, shift in leadership and
organizational philosophy—constitutes an example in which organizing
methods and contract provisions have also been shaped by the immigrant
composition of the workforce. The present study suggests that such shaping is likely to vary with the character of the immigrant influx, with the receptivity and the organizing principles of the union, and with the kind of
industry and occupations organized.

This case also suggests that recent immigrants are as—or more—
receptive to unions than are native-born workers, both because of their
prior experiences, and because they have more to gain and less to lose.
Thus unions need not anticipate a lukewarm reception from immigrants,
nor one that is unaffected by the experiences of work. However, the immigrant composition of the workforce is likely to affect the methods of securing and expanding member allegiance. As we have seen here, immigrant backgrounds significantly shape the social relations among workers
in ways that do not simply mirror their national backgrounds. Rather, nationality groups vary in terms of the preexisting characteristics, especially
language, that permit or encourage connections among them. In addition, the processes of work also structure the extent and form of intergroup affiliation. Thus in order to ground union solidarity in the natural
relations of acquaintanceship and trust among workers, and to oppose
managerial counterstrategies which are often based in these relations,
union organizers will need to attend to the varied ways that immigrant
backgrounds affect social relations at work.

Finally, we found that the social situations and concerns of immigrant workers are reconfiguring the language and provisions of labor contracts, extending a process that began with the civil rights and women's movements—that is, the expansion of labor union contracts beyond the narrow conditions of work in order to address the particular concerns and historical liabilities experienced by specific groups. For women and native-born minorities these have included such issues as nondiscrimination and child care. For immigrants they include a recognition of the special responsibilities and strains that immigrants experience as a result of their location within intergenerational kinship networks. They also involve an acknowledgment of the special demands placed on individuals and families by the extension of such networks across global space. In addition, they encompass a recognition of immigrants' vulnerable and changing status under U.S. immigration law, and their need for special protection and assistance. And they involve an acknowledgment and affirmation of immigrants' cultural differences, both their often limited facility with English and their multilinguality. Such acknowledgments, and their associated moral and material claims, arise from unions' commitment to rank-and-file organizing—a commitment that is imperative if unions are to recover from their decades-long decline.

5 Intense Challenges, Tentative Possibilities: Organizing Immigrant Garment Workers in Los Angeles

Edna Bonacich

The garment industry is the largest manufacturing employer in Los Angeles.[1] Garment workers are almost all immigrants, the majority of them women. In 1998, official statistics reported 122,500 garment workers employed in Los Angeles County (Employment Development Department 1998), but given that there is a large underground sector of unknown magnitude, experts estimate that the number could be as high as 150,000. Even using the official figures, the apparel industry accounts for 18 percent of all Los Angeles County manufacturing workers. Moreover, Los Angeles is now the largest garment manufacturing center in the United States, outstripping New York by over twenty thousand workers.

The apparel workers of Los Angeles are virtually unorganized. In 1995 the International Ladies' Garment Workers Union (ILGWU), for years the main union organizing in this industry, merged with the Amalgamated Clothing and Textile Workers Union (ACTWU) to form the Union of Needletrades, Industrial and Textile Employees (UNITE). The union has been losing membership since the 1950s and now represents only about four hundred garment workers in Los Angeles.[2]

This chapter explores the reasons why organizing garment workers has proven so difficult in this city, in comparison with other industries

1. This chapter is based on research conducted between 1989 and 1998, primarily for a book coauthored with Richard Appelbaum (Bonacich and Appelbaum forthcoming). Most of the assertions about the industry presented in this paper are documented there. Statements about the union and organizing strategies are based on almost ten years of experience working as a volunteer with ILGWU and UNITE, and spending many hours talking with organizers and observing their actions.

2. According to Laslett and Tyler (1998, 92), membership peaked at twelve thousand in 1948.

that employ immigrant workers, and in comparison with apparel organizing in the past. It also considers various possible approaches to organizing, and evaluates their prospects for success.

Given that garment workers are among the most exploited workers in Los Angeles, and that the ILGWU and now UNITE have been valiantly trying to help these thousands of workers organize themselves, one might expect that the garment industry would be at the forefront of the labor movement there. Instead, this industry has proven to be one of the most difficult to organize, primarily because of its flexible, global system of production. In many ways, the apparel industry is at the cutting edge of economic restructuring, forecasting what other industries will soon face. The restructured apparel industry poses a severe challenge to the labor movement to find new ways of organizing.

Structure and Organization of the Industry

The Los Angeles garment industry specializes in women's outerwear, the most seasonal and fashion-sensitive sector of the apparel industry. Los Angeles accounts for about 10 percent of all apparel production in the United States, but about one-quarter of women's outerwear (Wolff 1997). The fashion sector is the most volatile part of the industry, leading to efforts to externalize risk. Virtually all of Los Angeles' apparel manufacturers, therefore, contract out most of their actual production to small contractors who serve as the direct employers of the majority of garment workers. These contractors receive orders only when work is available, and have no long-term relationships with manufacturers or guarantees that they will receive work on a stable basis.

Garment workers, in turn, work on a contingent basis, with no security of employment. They are hired when work is available and get paid only for the available work. The typical method of payment is by piece rate; the worker makes as much money as she can by completing as many pieces as quickly as possible. Garment workers typically receive no benefits, no paid sick leave, and no paid vacations.

The law requires that workers be paid minimum wage and an overtime premium. Thus, even though workers are paid by the piece, records must be kept of their hours in order to ensure that they are being paid according to the legal prescriptions. However, contractors find many creative ways to avoid paying anything more than piece rate. For example, they will treat overtime as off-the-books work, paying workers in cash. Or they will make workers pay a cash kickback for any "extras" the contractor is legally compelled to pay them. The U.S. Department of Labor has extensive documentation of such evasive practices, leading to the charge that sweatshops have returned to the U.S. garment industry (Ross 1997).

Reports by a number of workers at UNITE's Garment Workers' Justice Center of their experience with the recent rise in the U.S. and California minimum wage is instructive here. At one shop the workers found that their piece rates remained unchanged, but the contractor told them that he would pay them $5.75 an hour, the new legally prescribed minimum, provided they could earn it through their piece rates. If they could not, he would fire them. In other words, they were forced to speed up their production or face termination. This contractor was thus able to run a "legal" shop without having to pay any extra money per garment in the face of the new standards.

Contracting in the apparel industry is a prototypical case of flexible production. The manufacturer not only minimizes risk by employing contractors only when he needs them, but can also shift work around to look for the best deal. Contractors underbid each other to get the work; some even pay kickbacks to production managers. The mobility of production extends far beyond the borders of Los Angeles; manufacturers employ contractors not only in other parts of southern California or the United States but in Asia, Mexico, Central and South America, the Caribbean, and many other territories. The degree of globalization may be exaggerated for other industries, but it is a fierce reality for this one. Since the 1960s, and especially since 1980, the industry has been moving offshore with great speed, leading to a loss of jobs in the United States and a rise in imports. The industry generally moves offshore to take advantage of low-wage, typically young, female labor in less-developed countries. The low wages paid by offshore contractors serve as a damper on wages and working conditions in the United States. Manufacturers who still produce locally must somehow meet the lower standards of the global labor market, and they do so by paying workers as little as possible.

This rush toward flexibility and mobility of production is a consequence not only of the risks of fashion and the increased ease of offshore production resulting from increased use of computers and containerization; it has also been accelerated by dramatic changes in retailing. Since the mid-1980s, apparel retailers have undergone a major restructuring. Giant retail chains have bought up other chains to form powerful consolidated companies, often through leveraged buyouts. Retailers have streamlined their operations so as to minimize their inventory, and their increased size and power have enabled them to place greater demands on the manufacturers in terms of cutting costs.

The consolidation of retailing has also led to increased competition among the few remaining chains. Despite the well-recognized fact that there are too many stores per consumer, each chain is expanding its store numbers in the hopes of knocking out its competitors. The effect is de-flationary, as stores unload excess inventory through markdowns which they then charge back to the manufacturers.

Retailers have also become formidable competitors of the manufacturers by producing their own lower-cost private (or store) label apparel. Many of these garments are produced offshore for the cheapest possible prices. Because of the hefty bulk of their orders, retailers can gain cost advantages over the manufacturers in offshore production. At the local level they can contract for production directly, eliminating the need for the middleman manufacturers. Another area of change in retailing involves the rise of giant discounters such as Wal-Mart. These very powerful stores insist on the lowest wholesale prices, forcing manufacturers to put price pressure upon the contractors who, in turn, squeeze the workers.

Capital hypermobility in the apparel industry, both locally and globally, makes union organizing very difficult. It is impossible for workers in a single contracting shop to organize because if they do, their factory will simply be boycotted by manufacturers and thus will quickly go out of business. Indeed, this problem even affects law enforcement: if a state or federal inspector finds serious violations in a shop, it will more than likely go out of business and the workers will find themselves without a job. Thus even the most elementary act of self-protection—reporting a violation to a government inspector—is fraught with danger for the worker. How much more dangerous, then, is attempting to organize at one's factory.

One way that ILGWU has traditionally tackled the problem, knowing that no contractor can be organized in isolation, is to attempt to organize a manufacturer and all of his contractors simultaneously. The manufacturer is the profit center from whom tangible gains can be won. Yet treating all of a manufacturer's contractors as a single production system poses major difficulties as well. For one thing, manufacturers are very secretive about which contractors they work with, and this information is not publicly available. Workers who are sewing for a particular label usually have no idea where their fellow workers are employed. Moreover, the list of contractors keeps changing from month to month. Even if the union can get a good list at one point in time, there is no way of knowing how long it will remain accurate. Most contractors work for more than one manufacturer, and the mix of manufacturers that they work for, and the proportions of work, keep changing. Thus an organizing committee in a contracting shop can be established at great effort and personal risk to the workers only to find that the targeted manufacturer is no longer sending work to that factory. The workers involved suddenly find themselves irrelevant to the organizing drive. Moreover, if the manufacturer is highly motivated to avoid unionization, as are all the apparel manufacturers in Los Angeles, he will move work away from that particular contractor if there is the slightest hint of worker organizing.

Garment manufacturing is not infinitely mobile, however. Some manufacturers develop longer-term relationships with some of their contractors. Some, although rarely, even invest in their contractors, tightening the relationship with them. It can be difficult to find a new contractor who produces up to the manufacturer's quality requirements. And it takes time to finish the jobs already in that contracting shop without significant losses. These points of friction in the system serve as loopholes in the finely honed mobility of apparel manufacturers, and can be used by the union to its advantage. In other words, a quick attack before they can move production may inflict a serious wound on a company, pushing it to make a deal.

Still, the difficulties abound. And when workers find that they lose their jobs as a result of an organizing effort—even though it is obviously not the union that fired them or closed down their shop, but the manufacturer in an effort to avoid worker empowerment—they become either more afraid of organizing or downright antagonistic to the union. Industry leaders opportunistically play up any factory closing connected with union organizing efforts, encouraging the view that the union is to blame for job loss.

Comparisons between Garment and Other Immigrant-employing Industries

How do these conditions compare with other industries that employ immigrant workers in Los Angeles? First, as a manufacturing industry, apparel differs from such service industries as janitorial services, health care, and hotels and restaurants, all of which are unionized to a significant degree in Los Angeles. Services are not in a position to move abroad, nor do they face direct wage competition from other countries. Moreover, because services typically deal directly with consumers, they cannot be secretive about their location, nor can they move about to avoid detection.

Janitorial services share the contracting system with the apparel industry and in some respects offer a close parallel (see Fisk, Mitchell, and

Erickson, this volume). The success of the Justice for Janitors campaign in the 1990s would seem to serve as a model for UNITE in its efforts to organize garment shops in Los Angeles. However, there are a number of noteworthy differences. First, janitorial services cannot move offshore. Second, the buildings that need to be cleaned cannot be hidden, even if the building owners *can* switch contractors when faced with worker organizing. Third, to the building owner who employs the contractor, the cost of cleaning services is a much smaller proportion of total costs than is the cost of sewing to an apparel manufacturer. The building owners can double the wages of their janitors and barely feel it. Apparel manufacturers, in contrast, calculate the cost of labor down to the last penny, and scrimp on every cent. A rise in the price of labor is perceived by them to be deadly, and they will fight against it to the end. Fourth, there is no equivalent in janitorial services to the giant retail chains that keep insisting on lower prices. Fifth, and perhaps most important, cleaning buildings is not a risky business subject to the fluctuations of style and season. Nor are janitors treated as contingent workers or paid by the piece.

This is not to say that UNITE cannot learn valuable lessons from Justice for Janitors. Its citywide approach to organizing may be the ideal way to organize garment workers as well, though the resources required for such an effort in a city with over 120,000 garment workers are large indeed.

Two other immigrant-employing industries that can be compared to apparel are construction and agriculture. Construction workers are subject to contracting and contingent employment similar to the garment workers. They also suffer from seasonal variations and job instability. As with services, however, the construction industry cannot move offshore, one of the most potent threats of apparel manufacturers; nor does local labor in construction face competition with lower-wage, offshore workers.

Another advantage in construction is that some workers are skilled. Craft unions have been able to protect construction workers by limiting access to training. Historically, the unions could maintain monopolies over certain skills, whereas garment workers are generally considered to be unskilled, performing simple, repetitive tasks at great speed. To be sure, many construction jobs are now being done by unskilled, nonunion immigrant workers, many of them day laborers hired on street corners. Despite the obvious difficulties involved in organizing this kind of casual labor, one key group of construction workers, the drywallers, have had amazing success in organizing themselves (see Milkman and Wong, this volume).

Agriculture is probably the immigrant-employing industry that most closely resembles apparel production. California agriculture faces intense competition from cheap imports, at least for some products. However, the land itself is an immobile form of capital, unlike sewing machines. Owners of agricultural land have a vested interest in its continued productive use, whereas apparel manufacturers have no such local investment to maintain.

Nevertheless, agriculture shares with apparel a high level of risk connected with seasons and the weather. Like apparel, agriculture has responded to risk by employing farm workers on a contingent basis and paying them by the piece. Indeed, agriculture and apparel share the dubious distinction of having the highest rate of labor standards violations in California.[3] That the apparel industry produces more violations of basic wage and hour and health and safety law than agriculture suggests that it is especially intractable both to state intervention and to union organizing.[4]

The manufacturing sector in Los Angeles does have at least one recent major organizing win to its credit, namely American Racing Equipment (see Zabin, this volume). As in the wheel industry, there are some sectors of apparel manufacturing where the advantages of being located in Los Angeles outweigh labor-cost considerations, and these might be attractive organizing targets in the future.

Conditions for Apparel Organizing: Past and Present

In New York City and elsewhere in the northeast, garment industry organizing was one of the great success stories of the labor movement in the

3. For this reason, the state Division of Labor Standards Enforcement joined with the U.S. Department of Labor in creating the Targeted Industries Partnership Program (TIPP). TIPP's goal is to combine limited enforcement resources in attempting to clean up these two industries. At a hearing of the Jewish Commission on Sweatshops, held in September 1997, TIPP officials reported that they have had far more success in cleaning up agriculture than the garment industry.

4. Under the leadership of state Labor Commissioner Jose Millan, TIPP is planning to expand its activities to other low-wage industries, including restaurants. However, we should note that apparel industry leaders have put considerable pressure on the state to take the spotlight off of garment industry transgressions, and when it does focus on apparel, to shift the blame from the established industry to the underground economy. This political battle has little to do with the realities of wages and working conditions, and everything to do with the control of image.

early twentieth century (Foner 1979; Howard 1997; Stein 1977; Tyler 1995). Early garment workers were mainly immigrant women, and their success in organizing demonstrated that both immigrants and women, groups viewed as having doubtful organizing potential, could successfully organize.

Immigrants and women remain the majority of the apparel workforce in Los Angeles today. So what has changed? Before examining changes in the workforce, let us consider changes in the structure of the industry. Though contracting out is not a new feature of apparel production, it is far more advanced today than it was in the early decades of the century. Moreover, the industry only began to move out of the northeast starting in the late 1950s (Bonacich et al. 1994). First it moved to the nonunion South, then to Japan, then to Hong Kong, South Korea, and Taiwan, and ultimately to the rest of Asia, especially China, where wages are one-tenth the U.S. level. Movement to Asia was followed by offshore production in Mexico, the Caribbean, and Central America, boosted by U.S. trade policies and the building of Export Processing Zones by destination countries promising controlled low-wage labor. The North American Free Trade Agreement (NAFTA) has accelerated the move of the industry to Mexico, now the largest exporter of assembled garments back to the United States.

The movement offshore has generated a tremendous rise in apparel imports to the point where, in 1997, 60 percent of U.S.-bought apparel was produced outside of the country (AAMA 1998, 4). Concomitantly, apparel employment in the United States keeps falling, from about 1.4 million in 1970 to 813,000 in 1997. Between 1978 and 1997, every state except California showed a decline in garment industry employment. New York, New Jersey, Pennsylvania, and Massachusetts lost over half their apparel jobs (AAMA 1998, 10). Only California (mainly Los Angeles) has shown a steady increase in employment, adding about fifty thousand jobs since 1978. These conditions have severely depleted the membership of the garment unions. In the early 1970s, the two component unions of UNITE represented 800,000 workers; by 1997 UNITE had less than 300,000 members.[5]

Los Angeles has grown as a center of apparel production for a number of reasons: Its focus on women's outerwear requires smaller lots produced in shorter lead times, making offshore production somewhat less

5. From U.S. House of Representatives Education Committee and Workforce Subcommittee on Oversight and Investigations hearings, "The American Worker at a Crossroads Project," Washington, D.C., August 6, 1998. They derived the data from U.S. Statistical Abstracts, and from U.S. Department of Labor data.

desirable, at least for the fashion sector. The industry was also attracted to the west coast as a way of avoiding the strong unions in the East. Finally, the availability of a low-wage immigrant workforce which, while not comparable to the Third World, is competitive with most of the rest of the country makes Los Angeles an attractive location. Let us now consider the character of the workforce and their potential for organizing.

The Workers

According to the 1990 Census, Los Angeles garment workers are about 75 percent Latino and 13 percent Asian, with the remainder from miscellaneous groups or unidentifiable in terms of ethnicity.[6] The largest group is from Mexico, followed by Salvadorans and Guatemalans. Asians include Chinese, Vietnamese, Thai, and other Southeast Asians. Based on the Census, about 75 percent are women.

An unknown but large proportion of Los Angeles garment workers are undocumented, and their position in the United States is especially precarious. The apparel industry is probably the premier employer of undocumented workers in Los Angeles; few if any immigrant-employing industries have as high a proportion.

As Héctor Delgado has shown (1993), lack of legal papers is not a fatal bar to organizing. But it certainly makes it more difficult, as workers fear that if they expose themselves they may face deportation. And since the ILGWU strike reported on in Delgado's book, conditions have worsened for undocumented immigrants. The 1986 Immigration Reform and Control Act (IRCA) made it illegal for employers to hire the undocumented. California voters voted overwhelmingly in favor of Proposition 187 in 1994, attacking basic rights of the undocumented and, even though many of its provisions have been struck down as unconstitutional, leaves no doubt as to the precarious position of these workers. Then in March and April 1998, the Immigration and Naturalization Service (INS) engaged in a series of factory raids aimed specifically at Los Angeles garment factories. They deported hundreds of workers, creating a reign of terror among the labor force. The INS has since moved on to other industries, but it has left a residue of fear in its wake. No comparable situation existed for the young immigrant women garment workers in New York, who rose up in 1909.

6. The portrait in this section is based partly on an analysis of the 1990 Census, and partly on working with the organizing department of the union and talking with organizers and workers over the years.

Garment workers in Los Angeles today face a number of other disabilities. Sewing in a garment factory is one of the jobs that many new immigrants find. Thus garment workers tend to be among the newer immigrants. Most speak little or no English. Though there is diversity among backgrounds, many of these workers come from small towns or rural areas. Many have limited formal education, and little experience in the wage labor force. In other words, they are first-generation proletarians. They come to the United States in part to support families back home and, despite pitifully low wages, still manage to send remittances. Some of the Latino workers are indigenous people for whom Spanish is a second language. Even when Spanish speaking, they tend to be dark-skinned, deriving primarily from the indigenous and mestizo populations of Mexico and Central America.

Partly because of their recent arrival in this country, and partly because of the spread-out character of Los Angeles, the degree of community organization among garment workers is limited. To be sure, there are enclaves of Central Americans, Mexicans, and the various Asian groups, but there is also considerable dispersion and consequent social isolation. Cristina Vasquez of UNITE and I recently interviewed the priests of five Catholic parishes believed to have a high number of garment workers. They were all struck by the lack of organization in the community, a need that the churches try to meet. One priest, who came from Chicago, pointed to the stark contrast between the strength of ethnic neighborhoods there and their weakness in Los Angeles. Again, the lack of strong community neighborhoods and institutions contrasts with northeastern cities in the early decades of the century.

Immigrant garment workers vary in their previous political experiences. Some of the Central Americans have had a great deal of experience with political struggles in their homelands, as have some of the Mexicans, especially those from Mexico City. On the other hand, many have been exposed to corrupt unions or to regimes that assassinate union leaders. These experiences, or the lack of any experience of political struggle, may handicap union organizing.

Another problem concerns the ethnic divisions among the workforce, most importantly that between Latino and Asian workers. Each of these larger groups suffers from internal divisions as well. The Asians are divided along lines of language, culture, and class, and their experience ranges from the infamous case of the Thai women who worked under conditions of semislavery in El Monte, to Asian workers who are favored by their co-ethnic employers and are given better jobs than their fellow Latinos. Some Asian workers are also able to use garment work as a stepping-stone to becoming contractors, a rarity among Latino workers.

None of this is to say that workers do not engage in any forms of resistance to their circumstances. They do. Typically resistance takes the
form of "weapons of the weak" (Scott 1985): workers constantly judge
and condemn their employers and supervisors, quit their jobs to look
for a more satisfactory position, and get back at their bosses in small
ways.[7] Occasionally workers engage in more militant action, especially
when faced with cuts in piece rates. Far more frequently, workers confront their employers after they have been laid off, or have not been paid
for weeks. Making a militant demand on a current employer is simply
suicidal, in terms of retaining the work, and so it occurs only in extreme
situations.

With some exceptions, garment workers are fully aware of their exploitation and would dearly like to change it. The problem lies not in their
consciousness but in their extreme vulnerability. At the drop of a pin they
can be fired or their factory can shut down. The possibility of job loss (and
deportation) inspires great fear, so that workers, quite reasonably, are reluctant to take actions likely to increase these risks. This fear is exacerbated by intense poverty, which gives them little room for maneuver.

Worker fear mitigates not only against union organizing but also
against the much-touted self-monitoring programs of the manufacturers.[8]
Workers know that if they report violations to company inspectors, either
they will be fired by the contractor or the manufacturer will cease to send
work to the factory and it may close. So they dare not report the truth.

Garment workers suffer from severe political disabilities, and the gap
between their powerlessness and the power of their employers may be
even greater than in other industries. Threats by industry leaders to flee
to Mexico grab the attention of local political officials who are constantly
offering new benefits to the industry in order to induce it to stay. The latest such effort concerns the granting of tax write-offs for being located in
Los Angeles' Empowerment Zones.[9]

7. The similarity between the situation of the Malaysian peasants studied by Scott and
that of the garment workers in Los Angeles is striking. Both groups of workers are faced
with declining industries in which any militance on their part is likely to speed up their
unemployment. Even though they understand perfectly well what is happening to them,
the opportunities for a frontal attack seem almost nonexistent.

8. The program of self-monitoring was developed by the U.S. Department of Labor in
an effort to get manufacturers to take more responsibility for conditions in their contracting shops. Unfortunately, manufacturers have turned this around to make the unwar-
ranted claim that they are now free of violations and have been more or less so certified by
the federal government.

9. A classic example was the mayor's creation of the California Fashion Association.
Although the CFA is now independently funded, it received a kick-start from the mayor's

Some UNITE leaders argue that in the face of industry flight it is better to be organized than unorganized. At least this allows workers to protest against the flight, and if there is a union contract, costly terms known as "liquidated damages" can be imposed on the manufacturer for moving. Unfortunately, the use of liquidated damages is now under investigation by a Congressional committee chaired by Pete Hoekstra (R-Mich), which is determined to eliminate one of the last vestiges of union ability to interfere in the free mobility of this industry.

The Los Angeles apparel industry is rabidly anti-union. This is true of other local industries as well, but apparel may exceed the rest in this respect, in part because of the market pressures the industry confronts. It faces a powerful retail sector that is putting intense downward pressure on prices, growing competition from offshore production, and imports from low-wage countries. It feels browbeaten by the U.S. Department of Labor, which insists that it ensures that contractors comply with the law. It fought against the rise in the minimum wage, and favored the elimination of the California eight-hour day. The industry is determined to keep the price of labor down to the barest minimum, and thus its anti-union animus is boundless.

Approaches to Unionization

The traditional approach to unionization involved representation elections supervised by the National Labor Relations Board (NLRB). Union organizers would meet with workers, discuss with them the pros and cons of unionization, and they would decide democratically whether or not they wanted to be represented by the union. This approach has become problematic in a number of industries; in the Los Angeles apparel industry it is virtually worthless. Even if workers in a given contracting shop did vote for a union and enter into a collective bargaining agreement with their employer, they would accomplish little since the real profit centers of the industry are the manufacturers and retailers. More important, the manufacturers would not be willing to employ a contractor whose price

---

office, and continues to maintain close ties with him. The purpose of the CFA is to promote the Los Angeles apparel industry and improve its image. Industry leaders are very sensitive to the charge that they operate sweatshops, and they hope that the reality can be masked by public relations campaigns. The CFA includes a Labor Committee, the chair of which is Stan Levy, formerly in-house counsel for Guess, Inc., and active supporter of the company. Neither the union, nor any worker, is ever heard from by this committee. The idea that a Labor Committee should have no representatives of labor gives some indication of the political state of affairs in this industry.

was one penny higher than the others, let alone one known to have "labor problems," which might threaten work schedules. The union contractor thus would be boycotted by all the manufacturers, would receive no work, and soon would go out of business. The workers would have won the election but lost their jobs.

Knowing that he would be driven out of business if a union election were won in his shop, the contractor is highly motivated to do everything he can, legal and illegal, to break the union. This is precisely UNITE's experience with NLRB campaigns in Los Angeles. In case after case, clear pro-union majorities have ended up in bitter defeat as the employer fired pro-union workers, threatened the others, called in the immigration authorities, and so on. Many of these actions are illegal, but enforcement is so slow and the sanctions so weak that the organizing drive is typically dead and buried years before any kind of redress—usually exceedingly minimal—is proffered. The fired union leaders simply lose their jobs, adding to the fear and intimidation that dominate the industry.

Apparel employers targeted by organizing efforts will sometimes call for elections, claiming that this is the only fair and American thing to do, that workers should have a free choice, and that they support a secret ballot. But these calls are disingenuous, arising only after the company has engaged in every union-busting practice in the book and feels confident that the workers will vote against the union. Recent history suggests that no apparel manufacturer or contractor in Los Angeles would simply allow a union election, without interference, to occur in his plant. And if a contractor did allow such an election, he would end up going out of business.

As is often suggested, legal and procedural reforms are needed in the NLRB process. However, such reforms would still not crack the nut of the apparel contracting system, which enables manufacturers—the real employers—to shift work away from unionized workers, thereby destroying any organizing effort in the long run, if not at the time of the election. Given these difficulties, UNITE has devised alternative approaches to the challenge of organizing garment workers, the two most important of which are jobbers' agreements and worker-centered organizing.

Jobbers' Agreements

The idea of a jobber's agreement comes out of the ILGWU's long experiences of organizing in the women's apparel industry in New York. The term "jobber" is still used from the New York context even though it does not apply to the Los Angeles industry. In New York, the term "manufacturer" is reserved for an apparel company that does in-house production, whereas a jobber is a firm that contracts out the sewing. Since in Los Angeles almost no apparel firms do their work in-house, the term "manufacturer" is used instead for all firms that design and arrange for the production of garments, even if they own no factory themselves. The Los Angeles usage is followed here.

A jobber's agreement holds the manufacturer responsible for conditions in his contracting shops by guaranteeing that he will only use unionized contractors, and will pay them the union scale and benefits. Under such an agreement, the manufacturer cannot boycott union contractors, but on the contrary is bound to use them. In such a context it is advantageous for contractors to be unionized because this gives them preferred access to that manufacturer. Indeed, jobbers' agreements tend to stabilize the highly mobile garment business, since they lead the manufacturers to stick with a particular group of union contractors.

To obtain a jobber's agreement, the union must organize the entire production system of a manufacturer at one time, including not only the workers who are employed in his headquarters (such as sample-makers, cutters, or warehouse workers), but also the workers in all the dispersed contracting shops. If the workers in these various locations can be brought together to unite around the issue of gaining a union contract across the entire system, then they may be able to succeed in getting the manufacturer and the contractors to sign.

The strategic approach that has been used to organize such a dispersed production system is to turn the manufacturer's benefits from contracting out into weaknesses. That the manufacturer does not have strong and stable ties with his contractors means that the links between the manufacturer and his contractors can be severed. The physical dispersal of production also opens up the possibility of interfering with the flow of garments between various plants. Because of the time-sensitivity of the fashion business, even temporary interruptions in the flow of production can be very costly, especially at the peak of the season.

Breaking the ties between the manufacturer and his contractors can be accomplished by a number of means. The workers in key contracting shops may go out on strike. Workers may picket certain shops or the company's warehouse, and may persuade truckers not to cross their picket lines. Contractors, who may work with other manufacturers apart from the one that the union is trying to organize, may decide to opt out of the latter relationship for the period of the labor dispute so as to avoid all the disruption; since the manufacturer has probably not been especially loyal to him, the contractor has little reason to see the manufacturer through these tough times. The union may also be able to get some contractors to sign "me too" agreements with the union, so that if they agree to cease working with the manufacturer temporarily, they will be able to sign the union contract on whatever terms are negotiated later—and obtain secure work.

Although the manufacturer may be able to move production to other shops in order to avoid those contractors where workers are organized, in the midst of a public labor dispute it is difficult for the manufacturer to find others who will work with him and risk being picketed. As soon as the union is able to trace the work to a new contractor, they can warn him of the consequences of working with a manufacturer who is fighting with the union. Thus the obvious advantage to the manufacturer of being able to shift production can be minimized during an organizing campaign.

The strength of the jobber's agreement lies in tying the manufacturer to the contractors so that workers can win significant gains. This approach is not without problems, however. First, it is extremely difficult to coordinate all the parts of the dispersed production system so that the union can take action on numerous fronts at once. Second, the union's need for secrecy is intense, since the employer will try mightily to kill such an effort before it gets off the ground, and yet secrecy impedes organizing and weakens the development of democratic structures among workers as the union is building membership. Third, such an organizing drive is most likely to succeed right away or not at all. The longer the struggle is drawn out, the more the employer is able to engage in evasive action, including devising methods for moving work away from contractors with strong union support. The manufacturer may build up the work load for his core contractors or move production to Mexico, among other options. This ability to shift production can be deadly to the workers' morale.

A fourth problem with organizing for a jobber's agreement is that it lends itself to top-down organizing. The contractor may sign with the union not because of pressure from workers but because he knows that a union contract will guarantee him stable work. The workers thus become irrelevant, and the contractor is motivated to sign whether the workers want a union or not. The agreement thus becomes one among the union, the manufacturer, and the contractors, with workers the mere objects of the agreement.

There is nothing inherent in a jobber's agreement that precludes workers' participation in the struggle to win it. Indeed, driving the manufacturer to the bargaining table may depend on strong worker activism of various sorts. Nevertheless, the situation lends itself to top-down agreements whereby workers find themselves as members of a union for which they did not fight. Under such conditions, the antagonistic relationship between the workers and their immediate employers is muted by the union contract, and the union often ends up dealing directly with the contractor rather than with the workers.

A fifth problem with the jobber's agreement approach is that the manufacturer who is so targeted will resist vigorously, in order to avoid being put in a weaker market position relative to his competitors. One way to deal with this last problem is to organize an entire sector as a competitive unit. Ideal sectors include those that have distinctive skills and machinery, that have a lower probability of flight to Mexico, that have a higher profit rate, or that occupy a strategic location in the industry such that union strength there will enhance future struggles. Of course, the resources required by such an effort are formidable.

An essential component of jobber's agreement campaigns, whether aimed at a single manufacturer or a sector, is the development of a corporate campaign. The labor movement as a whole has become much more sophisticated at researching firms it is trying to organize and finding points of vulnerability apart from their production systems. For example, stockholders may be dismayed to learn about company labor practices, and may be willing to exert pressure on the company to settle quickly with the union. When unions themselves are among the stockholders, this can be a potent weapon. The fashion industry would appear to be especially vulnerable to one such form of pressure, namely, an attack on a company's image. Fashion depends on the selling of an image, as much as on the selling of a product. The image-selling aspect of apparel has accelerated in recent years, as certain key brand names, supported by millions of dollars in advertising, have managed to create "identities" with which their consumers identify. Even without any interference, most apparel brands have a limited life cycle, and "hot" brands that cool off usually have a hard time revitalizing themselves. Unions (and other organizations concerned with labor abuses) can try to take advantage of the vulnerability of a brand's public image by developing negative associations with that name.

Corporate campaigns often attack a firm's sales in some form: by putting pressure on retailers to drop the brand, by getting consumers to question salespeople about production conditions, by calling for a consumer boycott, and so forth. If a company's sales are threatened, it is more likely to be willing to come to the bargaining table. These campaigns may also affect the value of a company's stock, in turn leading the owners to feel that action must be taken to end the damaging publicity—including possibly settling with the union.

Corporate campaigns are typically accompanied by community pressure, especially from union allies and supporters, including politicians, religious leaders, women's groups, students, artists, musicians, consumer groups, and sister unions. These supporters can participate in demonstrations against the company, publicize its labor abuses, and spread the word about a boycott.

Corporate campaigns and consumer pressure are especially suitable for holding accountable firms that move to Mexico (or elsewhere). If an apparel firm has shifted production offshore in order to escape unionization in Los Angeles, consumer groups can point to the even lower labor standards in the new location, and to the greed of the manufacturer in seeking even higher profits from the exploitation of impoverished workers. Such an approach is much more likely to succeed if workers in the new location join the struggle against the manufacturer, so that workers in both countries are calling for consumer support to end the abuses.

But a corporate campaign and community support can be problematic if they are not linked to a strong worker-organizing component. Pressure on a company may indeed hurt its sales or stock prices, which in turn may lead the company to cut prices and wages and lay off workers. In other words, workers may suffer from the consequences of a boycott (for example) and, if they are not actively involved in the campaign, may feel that these efforts by others to "help" them are very unwelcome. Without strong worker participation in the decision to boycott, without their informed consent and full knowledge that they may suffer some immediate repercussions, the approach can backfire, leading to the alienation of the very workers the union is trying to organize.

UNITE's Guess campaign is an example of an effort to organize around the jobber's agreement principle. Unfortunately, Guess retaliated in the predictable manner, by moving work away from contracting shops where strong workers' committees had formed and by moving a substantial proportion of its production work to Mexico. On the other hand, Guess has been vulnerable to a corporate campaign that contrasts its sexy and high-priced image with the sweatshop conditions under which its clothing is sewn. The outcome of this campaign has not yet been determined, and it will no doubt affect the future of organizing in the Los Angeles garment industry.

Worker-Centered Organizing

Instead of attempting to win a standard union contract with a particular employer, which is so difficult in this industry, another basic approach is to attempt to organize garment workers regardless of where they are employed (Hermanson 1993). This is the purpose of UNITE's Garment Workers' Justice Center in Los Angeles. The Justice Center offers services to garment workers with wage claims or immigration problems and helps to educate workers not only about their rights but also about the political economy in which they find themselves. In other words, it strives to provide workers with the tools they need to understand their world and begin to fight back.

The Justice Center also provides an environment where workers can engage in lower-risk political struggles rather than a full-fledged organizing drive. Such participation is radicalizing because it undermines the belief that the employers are all-powerful and that change is impossible (see Freire 1990). In sum, a workers' center can be the training-ground for the building of a general movement of garment workers who, regardless of where they work, are ready to fight when necessary.

Unfortunately, too often the Justice Center has been overwhelmed by trying to provide basic services to a very needy population, making it difficult to pursue the goals of developing an educational and political program. Still, the kind of worker-centered organizing it encourages is essential for building a *long-term* garment workers' movement in Los Angeles. The Justice Center can prepare workers for participation in organizing drives, provide worker-supporters for those drives, and give workers engaged in a particular drive a place to go and a support structure even if their factory has been boycotted by the manufacturer. The Justice Center can also provide a community for garment workers who too often live under conditions of social fragmentation and who need to build social support networks.

Worker-centered organizing finds a natural ally in community organizing, which involves organizing around the broader issues facing Latinos and Asians, including the political assaults on both legal and illegal immigrants. That garment workers are so poorly paid and work under such oppressive conditions contributes to the general impoverishment of the immigrant community, and the political oppression of Latinos, in particular, makes it much harder for all garment workers to protect themselves against economic exploitation. Their positions as workers, as women, and as immigrants under attack reinforce one another. The struggle to improve their situation thus extends beyond winning a union contract to winning political power for the community.

This approach is exemplified by the recently formed Coalition for Garment Workers, which brings together a number of community groups and the union with the goals of providing legal services, developing an educational program, and engaging in lower-risk political actions. The community groups involved include the Asian Pacific American Legal Center, the Coalition for Humane Immigrant Rights of Los Angeles, the Korean Immigrant Worker Advocates, the Mexican American Legal Defense and Education Fund, the Legal Aid Foundation of Los Angeles, Beit Tzedek (a Jewish group that offers free legal services), and UNITE's Justice Center. Each of the community groups has engaged in organizing and providing services, and has extensive experience in working with garment workers. This coalition is engaged in outreach to garment workers, providing them with legal services and encouraging participation in the Justice Center. The coalition hopes to relieve the Center of some of its responsibility for services, pooling the resources of all the organizations involved to develop an educational and political program.

Conclusion

Many criticisms can be leveled at UNITE for its lack of success in organizing Los Angeles' garment workers. The union is mainly run from the east coast. Its top leadership does not reflect the ethnicity of the majority of garment workers. It may lack a long-term commitment to organizing garment workers. It has been riven with internal conflicts, exacerbated by the merger. There has been far too much turnover in personnel and organizing leadership.

All of these criticisms have an element of truth to them. But many of them are *consequences* of the formidable organizing difficulties posed by this industry, rather than the *causes* of those difficulties. Virtually every staff member of UNITE in Los Angeles is highly dedicated. They work very long hours for low pay. They are smart, militant, and deeply committed to bringing about greater social justice. They work late into the night visiting workers in their homes. They drive workers to and from meetings. They spend endless hours planning points of attack. They are doing the best they can under extraordinarily difficult circumstances.

UNITE is faced with a declining domestic industry and declining membership. The union leadership knows that even if they succeed in organizing the apparel industry in Los Angeles, chances are that a substantial proportion of the work will move offshore. One can argue that this is not a good enough reason for not trying to organize now, and indeed the union continues to pour thousands of dollars a month into the Guess campaign. Nevertheless, the relationship between cost and likely benefit to organizational growth and strength is not highly favorable. One may condemn such a calculation as "business unionism," but the truth is that, without resources, the union can't help any workers very much.

New approaches are emerging to bring together community and union organizing, centered on developing the workers' own understandings and capacities to fight back. Cross-border organizing programs, where workers in the various countries of production join together in attempting to prevent being pitted against one another, are another promising possibility (Armbruster 1998). Social change in this arena is not going to be won overnight. The garment industry in Los Angeles, with its globalized, flexible industrial organization, is an immensely efficient engine of exploitation and poses a formidable challenge to union organizing.

6

Organizing Latino Workers in the Los Angeles Manufacturing Sector: The Case of American Racing Equipment

Carol Zabin

At the end of July 1990, over eight hundred workers at the American Racing Equipment Company (ARE), which manufactures automobile wheels, walked off their jobs. After three days the workers, who were almost all first-generation Latino immigrants, ended their wildcat strike but began long-term organizing to improve their working conditions. Six months later they voted in favor of union representation by the International Association of Machinists and Aerospace Workers (IAM), and in September 1991 they won their first contract. The workers are now working under their third union contract, which offers them significantly higher wages than in their pre-union days as well as employer-financed health insurance and union security.

Coming on the heels of the Justice for Janitors victory and shortly before the successful drywallers' campaign (both examined in this volume), the ARE victory helped build the case that immigrant militancy could lead a resurgence of organized labor in southern California. These three campaigns shared three important elements. In each case workers were very militant, and their participation in house calls, pickets, and street demonstrations was a central feature of the campaign—and a sharp contrast with organizing carried out mainly by professional union staff. In addition, the strong social and family ties among immigrants in each sector greatly contributed to creating the solidarity necessary to initiate and sustain the campaigns. And in all three cases organized labor made substantial resource commitments to strike funds, legal assistance, and / or the hiring of organizers.

I thank everyone we interviewed: the organizers, workers, and managers who were generous with their time and frank with their thoughts. Thanks also to the other members of our research team, Ruth Milkman, Luis Escala Rabadan, and Kent Wong.

Yet there were also significant differences between the ARE experience and the other two campaigns. The campaigns of both the janitors and the drywallers were industry-wide and carried out outside the National Labor Relations Board (NLRB) framework. In contrast, the ARE campaign used many traditional tactics of "hot shop" organizing and involved a normal NLRB election. The fact that ARE is a manufacturing plant also made it different from the other two cases, as capital mobility is not a threat in janitorial or construction work.

A number of scholars and union leaders (including the new leadership of the AFL-CIO) have argued that unions need to use innovative organizing strategies to unionize large numbers of new members (Sherman and Voss, this volume; Bronfenbrenner and Juravich 1998; Lerner 1991). The emerging conventional wisdom of this "new" labor movement suggests that unions should use a comprehensive approach that on the one hand emphasizes bottom-up worker participation and militance and on the other hand uses top-down tactics to confront employers on an industry-wide basis, as opposed to organizing in individual shops. These top-down strategies include corporate campaigns; negotiations with not only subcontractors who are the direct employers but also the companies who employ the subcontractors; and using neutrality agreements and card-check recognition instead of NLRB elections (see Sherman and Voss, this volume).

While the campaigns of the janitors and drywallers relied on both industry-wide organizing and what Bronfenbrenner and Juravich (1998) call a rank-and-file intensive strategy, the ARE campaign employed only the latter. The wheel workers themselves were a major force guiding the campaign, even long after the dramatic three-day walkout. The Machinists' Union employed bilingual organizers who respected the workers' ownership of the campaign and believed workers should participate in decision making. As in the Justice for Janitors campaign, key workers at ARE had previous political experience in their home countries and were imbued with a leftist ideology that saw unionization as part of a larger struggle for social justice. And as with the drywallers, although not to the same extent, organizing was aided by immigrant social networks based in common regions of origin in Mexico.

However, the ARE drive was a traditional one-shop campaign run within the framework of the NLRB. Though the victory shows that it is still possible to win the old-fashioned way, the conventional approach was precisely its weakness. For the ARE campaign missed an important opportunity for industry-wide organizing in the twenty-five wheel factories in the greater Los Angeles region. Even though several unionists suggested that IAM design a plan to spread the campaign to the other wheel factories, the union moved most of the organizers off the campaign once the election was won and pulled out the rest once the contract was signed.

The other factor distinguishing the ARE campaign from the janitors' and drywallers' campaigns was its vulnerability to capital mobility. Construction and building maintenance services by definition cannot move to another region, whereas manufacturing can and does relocate. When union strategists speak of "industry-wide" organizing, they refer to organizing all the competitors in a particular economic sector so that no particular firm is at a competitive disadvantage because it pays union wages. In construction and services, these competitors are generally found within a bounded geographic region. In manufacturing, however, "taking wages out of competition" means organizing everywhere on the globe that the product is produced. Thus industry-wide organizing in manufacturing is generally much more difficult than in services or construction.

Yet managers make decisions about where to locate a factory based on many factors, not just labor costs. In some cases, organizing all the employers in a manufacturing industry within a region can be possible without encouraging capital flight, as may be true for wheel producers in Los Angeles. A 1994 study suggested that at least a part of the wheel industry is anchored to the Los Angeles region and is unlikely to move in response to unionization. This industry segment produces wheels for the after-market—wheels that consumers use to improve the appearance of their cars—and is closely tied to Los Angeles' style-conscious car culture (Aizeki, Fujimoto, and Kramer 1994).

In addition to some level of local rootedness, two other characteristics of the industry make it a favorable target for organizing. First, workers are more highly skilled and less easily replaced by management than janitors or other unskilled service workers. Second, many workers in different wheel factories in Los Angeles know each other, either because of previous employment or family and social ties.

Since the ARE victory, several other unions have tried to organize some of the other wheel factories, but in an uncoordinated manner. None has been successful.

Background

With approximately 646,000 jobs in 1996, the Los Angeles region has become the largest center for manufacturing employment in the United States. However, while nondurable manufacturing has maintained employment over the last twenty years, durable manufacturing has declined precipitously since the employment peak of 1979 (Wolff and Zabin 1997). Much of the decline was due to defense cutbacks, but the automobile sector also shrank dramatically. Los Angeles was once a significant center for west coast automobile manufacturing with two General Motors and one Ford assembly plants and a thriving auto parts sector that served them (Morales 1986).

Like the other large wheel factories in Los Angeles, American Racing Equipment was established to produce wheels for the assembly plants. Started as a privately owned firm in 1963, ARE now has an aluminum wheel facility in Rancho Dominguez and a steel division in Gardena. Between 50 and 70 percent of ARE's wheels are still for the original equipment market (OEM) and are shipped to Chrysler in Detroit. Though there is no longer any reason for OEM production to be in Los Angeles, ARE has maintained market share through high quality and just-in-time delivery. The company has also opened factories in Kentucky and in Mexico, both of which produce for nearby Chrysler assembly plants. The rest of its production is destined for the aftermarket, an important niche market.

The production workers at the Los Angeles ARE facility are mostly long-settled Mexican immigrants; about 15 percent are Central American. Mexican immigrants have been the predominant workforce since the plant opened in 1963. Reflecting the Mexican immigrant population in Los Angeles overall (Zabin and Escala 1998), the workers came mostly from states in central Mexico, most importantly Zacatecas, Michoacán, and Jalisco. Many of the workers who were employed at ARE in 1990, the year of the walkout, arrived in the United States in the early 1980s. Most had families, and many of their children were born in this country. A large majority had become legal residents through the amnesty program of the 1986 Immigration Reform and Control Act (IRCA). In all these ways, ARE workers typify the wave of Mexican immigrants who came to Los Angeles in the late 1970s and 1980s and toil in manufacturing, construction, and service industries in southern California.

As in the Justice for Janitors campaign, some of the leaders who emerged during the struggle had been politically active in their home countries. Eucebio (a pseudonym), who became the main leader of the campaign and first president of the local, had worked in the steel mill in the town of Lázaro Cárdenas, Michoacán, and had been active in the dissident faction of the official union there. In fact, he left for the United States when he was blacklisted by employers for his activism and was unable to obtain work in Lázaro Cárdenas. Several other wheel workers knew him in Mexico. Another committee member had been an activist in a leftist party in the state of San Luis Potosi.

A number of committee members were also relatively educated. One leader had been a teacher and an oil field technician, and several others had studied in technical schools in Mexico. Unlike these leaders, however, most workers had more limited education and many came from rural backgrounds; few had experience with unions or with political activism in their home country. In this way as well, the ARE workforce was a typical cross-section of the Mexican immigrant community in Los Angeles.

Though from the outside the 1990 walkout looked spontaneous, ARE workers were not without organizing experience. According to a United Auto Workers (UAW) International Representative, the plant was unionized by the UAW in the 1970s but decertified a few years later. In 1984, International Brotherhood of Teamsters Local 952 tried to organize the facility (then called Modern Wheel), but lost the NLRB election 268–452. According to several workers, this attempt was sabotaged when the INS raided the plant and deported significant numbers of workers shortly before the election. Although many quickly recrossed the border and came back to work at ARE, the threat of deportation dampened support for the union.

In 1988, Teamsters Local 911 initiated a new organizing campaign at ARE. By this time most workers had obtained legal immigration status through the IRCA amnesty. According to the main Teamster organizer, the union targeted ARE because several of the workers had asked Hermandad Mexicana, a community organization that advocates for immigrant rights, for assistance in addressing their workplace problems. In the late 1980s, Hermandad helped thousands of immigrants gain their papers through the IRCA amnesty program, ran classes on immigrant and labor rights, and helped workers who were interested in organizing. The Teamsters worked closely with Hermandad and recruited one of its most active leaders to be the main union organizer for the ARE campaign.

Teamster resources for the 1988 campaign were quite limited. For much of it, there was only one full-time organizer who formed an in-plant committee of ten or twelve workers. Although the organizer was very talented and is remembered fondly by members of the committee, she was unable to cover twelve hundred workers, and the committee was strong only on one shift. Management developed an effective anti-union campaign and discredited the union by informing workers about the scandals and corruption charges that Teamster leaders were facing at the time. Even under these unfavorable circumstances, the union almost won the NLRB election, with a final tally of 516–609. The effort also educated a number of workers who would later become leaders of the successful campaign two years later.

The 1990 Campaign

The workers who walked off their jobs at American Racing Equipment on the last day of July in 1990 were deeply upset with their bosses. The company had been purchased the previous year by a Canadian transnational firm and was in the midst of a transition to new management. ARE had recently hired a consulting firm that carried out time-and-motion studies and recommended changes in operations to lower costs and increase productivity. New technologies were being introduced, but neither production workers nor supervisory staff had received extensive training in their use.

The walkout started on the second shift in the foundry, where work teams operate carousels that heat aluminum and pour it into molds to make the wheels. As part of the consultant's plan, new machinery had been introduced and the two-carousel work teams were reduced from thirteen to nine men. Frustrated by the speedup and worried that a smaller team would be unable to operate unfamiliar machinery safely, foundry workers on the second shift walked off their jobs. They were quickly joined by most of the workers in the machine shop, where workers drill the holes, place the valves in the rims, and check the wheels' dimensions. There was less immediate support in the finishing, quality control, and maintenance departments, but in the end all three hundred workers on the first shift walked off their jobs (Griego 1990). By the third day of the walkout, many workers from other shifts had joined them; at least eight hundred of the twelve hundred production workers had refused to enter the facility to work. Remarkably, no one person or group is credited with leading the strike; workers all say it just snowballed.

The main complaints of the workforce concerned the plant-wide speedups and the poor treatment of workers by their supervisors. Wages and benefits were also a concern, especially because after the changes in work organization workers were required to work harder but received no wage increase. In addition, dignity surfaced again and again as an important issue. Not long before the strike, workers had been presented with a list of ten new work rules, and they were particularly irked by the one requiring them to ask permission from a supervisor before they could go to the bathroom. Workers also complained that supervisors routinely granted promotions, better shifts, overtime opportunities, and other favors to their relatives or friends. Supervisors commonly recruited or promoted workers who were relatives or *paisanos* from their home towns in Mexico or other Latin American countries. Workers outside these networks felt that favoritism, rather than merit, guided supervisors' decisions.

The spontaneous eruption of discontent created an extremely powerful basis upon which to begin a union organizing drive. During the three-day walkout, representatives from a number of unions approached workers outside the plant wearing their union jackets and passing out handbills and union cards. To Eucebio, who later became the president of the local, it seemed like "all the unions in the United States showed up." An AFL-CIO official later described the situation:

> The reason this thing got so much attention was that the workers themselves had organized the wildcat strike. Now any time nonunion workers can take ninety-some percent of themselves out on strike for four or five days indicates to me that there is strong leadership and strong organization already in the plant. The second most apparent thing was that there were some very serious grievances that had not been addressed and that there was a schism as wide as the Grand Canyon between workers and management. So these were all the makings of what we call traditionally a hot shop.... So it's kind of like having big chunks of gold pop up at a cave you walk into. You know there's a heavy lode in there somewhere.... We embarrassed ourselves. About four or five international reps all went out there shoulder to shoulder with their handbills trying to convince the workers.

But the workers rejected help from established unions at first. On the second day of the walkout, a Teamster representative asked Eucebio, whom he had known from the 1988 campaign, to convince the workers to go with IBT. Eucebio described the scene outside the plant:

> The second day of the strike I got up on top of a car, and there were about three hundred workers of the night shift there, and I said to them, "This is the moment when we have to get organized, and we need a legal representative because they're going to fire us if we stay out more than three days. Who better than the Teamsters, because they've already dealt with us, they have a history with us, they have everything."...When we asked if they wanted support of the Teamsters, someone in the crowd yelled, "No, we don't want them because they are *bien rateros* [real thieves]."

The other unions were no more successful. The majority of the ARE workers decided that they were better off without a union. They formed a committee of representatives from each department on each shift to negotiate with the company directly. Management agreed to an immediate 5 percent increase in wages, another 5 percent increase in six months, and full pay for one of the three days of the walkout. In addition, ARE's president promised to meet every Monday with the committee to discuss ongoing problems in the plant. The workers elected to go back to work under these conditions rather than risk getting fired for exceeding the maximum three days of absenteeism allowed in the individual contract that each worker had signed when hired.

Meanwhile, several days after the walkout ended, representatives of IAM District Lodge 94 began talking with a small group of workers who were not on the committee meeting with management. The Machinists became involved after a retiree heard about the strike:

> My wife and I were sitting at the table, having our coffee in the morning, and all of a sudden she says to me, "Here, these people need help!" and she hands me the Metro section of the *Times*, and I read it, where these individuals had pulled a wildcat strike. Now, you realize that a wildcat strike in this day and age means immediate termination. But they went out in mass, and the company offered to meet with them, as the article states, and set up a committee to air their grievances. So I said, "My God, there's going to be unions out there like sharks at a feeding frenzy," so I picked up the phone and called [an IAM representative], and I told him... "Here's the address, get out there immediately and start talking with these people."

The retiree also went out to the plant himself. A Chicano, he introduced himself to a worker in Spanish and offered the assistance of the International Association of Machinists. The worker said he should talk to Eucebio, who had just gone in to work and wouldn't be out until midnight. The retiree came back at midnight with an IAM representative in tow, and met Eucebio and three other workers by *la bolita*, a tree near the lunch wagon where the workers gathered to eat and chat. One of them had a relative in the Machinists' Union, and this helped the union representative gain credibility.

The meetings between the union and the small group continued. According to the retiree:

> So, for the subsequent five days we kept meeting with [Eucebio] after work, and little by little, it grew from twenty fellows to fifty fellows, and

pretty soon we decided that we'd better meet someplace away from the company, 'cause it was obvious to the company to see a group of people, and we wanted to keep this undercover as much as possible.... Denny's has a restaurant, at Long Beach Boulevard, that closes at midnight. So we drove over to their parking lot, and pretty soon it had got up to two hundred fellows, meeting out there, and going through orientation, telling 'em, explaining what we can do, how we can do it, and with that meeting, where I counted two hundred fellows, I called up ... the coordinator of organizing, and I said, "You better get down there, this is ready to go." I said, "We can't keep it in the street, we gotta establish a place to meet and start working on it." So [he] showed up at one of the meetings, and at that meeting we had 250 people, and he said, "My God, I've never seen anything like this! ... We're ready."

The AFL-CIO regional office also became involved almost immediately. The Los Angeles and Orange County Organizing Committee (LAOCOC) called a meeting early on so that all the unions who were still interested in chasing this "pot of gold" could come to a consensus over who should be allowed to pursue it. Over the years, LAOCOC had gained substantial credibility in resolving this kind of jurisdictional conflict between unions. As its director noted:

[LAOCOC was] able to get people to come together, cooperate, recognize each others' causes and if there's a dispute over them to mediate those situations. I always used to describe it as a traffic control system, like traffic lights. We just had to direct the traffic of the labor movement to keep people from running into each other. Now this [the ARE walkout] was a classic case of a potential intersection collision.

A number of unions, including the Teamsters, the Steelworkers, the International Union of Electronic, Electrical, Technical, Salaried and Machine Workers (IUE), and the Machinists attended several meetings, but it was clear that the Machinists had already made some progress with the workers and that their International was ready to commit significant resources to the effort. As LAOCOC's Director said, "At the end of the day when everything was said and done, the Machinists laid a quarter-million-dollar commitment on the table and laid a commitment of four full-time representatives to do the organizing. Then the other unions said, well, we can't match that commitment. So there was an agreement [among the unions]."

By the middle of August there were six or seven organizers working full-time on the campaign, including two from the AFL-CIO's regional staff. The organizers continued to meet with Eucebio and the other workers, building a collaborative relationship between the union staff and the workers. One organizer described his approach to the workers as "a two-way thing. [I said to them], 'Look , you guys get a majority of cards and we'll lease an office and a hall.... We will invest into this thing but we've got to see a little bit more than what's there already.' " When the meetings at Denny's grew to several hundred workers, the Machinists rented an office a few blocks from the plant. Organizers immediately began building the workers' committee and collecting cards.

The original in-house committee continued to meet with management for a number of weeks but made little progress. At some point, a number of workers walked out of the meetings. According to Santiago (a pseudonym), who was on the committee, "A moment came when the management changed, and said to themselves, 'I'm not going to give anything more, the workers aren't going to do anything.' They weren't afraid either of the union or of the strength the committee had at that moment."

Throughout this period, tremendous tensions developed between IAM's volunteer worker committee and the elected in-house committee that continued to meet with the company. Each had a strong leader, and some of the discord was due to personal rivalry. But there were also substantive differences in the groups' approaches. As a union organizer put it, Eucebio characterized the other group as "a bunch of company union guys," whereas Rodrigo (a pseudonym), the leader of the more conciliatory group, felt that his committee had been elected by the workers and "had to show the folks that sent us here that we can't get anywhere, and that we have to exhaust the system" before walking out of the process. At one point, the tensions almost erupted into a fistfight among the workers.

The IAM organizers realized the danger of this divisiveness and the necessity of bringing the two groups together. They used the card-signing effort as a vehicle for this. During the first month of the campaign, the union committee was quite successful at getting union cards signed, but in the second month sign-ups tapered off. One of the organizers explained to the union committee, "Look folks, they [the other group] are not the enemy and frankly, you guys are bringing us cards but we're still not where we need to be. We need them. They have a constituency, they're going to bring in people."

The company's intransigence also helped bring the two worker factions together. One worker who participated in the in-house committee but later became a union supporter recalled:

> The company committed a lot of errors, not knowing how to treat people,
> the arrogance that people who are heads of companies often have.…
> After five or six weeks of negotiating with the company, when we were in-
> side of the company and the [union] committee was outside… there
> came a time when we couldn't get any further, and they couldn't either.
> So we had to make a break from the company and the company paved the
> way for us, they broke it up themselves, they gave us a motive for leaving
> the table. [This was] an error that they committed because if they had
> given us what we asked for, the [union] movement wouldn't have gone
> forward.

On September 16, Mexican Independence Day, the union finally managed to get the two groups talking together, and the campaign gained momentum. An organizer described the result: "That's when it broke and we were able to move them and then once this group came on, the cards came. They flowed and they moved. And that's when we filed [for an election] in October."

The campaign intensified in preparation for the election. A big selling point that the committee used to convince their co-workers of the need to work with the IAM was the information it could provide about the procedures required to form a union under the National Labor Relations Act (NLRA). The union organizers spent hours and hours teaching workers about how unions work in the United States, and training them as organizers. They made a list of ARE workers and teamed up with workers to make dozens of house calls. Weekly committee meetings, often attended by eighty or more workers, were held on Sunday nights at 9:00 p.m. and would often last three to five hours as workers debated tactics and strategy. In addition, weekly meetings were held for each of the three shifts.

The union office was staffed twenty-four hours a day so that union staff could respond to workers coming from or going to any of the three shifts. Organizers pinned photos of committee members on the wall of the hall to emphasize that it was their campaign, and so that new supporters could gain confidence by seeing how many people were already on board. The union sponsored *carne asadas* (barbeques) for the workers and their families and cooked a turkey dinner for the workers on Thanksgiving.

Management responded by hiring an anti-union consultant who held captive-audience meetings and tried to organize opposition to the union among the workforce. The union sought to "inoculate" workers by letting them know what to expect and how to behave in these meetings. The organizers trained the workers using role plays that simulated captive-audience meetings, with one worker playing the union buster and another a worker. They warned workers that the consultant would tell them that the union would make them pay high dues, that the union was out to get their money, and that the organizers were paid much higher wages than the workers. Organizers gave workers suggestions about how to respond during captive-audience meetings, such as clapping while the consultant spoke, asking the consultant how much money management made, and using other disruptive tactics.

According to a number of organizers, management made a lot of mistakes, and its anti-union campaign was quite clumsy. One organizer said he knew they weren't facing that formidable a challenge when he did his first handbill depicting the boss at home with his tennis court and pool while the workers were slaving away in the factory. The manager responded with his own ineffective handbill stating that he didn't have a tennis court.

The workers also had fun during the campaign. At one point, the organizers made a flyer depicting the consultant as a Judas goat with a suit and a briefcase stuffed with dollar bills. A Chicano union organizer explained:

> We translated it into Spanish and to me it had no meaning. You know, "*Chivo Judas*," the Judas goat, that makes sense in English but in Spanish, it just didn't make a connection.... Well, they [the workers] looked at it and they got a kick out of it. So they started calling [the anti-union consultant] "*El Chivo*." It just picked up, and... to ridicule this guy became the greatest thing because he lost it after that. So in the meetings, you know, they would kind of look down and they would go "baaaaa." When he was walking on the floor in the foundry or in the machine shop... guys would turn around and go "baaaaa," and the thing is that they'd get to him.

One union official had a small ranch with farm animals, including a goat. He sometimes brought the goat to the factory and put a necktie around him, and the organizers debated him as if he were the real *El Chivo*. This undermined the ability of the consultant to intimidate the workers and control the captive-audience meetings.

The committee also kept a finger on the pulse of their co-workers. When a company tactic appeared to be getting through to some of the workers, the committee and the union would organize a rally outside the plant gates in order to show the strength of the pro-union workers. Before and after their shifts, pro-union workers distributed handbills outside the plant. In the last couple of weeks preceding the election they often slept in the union hall, devoting all their waking hours to the effort.

On December 20, 1990, the election was held. Out of 1,058 votes, 655 were in favor of representation by the IAM. Unlike many employers who use NLRB appeals to delay bargaining, ARE chose to recognize the elec-

tion results. Eucebio attributes the victory to the workers' taking ownership of the campaign: "I think the difference in 1990 compared to the
earlier campaign was that we began to see the movement as our own, not
like a movement of the union...but rather [that we had to] start to improve our workplace in order to be able to improve our community...the
workers decided to fight for themselves."

One of the negotiators for the company concurred that the workers
"had spoken" and had demonstrated their strength through the walkout.
He also commended the Machinists' organizing campaign and their conduct during the negotiations. In his view, conditions in the company had
been very poor while it was privately owned. After it was purchased by the
Canadian parent company, conditions were improving, but not fast
enough to convince the workers that management's record of broken
promises would change. Workers who were involved in both the 1988
Teamster campaign and the 1990 IAM campaign perceived management
as less hostile to unionization in the latter period.

As is commonly the case, however, the battle was not over once the
election was won. In fact, a contract wasn't ratified until nine months
later, in September 1991. Quickly realizing that the negotiations were
going to be difficult, the Machinists kept organizing. The workers not
only elected a negotiating committee but also, with the union's help, created a temporary local union structure with stewards and a grievance-
handling procedure.

One organizer who stayed on the campaign after the election noted,
"It's the small little victories. We got some people back to work, we were
able to resolve some stuff and we were bargaining at the same time." The
union invited trainers from the UCLA Labor and Occupational Health
Program to train ARE workers to understand the risks in their workplace
and to discuss risk-reduction strategies. They linked this training to organizing, showing workers that under federal occupational health and
safety regulations they had the right to obtain information from their employers. When the committee was able to obtain Material Safety Data
Sheets from ARE management which explained the hazardous materials
in their workplace, workers saw the concrete benefits of unionization.
The union also was able to get several workers back to work after they had
been fired. In a couple of cases they had been fired for union activity, and
the Machinists were able to win Unfair Labor Practices complaints. In another case, a worker was reinstated after informal negotiations between
the union and management.

Another tactic developed by the workers to maintain pressure on
management was to control the speed of production. Over several days,

workers would speed up production and exceed their quotas. Afterwards, they would slow down production and go below their quotas. As soon as the supervisors noticed, they would speed up production again. These actions were orchestrated in such a way that managers could not obtain evidence of an illegal slowdown, yet they intentionally underscored the discipline of the workforce and their ultimate control of the production process.

Fearing that the negotiations would not result in a closed union shop, IAM also urged the committee to get their co-workers to fill out a membership application. Once they did so, they became associate union members through the AFL-CIO's California Immigrant Workers' Association (CIWA). The IAM constitution required that to be eligible for strike benefits, a worker had to be a member with three months' paid dues, but ARE workers were given special dispensation and paid only a small portion of the regular monthly dues. By the time the contract was signed, the membership list had reached about 70 percent of the workforce.

The first contract included wage gains and employer-financed health benefits with relatively low copayments for workers. Though the wage gains weren't dramatic, workers received steady increases amounting to 12 percent over the three-year life of the contract, in addition to the 5 percent they received immediately after the walkout. Moreover, the union contract assured that everyone received the same wage increases. "Before, they only gave raises to the brownnosers, or to the supervisor's nephew or cousin," a worker recalled. In addition, thirteen supervisors were fired after the first contract was signed.

The contract also had some weaknesses, most importantly in regard to union security. It specified a modified agency shop, in which all new hires and anyone who filled out a union membership application became part of the union. However, anybody who had worked in the plant before the contract was ratified could choose not to be a union member and was not required to pay dues. It was only in 1997 when the third contract was signed that this clause was eliminated and the facility became a union shop.

ARE management thus came to accept unionization at its aluminum division. The 1990 union drive occurred only a year after the company was bought out, and in the immediate context of a restructuring effort. Current management recognizes that the walkout was in part a response to years of poor treatment by the previous owner and not just resistance to the changes instituted by the new parent company. The human resource director asserts that the company now has much better relations with its workforce, as well as a good relationship with the union. However, he also noted that "our mentality is that we want to maintain a nonunion status with all the facilities that are nonunion." ARE's steel division remains nonunionized, and management is careful not to interchange workers between the two plants.

ARE's management does recognizes that unionization has brought some benefits. The higher wages at the aluminum division are associated with very low turnover rates among the production workforce. According to ARE data, turnover at the nonunion steel facility in neighboring Gardena was about 22 percent in 1997, while at the unionized Rancho Dominguez aluminum division it was slightly over 7 percent. Since the company does invest several weeks training workers in most of ARE's departments, turnover is costly. Management plans to increase wages in the steel division for the express purpose of lowering turnover, and it is currently analyzing jobs and writing job descriptions in that plant in order to "rationalize" workers' pay.

The workers at ARE now have their own local within IAM District Lodge 94. Named for the year the Mexican Revolution began, Local Lodge 1910 was created at the request of the ARE workers, who were concerned that they would not be able to remain in charge of their union if they were incorporated into another local. The incorporation of Local Lodge 1910 into District Lodge 94 attracted a lot of attention within the IAM. The new members were mostly monolingual Spanish speakers whose only knowledge of U.S. unions had been gained through their almost two-year struggle for representation. Their wages were significantly lower than other District Lodge members, and the IAM leadership granted them special dispensation on their per capita dues to the district and the International, a subsidy which has only recently been eliminated.

Although it took over five years, the IAM eventually brought onto its staff two of the leaders of the ARE campaign. One works directly for the International and the other is on the District staff, both as organizers.

Organizing the Wheel Industry

The IAM clearly ran a very successful campaign using the rank-and-file intensive strategy promoted by the "new" labor movement. It devoted extensive resources and employed dedicated and skillful Latino organizers who could develop rapport with the workers. It also gained the workers' trust by allowing them to carry the campaign as their own, to participate actively in strategic decisions, and, finally, to create their own local. It carried out training and education to build a solid union structure, and it continued organizing after the election was held in order to keep the pressure on the company during contract negotiations.

With hindsight, however, it is apparent that the IAM leadership missed an important opportunity to organize a greater part of the wheel industry in Los Angeles. Staying within the parameters of the NLRA, the union focused exclusively on winning the election and contract in one factory. As one AFL-CIO official said, "What the board [NLRB] does is, it forces you to think small. It forces you to look at it shop by shop.... We're trying to get the labor movement back to thinking on a large scale." The IAM leadership, in contrast, considered the battle won after the contract was signed.

After the victory, the Machinists' Union and the AFL-CIO moved the ARE organizers to other campaigns. Though there was talk of organizing other factories in the wheel industry, IAM did not commit resources exclusively to the effort. One organizer started to work with workers at another wheel factory and was able to get twenty workers to organizing meetings, but then he was reassigned to an unrelated campaign. ARE worker leaders also developed several contacts at other wheel factories, but were never able to work full-time on a campaign.

Since the ARE victory, the United Electrical, Radio and Machine Workers of America (UE), the Laborers, and the Teamsters have all tried to organize other wheel factories in the Los Angeles area. The UE lost a very closely contested election in one of the other large factories. The other two lost their elections by wide margins. There was no coordination among the unions, and in several instances two unions were developing contacts at the same factory at about the same time. These organizing efforts might have been much less difficult if the unions had been able to take advantage of the extensive social and familial contacts that ARE workers had with nonunion workers in other wheel plants. Unfortunately, the unions seem to have gotten in each others' way more than they helped each other out.

Several characteristics of the industry suggest that organizing the other Los Angeles wheel factories was in fact a viable strategy, though of course a risky one. First, though wheel production is a national and even global industry, there is some evidence to suggest that Los Angeles wheel factories are anchored to the region and would not relocate or close in response to union pressure. Los Angeles wheel factories produce for two different markets, as table 6.1 shows. The aftermarket is a niche market consisting of custom and hot rod wheels, while the original equipment market involves the production of wheels for new vehicles in the large automobile assembly factories. All Los Angeles wheel factories produce for the aftermarket, but the larger firms also sell a large portion of their output in the original equipment market.

According to the Specialty Equipment Market Association, custom wheels are the most popular modification that car buyers make to improve the appearance of their cars. The trend started in Los Angeles in the early 1970s when car owners began to chrome-plate their wheels. Wheel manufacturers soon began to produce customized steel and aluminum wheels with machined designs and plating, which now vary in price from eighty-five to five hundred dollars (Aizeki, Fujimoto, and Kramer 1994).

Aftermarket production boomed in Los Angeles during the 1990s, and several large firms have recently expanded their facilities. Ninety percent of U.S. aftermarket production is located in Los Angeles, the nation's trend-setter in car culture. Like apparel and furniture production, the wheel industry is style-conscious, driven by firms' desire to create or capture the latest fashionable look. Wheel manufacturers in Los Angeles develop as many as fifteen new styles a year, and commonly carry twenty or thirty styles. New styles can become unpopular quickly, and the ability to respond rapidly to changing fashions is a key competitive advantage (Aizeki, Fujimoto, and Kramer 1994). This aspect of production limits firms' ability to move offshore.

The original equipment segment of the industry, in contrast, is directly dependent on the automobile assembly plants, and its location in Los Angeles is a product of historical rather than current business logic. The four Los Angeles companies that produce for the OEM ship their wheels to car assembly plants in the Midwest, northern California and overseas, and are at a competitive disadvantage compared to wheel producers located near assembly plants.

This market and employment structure shapes the prospects for unionization in the wheel industry in several ways. First, the most strongly rooted firms are relatively small, making them more costly targets for or-

Table 6.1. Selected characteristics of wheel plants in Los Angeles.

Plants by no. of employees	No. of firms	No. of employees	% of workforce	Market served	No. of unionized firms
Less than 100	11	349	7%	Aftermarket	0
100 to 200	8	965	20%	Aftermarket	1
200 to 500	2	675	14%	Aftermarket	0
Greater than 500	4	2850	59%	Aftermarket and OEM	1
Total	25	4839	100%		2

Source: Aizeki, Fujimoto, and Kramer 1994.

ganizing. Second, although the large firms that depend on the OEM are currently profitable, they are not likely to grow in the future as new OEM investments take place in regions with large automobile assemblers. Although this limits the life span of existing wheel jobs, unionization alone will not drive these factories out of Los Angeles; proximity to assemblers seems to be much more important than labor costs in plant location decisions for OEM wheel factories.

The contrast between the aftermarket and OEM industry segments complicates, but does not eliminate, the possibility of a future industry-wide organizing campaign for wheel factories in the Los Angeles area. Though the IAM missed an opportunity in the early 1990s, the strong contract and continuing militance of the ARE workers may yet become the basis for building a drive in the other wheel factories.

Lessons from the ARE Organizing Campaign

Is the success of the ARE campaign replicable in other manufacturing industries in Los Angeles? Although unions cannot create hot shops, the general conditions that led to the walkout are not uncommon in southern California factories, especially those in which immigrants are employed. And unions can in fact replicate some of the other elements that led to the ARE victory.

First, they can conduct research to target other industrial subsectors that are unlikely to relocate in response to wage increases and that employ a workforce with some specialized skills. Although not all manufacturing in Los Angeles shares a rootedness in the area and a demand for semiskilled workers, some portion of it does. Manufacturing has maintained high levels of employment in Los Angeles not only because of the area's inexpensive immigrant labor force but also because of its huge consumer market, its role as a fashion and design center, and its extensive base of suppliers with experience and knowledge of a wide range of manufacturing technologies.

Second, although the effort may seem risky in the absence of strong spontaneous action by workers, unions can devote resources to carry out rank-and-file intensive campaigns. They can hire bilingual organizers and promote participation and leadership development among workers. They can build upon the social relationships and solidarity among immigrants and work with community organizations that have built ties with the immigrant population over many years. Though these strategies never assure unionization, the immigrant organizing experiences in the early 1990s suggest that they increase the chances of success.

The ARE case, along with the janitors' and drywallers' victories soon after, raises a key question, namely why the early 1990s was a period of such great immigrant labor victories, a trend that was not sustained in the following years. One tentative hypothesis is that the 1986 IRCA amnesty program created a window of opportunity. By 1990–91 a large number of previously undocumented workers had gained first temporary and then permanent legal residency in the United States. In doing so they gained a measure of security previously unknown to them. Many amnestied immigrants used this occasion to bring their spouses and children to the United States from Mexico, and in the process took a stronger step toward permanent settlement. In addition, through the process of obtaining amnesty many came in contact with community groups and nonprofit agencies that actively advocated Latino empowerment. Some of these, such as Hermandad Mexicana and the California Immigrant Workers' Association, explicitly promoted labor rights. This combination of elements may well have created a sense of hope that things could be better and perhaps made some immigrants more willing to make sacrifices to try to win a better future for their families in the United States.

This window of opportunity was soon shut by an economic downturn. For immigrants, the downturn was exacerbated by the flooding of the low-wage labor market in the late 1980s and early 1990s that ironically occurred partly as consequence of IRCA (Cornelius 1992). Thus while IRCA afforded Latino immigrants more legal security, it simultaneously helped usher in a time of growing economic insecurity. For a short period, the optimism from the amnesty may have made immigrants more willing to take the risks that an organizing drive requires. This hypothesis is not meant to contradict Delgado (1993), who disputes claims that undocumented workers are impossible to organize. However, it does highlight legal status as one of a host of factors affecting workers' willingness to take the risks necessary to unionize.

If the hypothesis that the IRCA amnesty helped unionization is correct, the next few years may offer a new window of opportunity for organizing among immigrant workers. Latino immigrants are becoming citizens in unprecedented numbers, and citizenship offers them new legal protections. As they go through the process of naturalization, they once again are coming into contact with nonprofit groups which help them pass their citizenship classes and fill out their forms, and which in the process sometimes encourage them to participate more actively in U.S. society. Moreover, unlike the period following amnesty, now the economy is growing and unemployment is low, creating tight labor markets and, perhaps, a better climate for organizing.

7

Organizing the Wicked City: The 1992 Southern California Drywall Strike

Ruth Milkman and Kent Wong

On June 1, 1992, after months of preparation, thousands of Mexican immigrant construction workers in southern California went on strike for higher pay and union recognition. They achieved both goals later that year, in one of the largest union organizing successes involving Latino immigrants in recent memory.[1] The five-month work stoppage involved drywall hangers, workers who install the Sheetrock panels that make up the interior walls of modern buildings. Their strike shut down residential housing construction throughout the region, from Ventura County (just north of Los Angeles) to the Mexican border.

Construction in the area had once been highly unionized, but in the late 1970s and early 1980s the builders and developers mounted a vigorous offensive which, combined with a severe recession, virtually eliminated unions from the residential segment of the industry. As wages fell

We gratefully acknowledge the financial support of the Institute for the Study of Labor Organizations at the George Meany Center for Labor Studies, the Rosenberg Foundation, UC Mexus, and the UCLA Academic Senate for the research on which this chapter is based. It draws on published materials, as cited herein, as well as eighteen interviews we conducted in 1997 with twenty-three individuals involved in the strike, including workers, contractors, union officials, community activists, and attorneys from both the labor and management sides. Unless their names appear in published accounts of the strike, they are not identified by name here in order to protect their privacy. Some of these individuals also provided us with unpublished documents related to the strike that proved very useful in our analysis. We also wish to thank Diane Layden for sharing her extensive collection of newspaper clippings on the strike as well as other documentary materials she generously provided; Luis Escala Rabadan for research assistance; and Jeff Hermanson and Michael Burawoy for comments on an earlier draft.

1. Estimates of the number of strikers vary in journalistic reports, with four thousand the most commonly cited figure. The best accounts of the strike are Grieder 1993, Brody 1995, De Paz 1993, and Sisco and Thornburg 1993.

precipitously and fringe benefits evaporated, Latino immigrants—previously a small minority of the industry's workforce—rapidly replaced white native-born "Anglos" in drywall hanging and other trades in residential construction. Anglos either left the industry altogether or moved into its commercial branch (building office towers, shopping centers, and the like), where unions retained a substantial presence. The deteriorating pay and conditions in residential construction sparked a few wildcat strikes by drywall hangers during the 1980s, but these fleeting efforts only underscored workers' vulnerability, and wages fell even further in the recession that gripped southern California in the aftermath of the Cold War.

Against this background the well-organized, massive 1992 drywall strike was a stunning development, culminating in a major labor victory after a grueling and occasionally violent campaign. Employers, especially the large builders and developers, were intransigent in their resistance to the strike, which threatened to reverse their successful effort a decade earlier to eliminate unionism from residential construction. There were hundreds of arrests and other police actions against the strikers, as well as scattered efforts to deport the undocumented immigrants among them. Yet the strikers overcame these formidable obstacles. Local Latino community groups rallied to the workers' defense, and strikers' wives and other family members participated in various support activities as well. Even more crucial was the extensive financial and legal assistance provided by organized labor, all the more remarkable given the fact that the strikers had no formal affiliation with any established trade union.

In a region where the working class is increasingly dominated by foreign-born Latinos, the drywallers' success had enormous potential significance for the besieged labor movement. Following two other major organizing victories among Latino immigrants in the Los Angeles area—the Justice for Janitors triumph in the summer of 1990 (see Waldinger et al. 1998; Fisk, Mitchell, and Erickson, this volume) and the wildcat strike at the American Racing Equipment wheel factory (see Zabin, this volume), where workers won union recognition in 1990 and a contract in 1991—the drywallers seemed to be riding a wave of immigrant unionizing successes.

A significant peculiarity of the drywall strike was the lack of any official union involvement. The drywallers met regularly in the local Carpenters' union meeting hall in Orange County, and about 2,400 of them eventually affiliated with that organization. But the work stoppage itself was a rank-and-file undertaking, in which no established union had an active role. The strikers did receive extensive financial help from the Carpenters as well as other AFL-CIO affiliates, and also relied heavily on legal assistance from the California Immigrant Workers' Association (CIWA), an AFL-CIO-sponsored organization. Community and church groups helped support the drywallers with donations of food and other necessities. And a series of CIWA-funded lawsuits against the firms being struck, alleging extensive and systematic violations of the overtime provisions of the Fair Labor Standards Act (FLSA), by all accounts played a pivotal role in the strikers' ultimate victory. Yet it was grassroots organizing among the drywallers themselves that stimulated all these support efforts from organized labor and the community, and that led the strike to develop in the first place.

On November 10, 1992, the Pacific Rim Drywall Association (PRDA), a group including all the major southern California drywall firms north of San Diego and employing the bulk of the drywall workers in that area, ratified a union contract. It recognized the Carpenters' Union as the drywallers' representative and provided piece rates almost twice as high as when the walkout began, as well as medical benefits and preferential hiring rights for the strikers. The settlement did not include San Diego County, however, where the employers instead sued the union in late November 1992 under the Racketeer Influenced and Corrupt Organizations (RICO) Act (see Brody 1995). The suit was eventually settled out of court, but in San Diego the residential drywall industry remains intransigently nonunion to this day. Nor did the success of the strike elsewhere in the region spark the wider process of union revitalization that some hoped (and others feared) it would, either in the heavily immigrant-employing construction industry or among southern California's vast population of foreign-born workers more generally. Nevertheless, the history of the 1992 drywallers' strike offers a glimpse of the potential for and limits on union organizing among immigrant workers.

Background

As an extremely competitive, cyclically sensitive industry that often attracts speculative investment, construction typically offers highly irregular and insecure employment. Moreover, flexibility is an inherent requirement of labor deployment in construction, in which production is vulnerable not only to market uncertainties but also to vagaries of weather and seasonality. With its specialized products and complex labor processes, construction has long relied on elaborate subcontracting arrangements involving highly skilled workers, who themselves undertake to acquire any necessary training and who own the tools of their trade. Contracts are negotiated with practitioners of various crafts to secure the performance of specific tasks, spreading market risk across many different parties. Thus the modes of bureaucratic organization typical of modern mass-production manufacturing never took hold in this industry (see Stinchcombe 1959). Instead it has preserved older systems of work organization, of a sort recently revived in other settings and famously celebrated by Piore and Sabel (1984) as "flexible specialization."

Although labor migration is often a feature of the construction industry—both geographical migration and movement between construction and other sectors of the economy in which the same skills are in demand—the production of buildings is inherently local: capital mobility is minimal even in periods of accelerating economic globalization. This simple fact, along with employers' dependence on skilled labor and their vulnerability to costly delays as a result of work stoppages, has long facilitated the organization of trade unions in the industry. In the United States, unionism has been an important presence in construction for two centuries, although it has fluctuated in strength over time and space, suffering from the same volatility that plagues the building industry itself. In times and places where construction unionism has been successfully established, unions have been the single important source of stability in what is fundamentally a highly unstable industry. In their absence, cutthroat competition flourishes, particularly at the subcontractor level where capital requirements are low and small enterprises (often founded by individual craft workers) are constantly seeking a foothold. But insofar as they succeed in "taking wages out of competition" by organizing the bulk of a regional market and establishing uniform wage rates, building trades unions become an asset prized not only by workers but also by employers. As economist Daniel Quinn Mills has pointed out, "The peculiar economic conditions and characteristics of employment in construction dictate that employers and unions are placed in a much more intimate relationship than in many other industries" (1972, 17). Indeed, the unionized drywall contractors we interviewed spoke about the union in the first person, as if they were members rather than parties to a labor agreement with it.

Building trades unionism has always been among the most locally oriented sector of organized labor, even in the context of the highly decentralized U.S. labor movement, and regional variations in the strength of construction unions have often been a feature of the industry. Although the Carpenters' Union—and, indeed, organized labor more generally—enjoyed great strength in northern California in the early twentieth century, the southern part of the state, and Los Angeles in particular, remained a stronghold of the open shop even after an energetic effort by the northern California construction unions to organize their brethren in Los Angeles in the 1910s. "We know that Los Angeles, in spite of its name, is a wicked city and sadly in need of someone who can point out the benefits of trade union organization and the iniquities of rampant capitalism," exhorted the San Francisco building trades newspaper *Organized Labor* in 1910 (cited in Kazin 1987, 202). The ensuing southern organizing drive was a failure, however, and a decade later the building trades lost ground in northern California as well, in the face of a massive open-shop offensive (Kazin 1987, 202–208, 234–69).

In the boom years during and after World War II the union recovered, with marked growth throughout California, and by the mid-1950s construction was California's most highly unionized industry, with over 325,000 union members in 1956—a figure even greater than the 316,000 wage and salary workers employed in the industry that year.[2] As table 7.1 shows, building trades union membership in the state continued to rise over the following decade, peaking in 1965 at an all-time high of 376,700 union members—more than 115 percent of the number of construction wage and salary workers. Patterns of unionism for drywall installers have paralleled those for construction generally, although in the recent period of declining union strength drywallers have been somewhat less organized than construction workers overall.[3] In southern California during the 1960s and 1970s, virtually all drywallers in commercial construction and about 80 percent of those in residential were unionized. "If you weren't union , you didn't work," one drywall contractor recalled. "There wasn't a lot of work you could do that involved large residential tracts of homes and not be union. It was unheard of."

Wage levels were high in this period, with drywallers receiving about nine cents per square foot of Sheetrock installed, plus premium pay for difficult jobs, and extensive fringe benefits. The trade was a prized working-class job, often passed down from fathers to sons. "My stepfather had been hanging [drywall] for thirty-some years, and my dad and my uncles, I mean my whole family did it," one drywaller recalled. "It was a good thing to come into, because the money was excellent. The first year I got

2. The reasons for this apparent anomaly—more union members than workers—include the fact that the enumeration of workers omits those employed by government agencies and others who maintain active building trades union membership while employed in other industries, or while self-employed or unemployed.

3. In the United States as a whole, according to Current Population Survey data, 18 percent of drywall installers were covered by union contracts in 1986, compared to 25 percent of all construction workers. In 1996 the figures were 14 and 21 percent respectively. See Hirsch and Macpherson 1997, 82, 98, 113, 137.

Table 7.1. Union membership in construction, California, 1956–1987, selected years.

	Union members in construction	% of wage and salary workers in construction
1956	325,900	103%
1965	376,700	116%
1968	341,500	113%
1977	332,200	90%
1979	350,500	74%
1981	349,900	81%
1983	309,300	85%
1985	309,400	61%
1987	313,200	54%

Source: Union Labor in California, various years, California Department of Industrial Relations, Division of Labor Statistics and Research.

into it, I could bring home twelve to fifteen hundred dollars a week out there in residential."

In the early 1980s, however, these halcyon days abruptly ended as employers went on the offensive, in keeping with the nationwide attack on unionism that marked this period of deep recession and conservative politics. Starting in the 1970s, there was a national open-shop offensive in the construction industry, led by the Associated Builders and Contractors (ABC), the largest single chapter of which was in Los Angeles in the early 1980s (Galenson 1983, 381; Bourdon and Levitt 1980, 114–16). "Double-breasted" firms (encompassing both union and nonunion operations under a single owner) became widespread in the industry, and labor laws were reinterpreted so as to legitimate this practice. Nationally, union density in construction was cut almost in half between 1970 and 1990, from 42 to 22 percent. Residential construction, where unions historically had been weaker than in the commercial sector in many parts of the country, was particularly hard hit (Allen 1994; Bourdon and Levitt 1980, chap. 2). As table 7.1 shows, both the absolute number of union members and union density began to decline in the state's construction industry after 1965, and by 1987 union density in construction was at less than half the 1965 peak. Although detailed data on union density in construction for the southern California region are not available for this period, the *absolute* number of construction union members in the Los Angeles–Long Beach metropolitan area fell over 30 percent between 1973 and 1985—even though employment in the industry was growing rapidly in this period (California Department of Industrial Relations, various years).

Although the unions did maintain their grip on the region's commercial construction industry, the ABC-led open-shop movement triumphed in the residential sector. In southern California the union did not experience this as a major crisis, however, since its membership readily found new work in the burgeoning unionized commercial sector. "In the 1980s we had tremendous growth in the commercial industry," a union official explained. "We were building twenty-, thirty-story buildings, it was just work for us and that's all we cared about. [We thought residential] is a lost industry, we'll just concentrate on commercial."

Not surprisingly, deunionization led to steep declines in wages and benefits in the residential sector, where drywallers' piece rates were cut by as much as half over the 1980s. At the same time, unscrupulous and illegal practices that were relatively rare in the era of high union density began to spread, as competition among contractors spun out of control. Reports emerged of workers being paid on an all-cash basis, and there were even some accounts of payment in drugs. A union contractor explained the economic logic of payment in cash to the Orange County Human Relations Commission in 1988:

> The average $10-an-hour employee may take home $8 out of that $10 that he earns after the taxes and the FICA and so on is deducted. Well, the typical cash-paying employer will say, "Look, I'll pay you $8.50 in cash, you're going to be $.50 better off." That saves him $1.50 right off the bat. That's just the tip of the iceberg. What else is he saving? He saves all his share of the payroll taxes that go on top of that: workers' compensation insurance and the other legal requirements, easily another $2.50. By not putting this work on the books, he's saving his obligation to the State and Federal taxes that he owes, easily another $1.00. You're talking $6.00 an hour in savings. I want to ask any subcontractor out there if he can work on 60% of his labor payroll....you can see, obviously, that you cannot compete with him. (Orange County Human Relations Commission 1989, 16)

This type of cost-cutting was especially common in the labor-intensive drywall and carpentry trades. "The carpenters is typically where contractors are really going to try and cheat," one unionist explained:

> There's so much man-hours concentrated in the average stick-built job on carpenters, that's where they can chop the dollars out of a job. In other words, "Let's make a decision, we won't cheap it on the electricians and the plumbers, that's where we get our lawsuits flowing from, and if those

things go wrong, you got a problem. But who knows bad drywall? Who knows the framing doesn't have enough nails in it?" you know. That will pass inspection now anyway, inspectors are getting looser. So they [the carpenters] take a big hit.

Under these conditions, native-born union workers began to leave the residential drywall trade; indeed most never returned after the 1980–82 recession.

As we shall see, some workers and union officials blamed the union's decline on the availability of cheap immigrant labor. But when we compare southern California to other parts of the nation, this view loses credibility. The deunionization process was national, yet in most parts of the United States immigrants were not a significant presence in the construction workforce in the 1980s. Nationally, 90.6 percent of unionized construction workers were white in 1977–78 and 89 percent in 1989; similarly, nonunion construction workers were 91 percent white at both dates (Allen 1994, 415). Native-born white workers exited residential drywall jobs in southern California in response to the changes induced by union decline, rather than the converse. Natives moved into commercial drywalling, where unions maintained a presence and where in the aftermath of the 1980–82 recession an office-building boom generated plentiful job opportunities. Meanwhile, in the residential sector, the union had been crippled, and the workforce had come to be dominated by low-wage immigrant Latino labor organized under a crude and highly exploitative system dominated by "labor barons."

The Immigrant Influx and the Labor Barons

U.S. Census data tell the story of the mass influx into the drywall trade—and into the construction industry generally—on the part of immigrant Latino workers. In the five-county area surrounding Los Angeles, as table 7.2 shows, native-born workers made up 87 percent of all drywallers as late as 1980 (down from 95 percent ten years before), with foreign-born workers accounting for only 11 percent. The vast majority of the native-born workers were white, although there was a substantial group of native-born Latinos as well as a few blacks. By 1990, when the total number of drywallers was triple the 1970 level, foreign-born Latinos comprised 35 percent of the occupation and native-born whites' share had declined dramatically, to 43 percent. Nevertheless, the absolute number of native-born whites employed in the occupation rose steadily during this period of dramatic expansion in construction employment, for there was plenty of room for all ethnic groups, natives and immigrants alike. The trend toward increasing reliance on immigrant labor was apparent not only for drywallers but in the construction industry as a whole, as table 7.2 also shows.

Unfortunately, separate employment figures are not available for residential construction (the data in table 7.2 include both commercial and residential work).[4] Virtually all industry observers agree, however, that by 1990 residential drywall workers in the region—and residential construction workers in many other trades—were nearly exclusively immigrant Latinos. Ethnic segregation became the norm in the 1980s, with native whites concentrated in the more unionized commercial sector and immigrant Latinos in residential construction, which by the mid-1980s was already solidly open-shop territory. This pattern of segregation was reflected in the huge income gap between the two groups: in 1990, foreign-born Latino drywall hangers in the region had wage and salary incomes that averaged only 57 percent of those of native-born white drywallers.[5]

As experienced drywallers exited the residential sector, Mexican and Central American immigrants moved in. "It was like an atomic explosion going on," one contractor recalled. "I mean, one guy would get in and he'd bring two or three relatives, make a crew, and then one or two guys would split off that crew and make two new crews, and before you knew it you had this huge amount of people here." Most immigrant drywall hangers in the Los Angeles area (86 percent) were Latino by 1990; and within this group by far the largest group was Mexican (90 percent), with another 5 percent from Central America. Most were recent arrivals to the United States: among the Mexicans, three-quarters had arrived during or after 1980, as had over 90 percent of the Central Americans. Most of these immigrant workers were from rural backgrounds and had little formal education. According to the 1990 Census, the average foreign-born Latino drywaller had less than nine years' schooling.

Employers now were relieved of the burdens of labor recruitment, as a cadre of "labor barons" (also known as labor brokers, coyotes, *contratis-*

---

4. In the state of California in 1992, 34 percent of the value of construction work was made up of residential projects (including single-family houses, townhouses, and apartment buildings); 29 percent involved office buildings and other commercial projects, with the balance comprising highways, streets, sewers, and other nonbuilding projects (presumably employing no drywallers). See U.S. Department of Commerce 1996, CA-3.

5. These data and all others in this section are derived from the 1990 U.S. Census, Public Use Microdata Sample. Unless otherwise noted, data are for the following five counties: Los Angeles, Orange, Ventura, San Bernardino, and Riverside, which together constitute greater Los Angeles.

Table 7.2. Nativity and ethnicity of construction workers in five-county Los Angeles area, 1970–1990.

a. Drywall Hangers

	1970		1980		1990	
	Number	% of Total	Number	% of Total	Number	% of Total
Native-born whites	3600	77%	5640	71%	6564	43%
Foreign-born whites	100	2%	240	3%	281	2%
Native-born Latinos	400	9%	1020	13%	2148	14%
Foreign-born Latinos	**200**	**4%**	**620**	**8%**	**5345**	**35%**
Native-born Blacks	400	9%	220	3%	667	4%
Other	—	—	260	3%	278	2%
Total	4700	100%	8000	100%	15,283	100%

b. Wage and Salary Blue-Collar Construction Workers

	1970		1980		1990	
	Number	% of Total	Number	% of Total	Number	% of Total
Native-born whites	57,800	75%	106,200	60%	134,258	42%
Foreign-born whites	5,000	6%	6,740	4%	8,798	3%
Native-born Latinos	5,600	7%	24,820	14%	40,584	13%
Foreign-born Latinos	**2,700**	**4%**	**26,420**	**15%**	**113,646**	**35%**
Native-born Blacks	5,300	7%	9,340	5%	13,206	4%
Other	8,000	10%	4,640	3%	10,572	3%
Total	77,200	100%	178,160	100%	321,064	100%

Source: Public Use Microdata Sample, U.S. Census.

Note: The group categories shown are mutually exclusive: "whites" includes only non-Hispanic whites; "blacks" includes only non-Hispanic blacks.

tas, or patrons) came to replace the union as a source of labor supply. These Latino entrepreneurs, experienced drywallers themselves, bridged the language gap with the employers and recruited and trained workers, drawing on extensive social and kinship networks in the immigrant community. "They [immigrant workers] didn't speak English, or very little," one contractor explained.

> You had the rise of the Hispanic that was bilingual, was a little sharper than the rest of them, and he very quickly realized that he could put himself in the position of being a labor baron and not have to touch a tool and make a lot more money than anybody working. So he was the guy that would contact the drywall contractor and say, "Gee, I control fifty drywall hang-

ers, you know. I'll run your work for you."...I have no respect for them
[labor barons]. They cheat their people, they cheat the drywall contractor,
they cheat everybody. In many cases they will add people to the payroll that
don't even exist, just put dead men on the payroll. And then they just take
the check down to the local check-cashing place where they'll cash anybody's check and, you know, pay the small fee, and they'll cash five or six
checks in different names. Other times they'll have guys take a check for x
number of dollars, cash the check, and give them back a certain amount of
it in cash. It's very hard to control. Obviously we cannot follow a man down
to cash his check and make sure he puts the money in his own pocket.

A union staffer described other abuses that were common in this period:

> They were controlling pools of thirty and forty people, living off these
> guys. They would give them twenty, thirty bucks a day. They could get away
> with this, because in Mexico you're lucky if you were making thirty dollars
> a week. And to come here and make thirty dollars a day, you're a king, you
> know. And some of these patrons had a big house and he had them live
> with him and he'd charge them rent. So he's whacking 'em twice. He
> charges 'em gas to go to work and he charges 'em for living with him.

The labor baron system was not entirely new; such arrangements had
existed before on the margins of the industry, even when the workforce
was largely native-born and white (see Haber 1930, 217, 511). But in the
1980s, with the collapse of the union and the shift to immigrant labor, it
became pervasive in the mainstream of the residential construction industry. The whole setup had many advantages from the contractors' point
of view. Not only were they spared the tasks of labor recruitment, but they
could also externalize risks. As one contractor explained, "If you're going
to bid so much money to do an operation and you don't use a labor
baron, and you pay out these dollars, you may run over cost. Where if you
just put it out as so much money and let them worry about getting it
done, you've already locked in your margin." In a business where labor
accounts for more than half of total production costs, the system was attractive to many employers.

Though the union made some halfhearted efforts to recruit the new
immigrant workers who came into residential drywalling early on, as
wages fell and nonunion contractors proliferated the entire sector was
lost, and masses of immigrants poured into it during the construction
boom of the 1980s. Although some Anglo drywall workers blamed the
union's rout on the influx of immigrants, the staff and leaders of the Car-

penters, at least with the benefit of hindsight, blame themselves. "These
Mexicans didn't do it to us. We did it to ourselves," Douglas McCarron,
then secretary-treasurer of the Carpenters' Union's regional district
council (and today the union's International President), told a journalist
in 1993. "We didn't stand and fight" (Grieder 1993, 36). Another union
staffer made a similar assessment:

> What did the leadership do? They deserted. First of all, they could not in-
> teract with the workforce that was coming in here. And at the beginning
> they thought, they're going to come here, make some money, and go
> home. And all the stereotypical things that you've always heard: "They're
> lazy. They're uneducated. They don't speak the language. They're just
> going to come here and take the money and run." I mean all those things
> were said.

No one really expected the new immigrant workers to be able to
unionize. "When you get the Hispanics, they don't have a history of
unionization, and so when they came up, nonunion contractors needed a
labor source that did not identify with unions, and that was their labor
pool," a drywall contractor noted. There had been a two-week wildcat
strike by these workers in 1987, which fizzled after the contractors
granted them a raise—only to cut wages again shortly after the strikers returned to work. Then, in the early 1990s, squeezed by a new construction
slump in the region in the aftermath of the Cold War, the immigrant drywallers launched a successful organizing drive, culminating in the 1992
strike.

Organizing the Strike

The story of the strike begins in October 1991, when Jesus Gomez, an immigrant from El Maguey, a small village in the Mexican state of Guanajuato, complained of being cheated out of some of his pay by a drywall contractor. Residential construction was severely depressed at the time; the
piecework rates at which drywall hangers are paid had fallen to an all-
time low of about four cents per square foot, and premium pay for difficult work had been eliminated. An experienced worker earned only
about forty to seventy-five dollars for a ten-hour day (*Construction Labor
Report* [hereinafter *CLR*] 7–1–92, 469; *CLR* 7–22–92, 528). Those working
under labor barons presumably earned far less.

Gomez, then thirty-three, had lived in the United States for many
years and had been hanging drywall since 1975. Along with several other
highly experienced drywallers who would emerge as leaders of the strike,

he had watched the union's decline in the 1980s and the steady erosion of pay and working conditions. In October 1991, when his employer paid him sixty dollars less than the meager amount he was supposed to receive for three weeks in a row, he decided it was time to fight back. "If someone is stealing out of your pocket, you have to do something," he said (Grieder 1993, 36). Gomez contacted some Carpenters' Union officials, who offered him meeting space in their Orange County union hall. He began visiting job sites and talking about organizing with drywallers he knew, including a number of old friends from his hometown.

The fact that at least a few hundred men from the tiny Mexican village of El Maguey worked in the drywall trade, and were bound together by close kin and friendship ties, was by all accounts an important source of the solidarity that emerged in the organizing campaign.[6] "That was the key, right there," recalled a drywaller who accompanied Gomez on some of the early organizing rounds. "Having that big group from one area. The first jobs he took [us to] were where he knew his friends were at.... He went right to the people he knew." Another participant in the early organizing agreed. "We used to have a committee of guys, you know, and they were all from El Maguey," he recalled. "That core group was a very vital, important thing. They were all friends, neighbors, relatives in some way or another."

In addition, some of the leaders of the organizing effort were or had been labor barons themselves. "Kind of ironic, isn't it," one contractor complained. "They in effect brought these labor barons in and started controlling the minds of the Hispanic worker out there and telling them how much more money they could make, how they could get health benefits, this, that, and everything else, if they would get involved." These leaders not only were central players in the immigrant workers' social networks but also were knowledgeable strategists. "They knew the inside of the industry very well," an attorney for the drywallers recalled. "They could see that the bottom was falling out of the industry and their choice was to either leave it or do something to make it better. They knew the weak points, how to talk to people. A lot of them had been here more than ten years and knew what it was like to live well off this industry."

The organizing got off to a slow start, but after a few months the Saturday morning meetings Gomez and his allies held in the Carpenters Local 2361 union hall were attracting hundreds of workers. As the campaign mushroomed, separate committees were formed in each of the

6. According to the Mexican Census, the population of El Maguey (San Francisco *municipio*, Guanajuato state) was 1,560 in 1990, including 734 children under age fifteen. INEGI 1990, vol. 11. Presumably as a result of disproportionately male migration to the United States, the ratio of males to females in the town's population was only 3:4.

counties involved (Orange, Ventura, San Bernardino, Riverside, Los Angeles, and San Diego). Although the Carpenters' Union made its halls available for these meetings, union members and staff—at this point still predominantly Anglo and fairly conservative, more or less typical of the building trades in both respects—were sharply divided in their views of the organizing effort. Many were skeptical about the prospect of organizing the new workforce. "Even some business agents from the drywall local, they were totally opposed," a union staffer recalled. "They said, 'No, you can never organize those guys. You're beating your head against the concrete.' "

The campaign, then, was a bottom-up affair. Although the Carpenters initially offered some modest resources to help it along, it seems clear that the union would never have initiated this effort, and initially the level of support was lukewarm at best. This proved quite fortuitous, however. The fact that these workers, who called themselves the "Movement of Drywall Hangers," were not affiliated with the Carpenters or any other union meant that they were not subject to the thirty-day legal limit on picketing for union recognition in construction (after which the National Labor Relations Act requires that a petition be filed for a representation election). When the militantly anti-union Building Industry Association (BIA) filed Unfair Labor Practice charges under the Act against the Carpenters, the complaints were dismissed for lack of evidence, precisely because the union was not an official sponsor of the strike (*Daily Labor Report* [hereinafter *DLR*] 7–30–92, A3; *CLR* 7–22–92, 527). Employers did get temporary restraining orders limiting picketing in many instances, but even this was more difficult than usual, thanks to the strikers' independent status. One drywall executive told us:

> There was some violence associated with it, some houses burned, windows were broken, some people were beat up. If the Carpenters were directly linked to it you could go get an injunction, a restraining order, and that would stop them from doing it. They could be liable if somebody actually got hurt. But more importantly, they would've been able to stop their activity. They would have to comply with all the picket laws.

> See, when you go out and if you're a laborer and you decide that you're gonna have a walkout and picket, there's no law governing you. You're basically just a worker. The courts really look upon you as, you're special, there's nothing that we can do to stop you. If you belong to a union, now I have legal recourse, now I can stop you. But as an individual there's no way to stop you because it's your freedom of speech and so on and so forth. So you get into a whole different ball of wax.

Indeed, as management attorneys pointed out later on, the "strategy of declining representation by a traditional labor organization in the early stages of the strike was an important tactic" (Sisco and Thornberg 1993, 14).

Initially the walkout was extremely successful, shutting down virtually the entire industry. "There is no drywall getting done," a PRDA representative told the press in late June 1992 (*DLR* 6–24–92, A5). There were widespread allegations of intimidation and violence from the outset. "The strikers are intimidating the non-(striking) people," one building executive complained to the *Orange County Register* in the strike's second week. "I've heard they followed them off the freeway, slashed their tires and smashed their (car) windows in" (Mouchard 1992). While it is difficult to know how extensively such tactics were used, they were particularly potent in the context of the immigrant networks in which most drywall workers were enmeshed. A drywall contractor explained in an interview:

> Unfortunately, the community, the Hispanic community is pretty tight, most of these people know where everybody lives....You may live next door to other people in the trade or on the same block. The guy down the street is a union supporter, you want to go to work, he sees you leave in the morning with your tools, uh, he's going to report you to the union thugs, that you're working. They're going to threaten you. There were people followed home, there were people shot at...we had a job where they actually kidnapped one of the guys and took him for a ride and dropped him off in the middle of the wilderness, basically threatened his life if they found him working again.

However, soon the employers began to fight back, winning court injunctions on picketing and actively recruiting "replacement workers" from out of state. Though the drywall contracting firms expressed some interest in negotiating with the strikers early in the dispute, the builders and developers were adamantly opposed to this course of action and urged continued resistance to the unionization effort (Flagg 1992a; field interviews). With no resolution in sight, as the strike entered its second month and it became clear that the dispute would be a prolonged one, some of the strikers began drifting back to work, increasingly desperate for income. "We were on a high at first, because we had 90 percent of the people come to the meetings," one drywaller active in the strike recalled. "And then, the reality was when the money went away, so did the workers." By mid-July, six weeks after the walkout began, another drywall movement leader estimated that 30 percent of the strikers had gone back to work, and employers claimed the actual figure was even higher

(*CLR* 7–15–92, 494). Under these conditions, there was an urgent need for funds to support the strikers who remained committed to the work stoppage.

Moral, Material, and Legal Support

After the strike had gone on for about six weeks, the AFL-CIO Regional Office established a Dry Wallers' Strike Fund, soliciting contributions of money to assist with strikers' rents, utility bills, and food and securing donations of pro bono legal assistance. Ultimately this appeal yielded over a million dollars from over twenty different unions, with the Carpenters' Union by far the largest contributor (*DLR* 11–23–92, C3; *California AFL-CIO News* 1992; field interviews). These funds played a critical role in sustaining the drywallers after the strike's first few weeks, when many strikers began to have difficulty paying their household bills. "They needed a lot, they needed the basics. They needed rent. They needed food," an organizer recalled. "In order to make the strike effective, we couldn't ask them to go out and get other jobs. We needed almost everybody to fan out in these teams and pull other strikers off the job sites."

Food and money were also donated by a range of community and church groups. A local Orange County restaurateur went so far as to sponsor weekly fund-raising parties, complete with dancing and raffle tickets, for which he provided all the food and entertainment. These were extremely popular with the strikers and their families and did a great deal to boost morale in addition to raising cash in support of the strike. The local Catholic church also offered both moral and material support. Food donations came from as far away as San Francisco. In mid-August a coalition of twenty-five religious, labor, and community groups delivered five thousand pounds of rice, beans, and tortillas to the strikers in a dramatic show of support (*Los Angeles Times* 1992).

Beyond helping sustain strikers' households, the AFL-CIO strike fund was also used to bail them out of jail, money for which soon proved to be in great demand. "The contractors were really raising hell with the police...every day they were jailing 'em," noted an organizer. "It was critical to keep our strike leaders on the ground, out of jail, out of the deportation tank." Nor were the arrests limited to strike leaders; by October 1992 some six hundred strikers had been arrested (Moran 1992). The single largest arrest occurred on July 2, 1992, a month after the strike began, when 149 strikers were arrested leaving a job site in the Orange County town of Mission Viejo on charges of trespassing and kidnapping—reportedly the largest arrest in the county's history. They were all jailed, with bail set at fifty thousand dollars per person. One of the attorneys involved in the strikers' defense recalled:

> It was a nightmare kind of situation, 'cause most of the people were major supporters of the strike and they felt that if these people were in a jail for a period of time, that large of a group, that it would wipe out the momentum. 'Cause Orange County was the center, the focal point at that time.... The whole idea was, we got to stop this strike right now, we know these guys are hoodlum, immigrant Mexicans, and we know how to take care of them. It was a very hot day. They put 'em in a bus and they kept 'em in the buses for hours, before transporting them. They took them over to the jail and processed them en masse. They were held in jail, some of them, for ten days, some of them without knowing what the charges were because they [the police] said they were investigating and finding out who was involved in the kidnapping and who wasn't.

Within hours, 250 people demonstrated in protest of the arrests outside the jail, most of them wives and children of the incarcerated strikers along with drywallers who were not arrested. The U.S. Immigration and Naturalization Service (INS) placed holds on eighty-eight of the arrestees, who were threatened with deportation after their cases were resolved (Weiner and Volzke 1992; Zoroya 1992; Hall and Flagg 1992).

Most of the legal work generated by the strike was coordinated by CIWA, which recruited a battery of volunteer lawyers specializing in immigration, criminal, and labor law to defend the drywallers against the employers' multipronged attack. CIWA had been founded in 1989 as an AFL-CIO experiment with outreach to Latino immigrants, and its staff played a key role in supporting the drywallers. "These were folks who are seasoned veterans in organizing [Latinos], speak the language, know the culture, and know the complexities of the immigration laws and the labor movement," recalled an organizer. CIWA's legal assistance proved quite effective in Orange County. After the 149 arrested strikers refused a plea bargain and insisted on their innocence and their right to a trial, forty-seven of them were released and bail was reduced for the rest. The kidnapping charges were dropped as well (see De Paz 1993; Saavedra and Collins 1992).

Thanks in large part to CIWA's work, the arrests did not intimidate the strikers and their supporters, but instead sparked intensified mobilization efforts. On July 9, a week after the arrests, three hundred people demonstrated at the Orange County courthouse, among them some of the newly released strikers, along with family members and supporters from Hermandad and other Latino community groups, demanding that all remaining criminal charges be dropped. The next day, another ninety-one workers were released from jail, but seventy-four of them were turned over to the INS for possible deportation. A few days later, another rally brought some five hundred strikers and supporters to Santa Ana's Civic Center Plaza. By late July all but twenty of the original group of 149 arrestees had been released, with some pleading guilty to minor charges, in a clear victory for the strikers (Martinez and Dizon 1992; García-Irigoyen 1992; Christensen and Legeon 1992; Reyes 1992; Christensen 1992; Reyes and Hall 1992).

Here the availability of money from the strike fund was also critical. "The thing that really helped us was being able to bail leaders out of jail and keep 'em on the ground," an organizer recalled. "That kept the morale going. As we accelerated the strike and pulled more workers off the job sites, it was the ability of those workers to look out there and constantly see their leaders willing to take the risk, going to jail." After these initial waves of mass arrests failed to squash the strike, and as publicity about the arrests generated extensive public sympathy for the drywallers, the Orange County police began to take a more cautious approach. In late July, another confrontation with strikers allegedly throwing rocks at a construction site ended with no arrests at all. Only a few strikers were arrested in Orange County in the following months, all on minor charges (such as spitting at security guards), despite continuing mass picketing and an ongoing police presence amid frequent allegations of vandalism, kidnapping a foreman, violence, and intimidation of strikebreakers (Legeon 1992a; Eaton 1992; *Orange County Register* 1992; *Los Angeles Times* 1992).

Just as the Orange County mass arrest cases were being resolved, the spotlight shifted to Los Angeles itself, when sixty-eight drywall strikers were arrested on July 23 in Hollywood in an incident that spilled over onto a nearby freeway, halting traffic. The strikers claimed the police forced them onto the freeway; the police claimed the strikers deliberately blocked the freeway (Malinic and Reyes 1992a; del Pilar Marrero 1992a). These arrests, not at remote construction sites in Orange County but at the epicenter of the nation's media industry, generated considerable publicity, much of it highly sympathetic to the strikers. "You don't really realize the difference between Orange County and Los Angeles until you see something like that," an organizer recalled. "Until you move into the media circus that's here [in Los Angeles] and then all of a sudden it becomes southern California, because of the media reach here in the major metropolis."

Once again the AFL-CIO and CIWA provided professional assistance on both the legal and public-relations fronts. Several hundred strikers demonstrated in front of Los Angeles Police Department headquarters six days later, demanding a meeting with newly appointed police chief Willie Williams, and extracted a promise that the Hollywood freeway incident would be investigated (del Pilar Marrero 1992a; Aldana 1992). This conciliatory approach reflected the fact that the Los Angeles police had been under heavy criticism in the preceding period and that the incident occurred only a few months after the Los Angeles "riots" in the spring of 1992, a context which the strikers played to their advantage. An organizer recalled:

> We said, "It's a Latino Rodney King. They're just beating the crap out of the people for no reason and all that kind of stuff." The police had spread out. They had the riot squad. They had cleaned the street, and the media had come in and they had heard about it too. The police were saying, these guys are drywall strikers and they ran into the freeway to block the freeway, so that they could get the attention to their strike, and we're arresting 'em—making these guys look like thugs. So we had to refocus the thing: "How can this happen and we have a new leader, Willie Williams?" Comparing it to Rodney King ended up making it a social justice kind of issue.

With the expert assistance of CIWA and of other groups supporting the strike, then, the police activity was largely neutralized. The one place where this was not the case was San Diego. Even as the police in Orange County and Los Angeles were backing off from the aggressive approach they had initially taken toward the strike, the San Diego Police Department (SDPD) escalated its efforts to control the situation. In mid-August 1992 the SDPD established a special Drywall Task Force which included some high-level police officers and which reported directly to the chief of police. The task force monitored the San Diego drywallers' organizing efforts closely and devoted extensive resources to surveillance of the strike leaders there. The intensity of this effort was probably related to the fact that the San Diego employers adamantly refused to sign the agreement which settled the strike in the rest of the region in November 1992 (a matter considered in more detail below). In any case, north of San Diego, by the late summer of 1992 the spotlight had shifted away from police activity and toward an innovative legal offensive that CIWA-funded attorneys had developed to increase the pressure on the drywall employers.

The Legal Offensive

In late July 1992, after the strike had been underway for about two months, the legal component of the strike support effort shifted from a purely defensive approach focused on keeping strikers out of jail to an aggressive multipronged attack on the employers. One element in this attack involved filing complaints with the National Labor Relations Board (NLRB) protesting the injunctions obtained by employers limiting strikers' picketing of job sites. A second involved complaints to the U.S. Department of Labor, soon followed by lawsuits, over drywall employers' violations of the overtime pay provisions of the 1938 Fair Labor Standards Act (FLSA). The third legal move involved a more obscure feature of the FLSA, the "hot goods" provision, which allows the government to stop sales of a product made in violation of federal labor law (in this case the FLSA's overtime pay requirements). Though all these efforts helped intensify the pressure on the drywall contractors, by all accounts it was the FLSA lawsuits that ultimately brought them to the bargaining table and led to the November strike settlement.

The FLSA overtime violation lawsuits were the brainchild of Robert Cantore, one of the attorneys who had been helping with the CIWA-coordinated legal defense of the strikers. He recalled:

> As I'd get to meet and talk with these guys, just to pass the time, I'd ask, "What were you guys being paid?" And, you know, I was hearing that they were making like three hundred dollars a week working six days, ten hours a day. I said, "Even with the overtime?" And they said, "Well, we're not entitled to overtime, we're pieceworkers." But the FLSA specifically provides for piecework and specifically tells you how to compute overtime....FLSA is a great statute; it's one of the most pro-employee statutes that's ever been enacted.

Realizing the huge potential liability of the drywall contractors, Cantore proceeded to document the overtime violations by means of a questionnaire (translated into Spanish) asking striking workers to record their hours and the employers they had worked for over the previous three years (the statute of limitations precluded any longer time period). Based on these data, he then wrote to the U.S. Department of Labor asking for an official investigation and indicating that he was prepared to file class-action lawsuits on behalf of all drywall hangers in the region, as indeed he ultimately did.[7]

By the time the strike was settled in November he had filed a total of forty-eight FLSA lawsuits (Saavedra 1992). The potential liability for the relatively small drywall firms involved was enormous, because the suits claimed not only back pay for overtime worked over the three-year statutory period by thousands of employees, but also double punitive damages and attorneys' fees. The "hot goods" section of the FLSA carried additional penalties. Indeed, these lawsuits were the turning point, finally bringing the employers to the bargaining table after over three months of intransigent resistance to entering into any negotiations. "We would have defeated the strike. It was the lawsuits," one drywall executive recalled. An analysis of the strike by the attorneys representing management made the same point in more detail:

> Despite the initial success of the strikers, by late summer the strike had begun to fail. Contractors continued to operate with employees who did not support the strike and with replacement employees from northern California or out-of-state. . . . the amount of work being performed by struck employers continued to increase, and it appeared that the companies and the strikers had entered into a costly war of attrition on the picket lines and in the courts. These dynamics changed when the strikers filed over forty class action lawsuits against the drywall companies for alleged violations of the FLSA. (Sisco and Thornberg 1993, 16)

And the owner of a large drywall firm explained:

> The unfortunate thing was that in the industry a lot of people did not keep good time records. . . . It's a pretty loose trade, and even some of the more sophisticated large companies did not have decent time records. Once those [suits] were filed, there were some people that had great exposure and some of those people with great exposure very quickly decided that maybe we should find a way to settle this lawsuit and the strike. It became in their interest to become a union contractor and have all this go away.

Starting in September 1992, the Pacific Rim Drywall Association (PRDA), a trade group comprised of nonunion residential drywall contractors which had been established a few years earlier but which previously had no involvement in labor relations issues, began meeting with

---

7. This complaint was filed on July 28, the same day that the NLRB unfair labor practices charges were filed. See *DLR* 7–3–92, A2–A3; Flagg 1992b.

strike leaders and with representatives of the Carpenters' Union about a possible settlement (Flagg 1992c, 1992d, 1992e; Murray 1992; Legeon 1992b). Some of the larger firms in the PRDA had been in the industry prior to the deunionization of the early 1980s and knew the Carpenters' Union leaders from those days, which facilitated the negotiating process. After the trade group amended its bylaws and established a "Labor Relations Member" status for those members who were interested in multi-employer bargaining, the PRDA proceeded to negotiate with the Carpenters' Union (see Sisco and Thornburg 1993, 18–19). By the time of the final settlement, the PRDA represented an estimated 75 percent of the drywall industry in the southern California counties north of San Diego.

Settlement and Contract

When settlement negotiations began, the Carpenters' Union, which previously had no involvement in the strike beyond offering meeting space and financial support, moved to center stage when it was asked to help negotiate a contract and represent the strikers. Now the PRDA-affiliated employers agreed to recognize the Carpenters' Union as the exclusive bargaining agent for the drywallers without a representation election; the drywall hangers became dues-paying members of the union; and on November 10, 1992, the employers and the union signed a two-year contract providing for higher wages and medical insurance benefits as well as a "Settlement Agreement and Mutual Release" that guaranteed withdrawal of the FLSA complaints and lawsuits. This second document was also signed by representatives of CIWA, Hermandad, and individual workers named as plaintiffs in the lawsuits.[8]

The contract offered dramatic improvements in the wages, conditions, and benefits for drywall hangers. It also provided a standard grievance procedure and arbitration clause. Piece rates were set at 7.25 cents per square foot of drywall hung, with higher rates for more demanding jobs, and employers agreed to pay half the costs of health insurance for the workers. The 7.25-cent base rate was almost double what workers had received when wages were at their nadir, just before the work stoppage began. Yet since the five-month strike itself had driven pay rates up already (because of the labor shortage it induced), the new rates were not perceived as particularly onerous by the contractors or builders. "By the time the strike ended, the rates were already up. So the agreement that

8. Copies of the contract and settlement agreement are in the authors' possession. See also *DLR* 11–13–92, A2; *DLR* 11–23–92, C1–C4; Flagg 1992f, 1992g.

we made with the union was almost invisible at that point to the builders," one drywall executive noted.

Although the contract represented a substantial improvement from the point of view of the immigrant workers involved, neither the wage rates nor the benefit provisions were comparable to what drywall hangers had enjoyed prior to the deunionization of the early 1980s. "It was a good agreement," an employer who had been involved in the negotiations recalled. "It did have health insurance, but the men had to pay for half of it. And there was no pension, none of the things that you normally associate with a union." The contract did guarantee, however, that strikers who signed the accompanying settlement agreement (withdrawing the FLSA lawsuits and complaints to the Labor Department) would be placed on a preferential hiring list, and that at least half the workforce of each signatory contractor would be drawn from this list over the two-year period covered by the contract. There was a delay of several weeks in implementing this part of the agreement because of difficulties in getting signatures from the numerous named plaintiffs in the FLSA suits (and thus delays in filing the settlement agreement in the courts), which caused some unhappiness among the rank-and-file strikers who were eager to go back to work under the terms of the new contract. Still, on the whole the settlement was a clear victory for the strikers.

PRDA leaders were acutely conscious of the risk that future growth in the nonunion sector would erode their profitability, and so they negotiated an unusual clause in the union contract linking wage rates to the market share held by the union. The contract provided that if the market share held by union firms dropped by 20 percent or more, the workers would automatically lose the 50-percent employer contribution toward their medical insurance, and piece rates would be determined by market conditions instead of by the contract. If the possibility of a reversion to nonunion wage levels that this clause contemplated cast a dark shadow over what was widely hailed as a major victory for organized labor, even more ominous was the fact that the drywall employers in San Diego County, who had resisted the strike vigorously from the outset, now declined the opportunity to join the PRDA-brokered settlement.

Holding Out in San Diego

From the outset, the San Diego drywall employers were far more strongly opposed to the strike than their counterparts to the north. Even in the context of the larger southern California region, with its long history of hostility to labor unions, San Diego is the extreme case. In 1991, on the eve of the strike, only 7.2 percent of private sector workers were union members in the San Diego metropolitan area, compared to 12.5 percent in the Los Angeles–Riverside–Orange County area (Hirsch and Macpherson 1997, 63, 66). The San Diego construction industry had once been heavily unionized, as in the rest of the state, but as deunionization took hold in the late 1970s the employers proved even more determined than those elsewhere to block any new organizing efforts. "They'd be damned if they were to ever have any unions come into their territory—as opposed to ours [L.A.-area employers], who were saying, 'Well, we held them off for ten years,' " a building trades unionist explained.

> San Diego's like a different state for construction workers. L.A. and Orange County are fairly homogeneous. Riverside and San Bernardino are a little different, a little less organized. You know, for as little control as we have here, they have less there. San Diego has no control. [California governor] Pete Wilson used to be the mayor of San Diego. He busted prevailing wages out of San Diego and wiped the unions out. And that was a big chunk of work, city-controlled work. And also it seems like the ABC's efforts, our anti-union group, was really concentrated in San Diego for a long time. So it's a whole different world down there.

The employers had extensive local support in their resistance to the strike, as San Diego's political culture is intensely conservative and anti-unionism is pervasive. The area has a vast network of military installations, and its immediate proximity to the Mexican border helps foster a strong anti-immigrant animus among employers and other members of the local elite. "As a county, it is to the right of Attila the Hun," one of the drywall strikers' attorneys exclaimed. As noted, police surveillance of the strikers was also far more energetic and unrelenting in San Diego than to the north. Several of our interviewees claimed that there were close ties between developers and the city's political leaders, and that these ties explained the high priority the police department assigned to the strike, although we were unable to document this directly.

Another effect of the relatively small size of San Diego was that contractors there formed a tightly knit community. "They are a much more closed society down there than we are," a Los Angeles-based contractor stated.

> Those contractors down there, a lot of them are second or third generation, their kids play on each other's baseball teams, and they just have a different mind set. It's kind of a "good old boy" school. There's only a couple, two or three material suppliers. So you can bump into the guy

every day or every other day. I mean, there's a lot of opportunities to see these people. You just don't have that here. You can't; we all come from different areas.

The employers in San Diego were organized by the open-shop-oriented ABC, which helped set up a labor recruitment system during the strike to supply "replacement workers" to contractors affected by the strike. Although there was at least one meeting between the representatives of the ABC in San Diego and the PRDA, "they wanted no part of the settlement," as one contractor put it. "They just didn't want to be under the control of a union." Another contractor was more critical. "The ABC got involved, a guy came up and talked to us at the PRDA and told us the things that we could do," he recalled. "And half the things he said were with an eye wink. I mean, basically what he was suggesting were things that if he said them out loud, they'd be illegal."

Just as the employer community was more closely knit in San Diego than to the north, the drywall strikers enjoyed less support in San Diego from the local labor movement and the Latino community than their counterparts in Orange County and Los Angeles. There was also rivalry between some of the strike leaders in San Diego (none of whom was part of the El Maguey network) and those in Orange County, which did not help matters. Moreover, immigrant drywallers, at least those without documents, were often geographically isolated in San Diego because of the many border checkpoints between that city and points north. "San Diego is like a jail for an illegal alien," one strike leader noted. "They can go nowhere but there in San Diego, because of the checkpoints. They stay there for years. People from here [Orange County] can go to work over there, but people from there can't come and work here. If they get caught by the border patrol, they're gone. And you know, it's getting tougher and tougher [to reenter the United States from Mexico]." Thus, as their employers organized more effective resistance than their counterparts to the north, the San Diego strikers were more easily intimidated and less cohesive.

The RICO Suit

The drywall firms in San Diego not only refused to be part of the strike settlement but went on the legal offensive shortly afterward, filing a massive lawsuit against the Carpenters' Union under the RICO Act and several other federal and state laws in November 1992. The civil suit accused the union of orchestrating the strike and the violence associated with it,

naming individual strike leaders active in San Diego as codefendants as
well (*DLR* 1–15–93, A5–A7). As David Brody has pointed out, RICO has
recently emerged as a powerful legal tool for anti-union employers facing
a militant strike:

> The law, as written in 1970, was intended to deal with a particular prob-
> lem: the penetration of legitimate business by organized crime. Captur-
> ing this kind of elusive activity demanded legislative crafting that was at
> once comprehensive and elastic, and this, in the hands of inventive pros-
> ecutors and lawyers, has made for a law of nearly endless applicability to
> alleged patterns of criminal conduct not remotely attributable to the
> Mafia. . . . Any hard-fought strike—the drywallers' strike, most certainly—
> will produce sufficient allegation of "a pattern of illegal activity" so de-
> fined as to pass the threshold, and hence may become a target for a RICO
> suit. (1995, 365)

The legal costs of a RICO suit can be mammoth for both sides, as the law
is extremely complex. The union was potentially liable for triple damages
plus costs and attorneys' fees—as well as punitive damages on the state
law claims—amounts that could easily total tens of millions of dollars.
And even if the suit proved unsuccessful, the legal costs of mounting a defense would be formidable. In fact, the San Diego drywall contractors
who were the nominal plaintiffs in this suit lacked the resources to finance it themselves; instead ABC—the national trade association that
had taken the lead in deunionizing the construction industry a decade
earlier—paid the bills. As Brody notes, "ABC leaders must have read the
drywallers' victory in just the same way as did the jubilant L.A. movement,
that is, as a breakthrough event for construction unionism. The RICO
suit was their counterthrust" (1995, 366).

The union's initial reaction was to move to have the RICO claims dismissed; although the court did dismiss them once, later it allowed them
to be reinstated. Matters dragged on for more than a year and a half before an out-of-court settlement was reached in September 1994. Although
the terms were not publicly disclosed, they included a "substantial payment" from the Carpenters' Union. Certainly the prospects of the
union's prevailing in a San Diego courtroom (just as the campaign for
the anti-immigrant Proposition 187 was beginning) were not especially
favorable, and the Carpenters presumably sought to cut their potential
losses (Brody 1995, 366). The strike continued in San Diego after November 1992, although with declining effectiveness. In June 1993, as they
grew increasingly desperate in the face of the contractors' intransigence,
the striking San Diego drywallers launched a hunger strike. By that time

they even had formed an affiliation with the Painters' Union, although they continued to use the Carpenters' meeting hall. In the end, the San Diego employers remained nonunion, the one exception to the strikers' victory in the wider region. Drywall hangers' wages did rise in San Diego, however, to a level comparable to those paid in areas where they had won a union contract.

Epilogue and Conclusion

If nothing else, this strike certainly demonstrated that immigrant Latino workers are "organizable," even under the adverse conditions characteristic of the late twentieth century. If such a strike could happen in the construction industry, where new organizing was, at least until very recently, a nearly forgotten art, it could happen anywhere. Many building trades unionists who became involved saw the strike as a peak experience. "You know, there are people who go through their whole careers as business agents, and they never see anything like this," one union official exclaimed. "It finally brought to view that organizing was possible, that it's not just some b.s. ethereal concept. It's like forever, from then on forward, whenever I bump up into a developer and they find out who I am, it's like 'Oh, you guys really can blow things up!' I think any craft that had the bucks could try something similar." The success of the drywallers' campaign depended on the unusual combination of bottom-up organizing by workers themselves on the basis of preexisting immigrant social networks, on the one hand, and the financial and legal support provided by the labor movement on the other. The absence of any active involvement on the part of a preexisting union, and the pervasiveness of illegal labor practices among employers—making them vulnerable to the FLSA lawsuits—were also key ingredients of success.

If the case offers some grounds for optimism, it also offers some cautionary tales. The victory depended on a massive expenditure of funds (including unusually generous support for strikers' living expenses) on the part of organized labor. The RICO suit, only one component of the financial burden, casts a dark shadow over future organizing in construction and elsewhere. Although many people in the labor movement hoped—and many employers feared—that the drywallers' victory would be the first of a series of efforts to reunionize the residential construction trades in the Los Angeles area, this has not yet occurred.

There was a large-scale strike by three thousand Latino framers in 1995, using some tactics similar to those that had worked for the drywallers. However, this work stoppage proved ineffective. The immigrant community did not rally to support the strikers as it had in 1992, and CIWA had been dismantled by the national AFL-CIO shortly after the drywall strike. In addition, the employers immediately sued the Carpenters' Union and won injunctions on picketing, minimizing the impact of the strike. Although the strike did yield a marginal increase in the number of residential framing contractors who signed a union contract with the Carpenters, most remained nonunion (*California AFL-CIO News* 1995; Burnham 1995; Lee 1995; *DLR* 6–19–95, A4–A5).

Not only has organizing failed to spread to other deunionized crafts in residential construction, but since the 1992 strike the Carpenters' Union has failed to sustain the share of the residential drywall industry it had at the time of the 1992 settlement. At the end of the strike well over three-fourths of the drywall trade was under union contract; five years later the union share had eroded to about 50 percent. Most of our interviewees—unionists and employers alike—blamed the union for this. "If the union doesn't stay strong and vigilant out there, then there gets to be more incursion of nonunion drywall," one building trades staffer noted.

> The fact is that they don't bring the hammer down on every developer that uses nonunion drywall, in the same way they did during the drywall strike. You got to spend another ten years [after the strike] policing it as militantly! That's the tough part. And our attention span is so short, we're so project-oriented, that it's tough to understand that whatever wrath of God you brought down during the strike, you got to do the same thing to every developer that wants to build a home.

A drywall company executive also expressed disappointment in the union. "They've done a really poor job of organizing," he said. "They don't seem to have any real muscle. I mean, they can send a couple of guys out and they can picket around in front of a job, but who pays any attention?"

As the union's weakness became evident, membership in the PRDA fell from thirty-four firms after the strike to only about a dozen five years later. The union contract has been renewed a few times since the strike, and the clause allowing wages to float with the market has not been a problem. Indeed, wages have remained high in both the nonunion and union sectors, thanks to a construction boom, but for union contractors the decline in the union's market share poses a serious problem. Although the buoyant economy has thus far allowed the union to keep its membership largely intact, the next recession could easily stimulate another open-shop offensive like the one in the early 1980s, once again threatening the union's hard-won foothold and putting downward pressure on wages.

The Carpenters did hire two of the strike leaders as staff members after the settlement, but there was no structure in place to educate the new membership. Indeed, one of these new staff members reported that very few of the workers are involved in the union: "Right now, all they want to do is work and work and work. So they don't come to the meetings. Just a few guys turn out." Moreover, the Carpenters' Union had no recent history of internal organizing. "There was a lack of union education back in the '70s and '60s," one union official recalled. "There was no need for it. Everything was unionized. People were very complacent. Union leadership was very complacent. The union workforce was very complacent. Everything was taken for granted. You know, 'I pay my dues, I have to because my employer is union; I have to be a union member.' And they really got totally away from the true concept of a union."

The challenge of consolidating the achievements of the 1992 strike, then, has yet to be fully confronted. And though awareness of this victory has reverberated through the building trades and the wider labor movement—particularly in California but to some degree nationally as well—thus far no one has built on the 1992 success. "It was an incredible opportunity that was granted to us, and we didn't seize the moment," said a longtime Los Angeles-area immigrant union organizer.

> The drywallers were like the $100 bills that you find in the street, it was handed to you. Now you have to build it up, you know, use that momentum and build the movement, and don't stop even if you get a contract.... No matter how big the drywallers' movement was, it was just a spark. The unions didn't capitalize on the momentum, so that spark failed to become a huge fire in the industry—and not because the workers were not ready, but because the unions were not ready to do something about it. They couldn't capture the movement, and here we are, you know, talking about the drywallers like it was ancient history.

The new AFL-CIO leadership has already demonstrated a commitment to organizing immigrants and other historically underserved groups of workers, based in part on the experience of this strike, and the building trades are very much a part of that effort. Doug McCarron, who was the head of the Carpenters in southern California during the 1992 drywallers' strike and is now the union's International President, has recently launched a number of new initiatives intended to enhance the union's ability to organize new workers. But only time will tell whether it can replicate the southern California drywallers' victory in other settings. In an economic, political, and legal environment that is extremely hostile to unionism, both organizing other deunionized sectors in the construction industry and consolidating union victories after successful organizing, as this example illustrates all too well, pose formidable challenges for the future.

8

Union Representation of Immigrant Janitors in Southern California: Economic and Legal Challenges

Catherine L. Fisk, Daniel J. B. Mitchell, and Christopher L. Erickson

The victory of the Justice for Janitors (JfJ) campaign carried out by the Service Employees' International Union (SEIU) Local 399 in Los Angeles in 1990 is often hailed—and deservedly so—as one of the major success stories of immigrant unionization.[1] Nearly a decade later we are now in a position to evaluate the degree to which the SEIU has been able to consolidate its achievements and extend its benefits. In this chapter we review the history of the Los Angeles JfJ campaign and examine some of the key organizational, economic, and legal challenges facing the union as it moves forward into the next century.

The Decline and Resurgence of Janitorial Unionism in Los Angeles

During the 1980s Los Angeles experienced an office building boom, particularly in the downtown area. After 1990, however, the California recession—which hit Los Angeles especially hard—brought this expansionary period to an abrupt halt. One might think that the building boom would have been favorable to unionization of janitorial workers, but in fact the 1980s was a period of deunionization of Los Angeles' building services.

Unionization of building service workers had developed in San Francisco in the 1930s, where the local union of what later became the SEIU played an important role in freeing the national union from control by racketeers. The SEIU had success organizing janitorial workers in Los Angeles during the period from just after World War II through the late

---

1. Parts of this chapter draw heavily on a previous paper in which two of the authors were involved. See Waldinger et al. 1998.

1970s, with membership in Local 399 peaking at about five thousand in 1978 and compensation in the union sector rising to twelve dollars an hour by 1982. But then the bottom fell out. Throughout the United States, the severe recession of the early 1980s was accompanied by falling unionization and union wage concessions to employers. By 1985, janitorial membership in Los Angeles had fallen to eighteen hundred.

As tables 8.1 and 8.2 show, the building service industry and the janitorial occupation in contemporary Los Angeles are decidedly low wage. The industry pays well below half the Los Angeles average wage. Nationally, the starting wage for union janitors was about one-fourth above the nonunion starting wage in 1995.

Table 8.1. Hourly wages for janitors Los Angeles–Long Beach, selected dates (in dollars).

	Oct. 1985	Dec. 1989	Dec. 1990[a]	Dec. 1992[b]	Dec. 1995[c]
Mean	$6.26	$6.10	$6.24	$6.49	$6.83
Median	$5.75	$5.00	$5.33	$6.00	$6.00
First quartile	$4.24	$4.50	$4.50	$5.00	$5.08
Third quartile	$7.55	$6.82	$6.75	$7.15	$8.00
Federal minimum	$3.35	$3.35	$3.80	$4.25	$4.25

Source: Area Wage Surveys and *Occupational Compensation Surveys*, U.S. Bureau of Labor Statistics.

[a] After Century City contract signed with ISS.
[b] After extension of contract to Bradford.
[c] After 1995–2000 contract signed with major firms.

Table 8.2. Annual wage in building service industry as compared with all-industry annual wage and number of building services employees, Los Angeles County, selected years.

	1985	1989	1990	1992	1995
Building services (SIC 7349)	$8,477	$10,631	$9,987	$12,761	$13,460
All industries	$21,537	$25,591	$26,379	$28,291	$30,001
Ratio: (%)	39	42	38	45	45
Building services employment	19,132	20,812	22,953	18,535	22,936

Source: County Business Patterns, U.S. Bureau of the Census.

Sources of union decline were twofold: changes in the industry and changes in the workforce. The industry's drift away from building owners managing janitors and toward cleaning contractors doing so had made for increasingly fragile relationships between janitors and their employers. The relationship is further strained by the fact that although cleaning labor costs as a fraction of total building operating costs are small, they are a major element of the cleaning services themselves. As figure 8.1 shows, *direct* labor costs—those attributable to employees actually cleaning or immediately supervising the cleaners—rise as a percentage of sales with the size of the cleaning firm; for the smallest firms, such costs absorb over half of sales revenue and for the largest, over three-fourths. The correlation with size is due to the spreading of overhead (administration, marketing, and so forth) over a larger sales volume for the bigger firms. Thirteen firms in the survey underlying figure 8.1 reported being unionized; eight of these were in the largest sales category (BSCAI 1996, 6–7).

Contracts between building owners or managers and cleaning service contractors are written to permit very short notice of termination, typically thirty days. Thus union members can lose work almost overnight if a

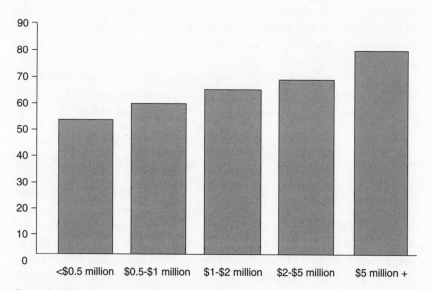

Source: Building Service Contractors Association International 1996.

Figure 8.1. Ratio of direct labor costs to annual sales volume, 1996 (percentage).

building owner switches from a union to a nonunion cleaning service. SEIU Local 399's past ability to improve or maintain conditions and compensation relative to nonunion standards motivated cleaning contractors to explore nonunion options by the early 1980s. The unionized part of the industry—made up of the larger, more heavily capitalized firms—was under particular cost pressure, as they suffer from discontinuous economies of scale. Once a firm reaches a certain threshold of assets (needed to cover payroll and insurance costs), there are few economies of scale, and none on the labor side, making it hard to pass on wage increases to building owners and yielding a fiercely competitive industry.

The last master union agreement prior to the JfJ campaign was signed in 1983; shortly afterward, all increases in wages and benefits were frozen in response to the city's slide toward nonunion building services. A desire to retain members led to a proliferation of concession side agreements by Local 399. Only downtown retained a unionized workforce of measurable proportions, and even there, union ranks barely attained 30 percent of major buildings. Countywide the situation was more dismal still, with under one janitor in ten a member of Local 399. Thus the replacement during the building boom of old, obsolete structures in the downtown area did not help unionization. Indeed, some of the new owner/entrepreneurs pursued aggressive union-avoidance strategies. Though the cost of janitorial labor was small relative to total costs, in major office centers the absolute dollars that could be saved were significant enough to tempt a building manager or owner to go nonunion.

One-third of Los Angeles' current office space was built after 1980. The building service industry—but not the union—burgeoned, employing 28,883 janitors by 1990, more than twice as many as in 1980 by Census count. The backgrounds of the workers were quite different in the 1980s and 1990s compared to earlier periods. Census data indicate that almost all of the new jobs went to Latino immigrants, mostly from Mexico and Central America, whose share of employment in the industry rose from 28 to 61 percent between 1980 and 1990. The industry's expansion meant that net black employment essentially held steady, but relatively, native-born blacks slipped badly, declining from 31 to 12 percent of the workforce; this trend also held nationwide, where the black share of janitorial employment dropped from over 30 percent in 1985 to about one-fifth in 1997. In Los Angeles, native-born whites also lost share, dropping from 24 to 11 percent.

The influx of immigrants coincided with a change in the gender composition of the janitorial workforce. In 1980, 60 percent of the Central

American janitors were women; the growth in janitorial employment over the next ten years left that ratio virtually unchanged. Women comprised 30 percent of Mexican immigrant janitors in 1980, and this grew to 43 percent a decade later. Meanwhile, among those black workers still in the occupation, the proportion of women actually fell, even as earnings for the shrinking pool of black janitors rose. Any campaign to reunionize the industry in Los Angeles would inherently be an immigrant-based endeavor, often focused on women.

In the mid-1980s, the national SEIU began to focus its efforts on its historical base—building services. Though the founding locals (Chicago, New York, and San Francisco) were still holding fast, the rest of the building service division was in deep trouble, losing ground to nonunion competitors and getting battered by unionized employers in search of concessions. What is now a codified set of campaign practices under the rubric of "Justice for Janitors" emerged gradually in the face of this crisis.

JfJ arrived in southern California in 1988. SEIU Local 399, which represented janitors, also represented health care workers, mainly at Kaiser, the giant health maintenance organization. It had largely written off recovery of its building service representation and had decided to focus on Kaiser and health care, in which most of its members now worked. JfJ was essentially imported and imposed by the national SEIU on the local—a process which contributed to later tensions.

The Los Angeles JfJ campaign began in the downtown area in the hands of union representatives inserted by the national SEIU into the local. The campaign had to deal with both representing the remaining union base and organizing nearby nonunion buildings. The plan involved targeting the nonunion wings of "double-breasted" cleaning service companies (firms with both union and nonunion operations under different names) and other nonunion operators. The union allowed unionized firms to hire new janitors at low wages with the understanding that they would move to union standards once half of the market had been organized. But the JfJ campaign also involved a variety of unorthodox organizing tactics.

Essentially, JfJ tactics focus on building owners and managers, even though the formal employer is the building service contractor. The objective is to pressure owners or managers to agree to use union contractors paying union-scale wages. Direct pressure on contractors is ineffective because they are so easily replaced by lower-cost nonunion contractors, even if they agree to union representation and terms. For reasons explained below, the approach to representation ensconced in

U.S. labor law—a National Labor Relations Board (NLRB) election at the formal employer—became ineffective once the management of building services employees was detached from building owners.

On the face of it, it might seem that organizing one nonunion cleaning service at a time would be impractical. There are many such services in the Los Angeles area; *County Business Patterns* for 1995 lists over a thousand "establishments" (not necessarily the same as "firms") under "building maintenance services" [Standard Industrial Classifications (SIC) 7349], employing about 23,000 workers. But few have large numbers of employees, and because the capital costs of operating in the building service industry are low—essentially vacuum cleaners and waxing machines—entrance to the industry is technically easy. However, the industry is surprisingly concentrated in the market for major buildings and complexes, which proved to be an important advantage for JfJ's tactics.

Figure 8.2 shows the distribution of employment among firms that were covered by the master union contract in 1995. These are American Building Maintenance (ABM), International Service Systems (ISS), and "19 others." The two largest firms account for over a fourth of janitorial employment, and the top twenty-one firms account for over a third (the proportion is even higher if only janitors at major buildings are included). Why is there such heavy concentration of employment in a few firms?

Essentially, the issue for building owners and managers is trust. Cleaning service personnel are given the keys at night to office buildings and others containing valuable equipment and records. Mom and pop operators cannot necessarily be trusted to do the job right and prevent theft or damage. Owners and managers want to entrust their cleaning services to firms with a reputation for good service. And since they often have properties in more than one city—even in more than one country—they look for building service firms with which they have dealt elsewhere. Thus, in Los Angeles, only two firms (and their nonunion subsidiaries) dominated the market for so-called Class A buildings, ABM and ISS (a Danish-based multinational). If agreement could be reached with these two firms, JfJ strategists theorized, other smaller contractors would follow and the city's major office centers could be reunionized.

ABM operates, primarily in janitorial services, in the United States, Canada, and Mexico, with revenues of over $1 billion and 47,000 employees. It has a variety of subsidiaries, including Bradford Building Services, through which it offered nonunion janitorial services in Los Angeles dur-

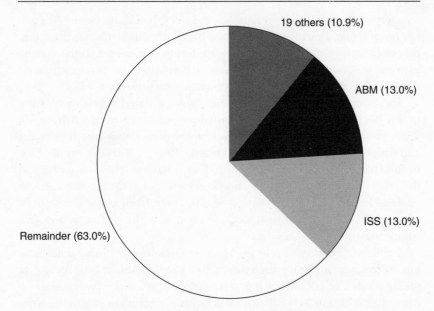

19 others (10.9%)

ABM (13.0%)

ISS (13.0%)

Remainder (63.0%)

Note: Based on an estimate of 23,000 janitors in Los Angeles County. ISS, ABM, and "19 Others" are firms covered under the 1995 Master Contractors' Agreement.

Figure 8.2. Composition of janitorial employment in Los Angeles County, 1995.

ing the period of deunionization, a classic example of double-breasting. The ISS Group operated until recently in twenty-one European countries and eight Asian countries plus the United States and Brazil. The U.S. subsidiary known as ISS, Inc. has about forty thousand employees and $800 million in revenues, and claims 4 percent of the total U.S. outsourced building maintenance market. About a tenth of California employees in the industry were reported to be employed by foreign-owned firms including ISS in 1992, the latest year available (U.S. Bureau of Economic Analysis 1992, 43).

The JfJ campaign made slow but steady progress. By April 1989, Local 399 had negotiated a master agreement, the first in downtown Los Angeles since the early 1980s. Then, in the summer of 1989, the campaign's focus shifted to Century City, a large Westside office complex employing four hundred janitors, of whom 250 were employed by ISS. JfJ marshaled a variety of tactics to put pressure on ISS. As it had done downtown earlier on, JfJ staged various "in-your-face" publicity stunts to draw the attention of Century City building tenants to the janitors' plight. Tenants complained to building managers about JfJ activities or even expressed sympathy for the janitors, indirectly intensifying pressure on ISS.

In late spring 1990, the pace of activity escalated sharply when the union decided to strike. A major turning point occurred on June 15, 1990, when Los Angeles police attacked a peaceful march of JfJ strikers and supporters as they walked from nearby Beverly Hills to Century City. In full view of the media and recorded on videotape, the police charged the crowd, injuring many including children and pregnant women. Organizers feared that workers would be intimidated, but at a strikers' meeting shortly after the event it became clear that the police action had strengthened workers' resolve.

Public outrage at the televised police attack brought local politicians into the dispute, including then-mayor Tom Bradley. And in New York, after seeing a video of police beating strikers, Gus Bevona, the powerful president of SEIU Local 32B-32J (who was facing a significant dissident movement at the time), took action. He had previously been unwilling to exert pressure on ISS, which was unionized in New York. But reportedly after seeing the video, Bevona called the president of ISS into his office and insisted that a deal be reached. The Los Angeles contract with ISS was signed that day and was subsequently extended to ABM and other operators.

The initial ISS contract resulting from the Century City events ran for twenty-two months and covered only two hundred workers. These workers averaged $4.50 an hour at the time. The contract provided for a 30-cent increase or a wage of $5.20, whichever was greater. A second increase of 20 cents or $5.50 was scheduled for April 1991. However, by the time the second increase was due the contract was superseded in March 1991 by an extended three-year agreement also covering ABM's nonunion Bradford subsidiary. Public sources estimate that this contract covered five to six thousand workers. The new agreement added dental and drug coverage to the health plan and provided increases of 20–45 cents per hour in each of the three years, depending on location.

These contract settlements were hailed as a major victory for the southern California labor movement and for immigrant unionism in particular. All did not go smoothly thereafter, however. We now turn to the question of the sustainability of the gains won by JfJ in 1990, focusing on three main challenges that later emerged: internal union turmoil, economic challenges, and legal challenges.

Internal Union Turmoil and Organizational Challenges

Not long after the initial JfJ organizing victory, SEIU Local 399 broke into factions. The split was partly between health care workers and janitors and partly along ethnic lines (many of the original JfJ organizers were Anglos, albeit Spanish-speaking). An alliance of disgruntled health workers and Latinos who referred to themselves as "Reformistas" challenged the leadership and focus of Local 399. One of the issues raised was the future focus of the JfJ effort. Should the union's attention now turn to day-to-day contract administration—the handling of grievances and services to the newly covered members? Or should it continue to be focused on new organizing, perhaps expanding to outlying areas and even to conservative Orange County? Ultimately, these internal disputes led the national SEIU to put Local 399 in trusteeship on September 14, 1995, and in the restructuring that occurred, the janitors were separated from Local 399 and joined to Local 1877, a San Jose local for janitors in Silicon Valley, Oakland, and Sacramento which also utilizes JfJ tactics.

The union achieved greater success in consolidation than in new organizing efforts. Before the trusteeship, a second contract was negotiated in 1995 with ISS, ABM, and nineteen other smaller cleaning service firms, covering about 8,500 workers—about three thousand each in the two major firms and the balance in the others. Table 8.3 and figure 8.3 summarize key economic terms of the contract. As can be seen, the highest wages and benefits specified prevail in the downtown and Century City area, known as Area 1. As the contract moves away from the core office areas, it permits lower wages. Indeed, in some outlying areas wages were below—and were superseded by—the California minimum of $5.75 which became effective March 1, 1998.

Another important aspect of the contract—which figure 8.3 graphically illustrates—is that over time it moves areas with wages below those of Area 1 toward the Area 1 rates. Also noteworthy is the application of Area 1 health insurance coverage in the final year of the contract to all workers except those in miscellaneous Area 5. The coverage provided in Area 1 is essentially a comprehensive Kaiser plan (including drugs) or an SEIU equivalent, plus a dental plan and a modest one thousand dollars in life insurance. The specified cost to Area 1 employers at the opening date of the contract is over $240 per month per employee. On the basis of a forty-hour week, this benefit would be equivalent to about $1.50 per hour, a substantial amount when compared with the cash wages paid to workers under the contract. Thus the contract is backloaded on the benefit side.

Table 8.3. Wages and wage adjustments specified in 1995–2000 maintenance contractors' agreement for cleaners.

	4/1/95	9/1/95	4/1/96	9/1/96	4/1/97	4/1/98	4/1/99	2/1/00
Area 1								
Start	$6.80	$6.80	$6.80	$6.80	$6.80	$7.00	$7.20	$7.20
Minimum	$6.80	$6.80	$6.80	$6.80	$6.80	$7.00	$7.20	$7.20
Increase[a]	$0.15	$0.00	$0.15	$0.00	$0.15	$0.25	$0.30	$0.00
Health	Yes	Yes	Yes	Yes	Yes	Yes	Yes	Yes
Pension[b]	Yes	Yes	Yes	Yes	Yes	Yes	Yes	Yes
Area 2								
Start	$5.40	$5.40	$5.50	$5.50	$5.65	$5.90	$6.30	$6.30
Minimum	$5.60	$5.60	$5.80	$5.80	$6.00	$6.30	$6.80	$6.80
Increase	$0.20	$0.00	$0.20	$0.00	$0.20	$0.30	$0.50	$0.00
Health	LT Area 1[c]	LT Area 1	LT Area 1	LT Area 1	LT Area 1	LT Area 1	LT Area 1	Yes
Pension	No	No	No	No	No	No	No	No
Area 2A								
Start	$4.70	$4.70	$4.85	$4.85	$5.10	$5.55	$6.05	$6.40
Minimum	$4.95	$4.95	$5.20	$5.20	$5.75	$6.30	$6.80	$6.80
Increase	$0.25	$0.00	$0.25	$0.00	$5.55	$0.55	$0.50	$0.00
Health	No	No	No	No	No	No	No	Yes
Pension	No	No	No	No	No	No	No	No
Area 3								
Start	$4.70	$4.70	$4.85	$4.85	$5.10	$5.55	$6.05	$6.40
Minimum	$4.90	$4.90	$5.10	$5.10	$5.55	$6.05	$6.40	$6.80
Increase	$0.20	$0.00	$0.20	$0.00	$0.45	$0.50	$0.35	$0.40
Health	No	No	No	No	No	No	No	Yes
Pension	No	No	No	No	No	No	No	No
Area 4								
Start	—	$4.45	$4.45	$4.45	$4.75	$5.15	$5.65	$6.15
Minimum	—	$4.45	$4.45	$4.75	$5.15	$5.65	$6.15	$6.80
Increase	$0.00	$0.20	$0.00	$0.30	$0.40	$0.50	$0.50	$0.65
Health	No	No	No	No	No	No	No	Yes
Pension	No	No	No	No	No	No	No	No
Area 5								
Start	—	$4.50	$4.50	$4.50	$4.65	$4.90	$5.20	$5.20
Minimum	—	$4.50	$4.75	$4.75	$5.00	$5.30	$5.65	$5.65
Increase	$0.00	$0.25	$0.25	$0.00	$0.25	$0.30	$0.35	$0.00
Health	No	No	No	No	No	No	No	No
Pension	No	No	No	No	No	No	No	No

[a] "Increase" refers to existing employee receiving minimum or above.
[b] Pension: minimum of $.10 or continuation of contributions of $.33 or $.35.
[c] "LT Area 1" means "less generous than Area 1."

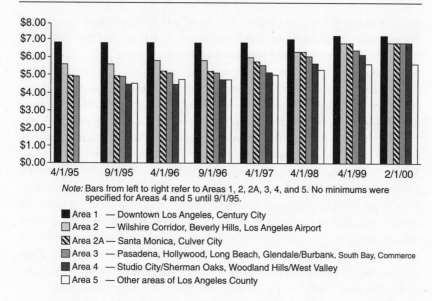

Note: Bars from left to right refer to Areas 1, 2, 2A, 3, 4, and 5. No minimums were specified for Areas 4 and 5 until 9/1/95.

■ Area 1 — Downtown Los Angeles, Century City
☐ Area 2 — Wilshire Corridor, Beverly Hills, Los Angeles Airport
▨ Area 2A — Santa Monica, Culver City
▨ Area 3 — Pasadena, Hollywood, Long Beach, Glendale/Burbank, South Bay, Commerce
■ Area 4 — Studio City/Sherman Oaks, Woodland Hills/West Valley
☐ Area 5 — Other areas of Los Angeles County

Figure 8.3. Minimum hourly wage for cleaners, 1995–2000 Maintenance Contractors' Agreement.

Although the new contract provided significant wage and benefit gains, substantial new janitorial organizing has not occurred since it was signed. Once the union had incorporated the major cleaning firms under its master agreement, it had roughly a third of all janitors in Los Angeles County under its jurisdiction.[2]

In 1997–98, the union did score a highly publicized win at the University of Southern California, which had earlier contracted out its cleaning service to a nonunion firm. And the union has continued its tactic of public demonstrations when attempts are made by building owners or managers to switch to nonunion cleaning contractors. Basically, however, no dramatic new organizing efforts have been evident. Mike Garcia, president of the newly reconstituted Local 1877, has stated publicly that an organizing campaign in Sacramento will take precedence over nonunion areas in southern California such as Orange County.

Tensions arose within the union between those who wanted to continue active organization of nonunion areas and those who wanted to con-

2. Table 8.1 suggests some widening of the wage distribution in 1995, perhaps due to the boost in wages provided to unionized janitors relative to nonunion. There may have been some spillover to the nonunion sector; table 8.2 indicates a modest increase in building services wages relative to the county average in 1992 and 1995, both bargaining years.

solidate prior gains and ensure that members feel adequately serviced. Progress has been made on the latter front. For example, the 1995 contract included an expedited grievance-arbitration system which appears to be working smoothly. About twenty grievances per year find their way onto the calendar of the panel of arbitrators designated to hear these cases. Some are settled, however, before actual hearings are held. Most disputes that come to the panel involve discipline or employee wage entitlements.

The professional arbitrators on the panel produce "bench" (immediate) decisions or decisions within forty-eight hours after the hearing. They are encouraged to assist in mediated settlements where possible. Lawyers are not allowed to present cases on either side. As a result, presenters are not always as polished as would likely be the case in traditional arbitration. However, the process benefits from lower costs and greater informality. Decisions made under the expedited process are not considered as precedent-setting. If management wanted to challenge the union aggressively, it could have taken grievances out of the expedited process and otherwise stimulated a backlog of expensive-to-process grievances. That it did not do so suggests it prefers that the union devote its resources to preventing erosion of the unionized sector of the industry.

The union has also addressed the issue of immigration status. Prior to the Immigration Reform and Control Act of 1986 (IRCA), employers were not in violation of the law if they hired illegal immigrants. This situation gave employers seeking to avoid unionization a potential weapon: they could call in the INS to remove union sympathizers or threaten to do so. Once IRCA made knowingly hiring illegal immigrants a violation of law, in principle employers were deprived of this weapon, for calling in the INS would be an acknowledgment that they themselves had committed an illegal act. (In practice, however, employees do not always know about the employer provisions of IRCA and may still be intimidated by threats concerning their immigration status.) The current union contract in Los Angeles deals with immigration issues in detail. It obligates the employer to notify the union by phone if an INS agent appears on or near the premises. Employers are forbidden to disclose information about employees to the INS unless required by law. Reinstatement is required for employees who are absent from work for up to seven days due to immigration hearings. Employees who lawfully change their names or social security numbers cannot be penalized. And there is a catch-all protection against discharge or discipline for absence for up to seven days due to circumstances beyond the employee's control.

Immigrants, who constitute the majority of the membership of Local 1877, have become an active part of the union leadership since 1990.

And, since the trusteeship, the member-elected Executive Council, which shares authority with the formal union leadership and contains some of the leaders of the dissident "Reformista" faction, has gained in influence. It appears that the tensions from the pre-trusteeship period have been largely resolved by the restructuring of the union.

Sustainability: Economic Aspects

Is the current union coverage of the Los Angeles building service industry economically sustainable? Even at the time of the Century City breakthrough, the Los Angeles economy—including its market for office space—had begun to turn down. And when the second contract was negotiated, the local economy was still in bad shape. U.S. nonfarm payroll employment was back to its pre-recession peak by 1993 and in California by 1996, but the Los Angeles-Long Beach area was still below peak in late 1998.

Building service employment fell during the Los Angeles slump, as table 8.2 shows. The poor local economy had two effects, both of which (paradoxically) could have helped sustain building service unionization. With high vacancy rates, many large buildings ended up in the hands of unhappy financial institutions that had previously lent money to developers. Some knowledgeable observers argued that these owners-in-spite-of-themselves did not mount a counterattack because they simply wanted to avoid labor trouble and offense to scarce tenants. Moreover, they were susceptible to pressure from their institutional investors and clients, which often included labor unions and other institutions likely to be sympathetic to the plight of the cleaning workers. Indeed, financial institutions were characterized in some of the interviews we conducted as potentially more vulnerable to union pressure than "real" owners would be. Cleaning services depend on contracts with building owners and managers, and if the owners and managers say they want unionized services, the services comply.

By 1995, employment in the industry had almost regained its 1990 level. As noted, when the 1995–2000 contract expires, office market conditions may be substantially better than when the first two contracts were negotiated. First, parts of Los Angeles, outside the downtown area have boomed in response to the growth of the entertainment and multimedia sectors. These include the Westside and the Glendale-Burbank areas. Other outlying areas began picking up in the mid-1990s, based on general industrial growth and demand for office space. Second, there is evidence that even the sluggish downtown area is picking up, in part due to incremental spillover from the hot outlying areas where rents are high and vacancies low.

A new ownership pattern has been establishing itself in Los Angeles. Real Estate Investment Trusts (REITs) are becoming the major players in the commercial real estate market, both downtown and in outlying areas. Some Japanese investment firms have remained, notably Shuwa. REITs, however, acquired major properties during the depths of the real estate slump from former owners and unwilling financial institutions at what may turn out to be bargain prices. It is unclear whether the new owners will be more resistant to union coverage than the financial institutions. Unlike the financial institutions, REITs want to be in the real estate business and they may thus see themselves in the local market for the long haul. So far, however, the REITs have not made any coordinated anti-union moves.

The newly restructured Local 1877 faces several challenges. First, it must continue to be vigilant about erosion of the union sector through conversion of union-cleaned buildings to nonunion. Presumably, its emergence from the earlier political turmoil and trusteeship should assist in this objective. In addition, Local 1877 has achieved a sufficiently amicable relationship with the major cleaning service firms that they are likely to bring to the union's attention conversions of buildings to nonunion status as they are contractually obligated to do. And the local has access to other sources of information, including reports from members, on such conversions. As long as nonunion conversions are detected and thwarted, the union can remain in its current locations.

However, there is a second form of erosion with which the union must be concerned. It must eventually begin new organizing in expanding outlying areas or face representing a diminishing share of the janitorial labor market, simply because of the outward expansion of economic activity away from the downtown area—a continuous historical tendency in Los Angeles. Los Angeles has tended to be a lower-density metropolitan area than traditional eastern cities, thanks to its ubiquitous freeways and the availability of cheap land on the perimeter. Population growth and traffic congestion constantly contribute to the development of regional centers away from downtown. Urban planners may decry these tendencies, but there seems little on the horizon—including the various rail transit projects—that will reverse them. Thus more and more janitors will be working outside the current union jurisdiction.

So the union faces a choice. It could live within its current boundaries. But if its mission is to upgrade the incomes of area janitors, it must eventually embark on aggressive organizing, even into Orange

County. And closer to home, there are many janitors in smaller buildings not under the master agreement. These concerns mean that the legal barriers to further organizing must be examined. Indeed, JfJ tactics used to avert building erosion to nonunion status would confront these legal issues even if the union were content to stay within its current boundaries.

Sustainability and Prospects for Expansion: Legal Issues

The National Labor Relations Act (NLRA) protects the rights of employees to form labor unions and bargain collectively. But it provides as many tools for employers to thwart organizing efforts as protections to employees seeking to organize. Building service is an industry in which labor law fails to protect the rights of workers to organize. JfJ shows how organizing campaigns can nevertheless succeed by rallying public support to neutralize the employer's many legal and illegal methods for defeating organizing efforts.

The fundamental employee protections in the federal labor law are found in sections 7 and 8 of the NLRA. Section 7 protects the rights of employees to join or assist labor unions, to bargain collectively, and to engage in "concerted activities for the purpose of...mutual aid or protection." Section 8(a) makes it an unfair labor practice for an employer to interfere with the exercise of the rights guaranteed in section 7; to dominate or interfere with the administration of a union; or to discriminate in employment to encourage or discourage union membership.

Employees are protected under sections 7 and 8 regardless of their immigration status. That many janitors are not U.S. citizens, and that many are undocumented, is irrelevant; the NLRA provides even undocumented workers the right to join unions and protects them against illegal employer interference with that right (*Sure-Tan, Inc. v. NLRB*, 467 U.S. 883 [1984]).

Two legal factors make janitors especially difficult to organize. First, in the modern cleaning service industry janitors do not work on their own employer's property but rather in a building owned or managed by their employer's client. The NLRA does not impose the same obligations on the client as it does on the employer, and it protects the client from workers' concerted activities to better their working conditions even though the client may as a practical matter exert significant influence over those conditions.

Because labor is the predominant cost in a cleaning contract, the wages the employer (building service contractor) can pay are determined by what the employer's client (the property manager or building owner) is willing to pay. Often, the client has the practical ability to oversee the work of the janitors and the contractual power to demand firings. Notwithstanding the influence that the client may have on the effective working conditions of the janitors, it is extremely difficult under current law to establish that the client is the "joint employer" of the janitors who work in its buildings. Unless the building owner or manager can be shown to be a joint employer, it owes no duties to the janitors.

The client can insulate itself from NLRA responsibility to the janitors by ensuring that the nominal "supervisor" of the janitors is an employee of the cleaning contractor, and the contract is carefully drafted to allow the client to direct only the "results" of the cleaning work and not the "means" by which it is accomplished (although there is little practical difference when it comes to janitorial work) (*Southern California Gas Co.*, 302 NLRB 456 [1991]). Thus the property manager or building owner is likely to be treated as a "neutral" or "secondary" employer who can be protected from labor protests that would be permissible if directed at the contractor, the "primary" employer.

The second legal obstacle to organizing janitors is that a property manager may legally terminate its contract with a unionized cleaning contractor in favor of a nonunion contractor simply because the nonunion company pays its employees less. As a consequence, the traditional organizing tactics of seeking an NLRB-supervised representation election or persuading the employer to recognize the union without an election will fail unless the property manager is also persuaded. Yet the law prohibits many types of union efforts to persuade the "neutral" property manager.

Secondary Boycotts

A secondary boycott is the use of pressure upon an entity with whom the union has no dispute in an attempt to persuade that entity to cease doing business with someone with whom the union does have a dispute. Specifically, it is an illegal secondary boycott under section 8(b)(4)(ii)(B) of the NLRA for a union or its agents "to threaten, coerce, or restrain any persons" with an object of forcing them "to cease doing business with any other person." If the union persuades a cleaning contractor to recognize the union as the representative of its employees and the property manager terminates the cleaning contractor as a result and hires a nonunion contractor, the union can do little to protest the property manager's action. Most forms of protest would be deemed to be illegal efforts to "coerce" the property manager to cease doing business with the nonunion contractor.

In ruling on the permissibility of JfJ tactics in the 1993 *West Bay* case (discussed in more detail below), the NLRB rejected the contention that the tactics were permissible primary pressure because the union had a dispute with the building owners and managers who chose nonunion firms. The NLRB determined that the principal target of the JfJ campaign was "to attack the non-union status" of the contractors "rather than the generic fact of subcontracting by the building owners and managers" (312 NLRB 715, 744). Many of the union's secondary boycott problems would likely disappear if in future cases the union could persuade the NLRB that its dispute is with property managers who choose nonunion cleaning contractors as well as with the nonunion status of the contractors themselves.

The penalties for violating the secondary boycott provisions, unlike many remedies under the NLRA, are severe and can be obtained swiftly. Any affected secondary parties—the property manager, building owner, or tenants in the building—can file an unfair labor practice charge with the Regional office of the NLRB. The NLRB gives handling of such charges priority over all other cases, which is a significant advantage to employers because the agency is understaffed and has a backlog of cases awaiting investigation. If the Regional Director determines that there is reasonable cause to believe that the charge is true, he or she *must* seek a federal court injunction against the ongoing alleged unfair labor practice. The NLRB acts expeditiously in seeking these injunctions and can obtain them in less than a week, which is less than one-tenth the time it takes to obtain an injunction against ongoing unfair labor practices by an employer. The NLRA also authorizes employers and any others whose business or property has been injured as a result of a secondary boycott to seek damages against the union in a civil suit.

Building owners and property managers have energetically invoked the secondary boycott provisions in response to JfJ activities, filing hundreds of unfair labor practice charges in Los Angeles and elsewhere. Most of these have not resulted in published decisions because the cases were settled or dismissed during administrative processing by the NLRB. But a number of published NLRB decisions have made clear that some JfJ tactics are illegal secondary boycotts. Among these decisions is *Service Employees Union, Local 87* (*West Bay Building Maintenance Company*), which found illegal many of the JfJ tactics used in a campaign in San Francisco in 1990 (312 NLRB 715 [1993]).

The *West Bay* Case

The JfJ activities at issue in *West Bay* were daily mass protests that typically began immediately after the building owner or property manager canceled a contract with a unionized janitorial firm and contracted with a nonunion firm. The protesters marched around at the entrance to the building chanting and carrying picket signs, flags, and banners that read: "Justice for Janitors—Local 87" and "Unfair Labor Practices—Local 87." Protesters distributed leaflets addressed to building tenants that explained that union members had lost their jobs because the building manager awarded the janitorial maintenance contract to a named nonunion contractor. One leaflet suggested: "You can help us and help yourselves by contacting your building managers and letting them know how displeased you are about this scam." Some days, protesters played guitars and sang about janitors "in a folk song-like manner." Some protesters shouted through bullhorns and blew whistles. At some points in the protests, the protesters gathered around the entrance to the building, making ingress and egress difficult. On a few occasions at various buildings, the protesters entered the lobby en masse. In one incident, two employees of a building tenant were accidentally caught up in the crowd.

The NLRB determined that the activities had a secondary object because the protests were neither confined to the times during which nonunion janitors were in the building nor to the doors reserved for the use of those janitors. Moreover, the signs and banners did not clearly disclose that the union's dispute was with the janitorial firm rather than with the building owner or the tenants. The NLRB also determined that the protest was coercive and thus illegal, even though it sought no labor stoppage.

In part, the NLRB's conclusion about coercion was based on the fact that some of the protest activity involved picketing, which the law regards as an especially threatening form of speech. The union argued that the other conduct—yelling, whistle-blowing, marching, blocking the entrance, and singing—was not picketing, but the NLRB deemed most of it coercive, too. Even when the mass gatherings involved flags and banners instead of traditional picket signs, the NLRB found unlawful coercion based on the excessive noise, the very large number of protesters, the patrolling, and the trespassing entries into the building.

West Bay, it should be stressed, does not establish new law, nor is it an expansion of the scope of the secondary boycott law. Rather, it applies to the JfJ context rules that had long since developed in other contexts. These rules limit the ability of the employees to pressure the entity that has de facto control over their working conditions when the de facto employer is not the entity that the law recognizes as the de jure employer.

Distinguishing Permissible Protest from Secondary Boycotts

The success of future JfJ organizing efforts will depend on the skill with which the organizers can steer clear of the secondary boycott limitations described in *West Bay*. The main avenue for legal protest is that described in the Supreme Court's decision in *Edward J. DeBartolo Corp. v. Florida Gulf Coast Building & Construction Trades Council*, which held that some labor appeals to customers are exempt from the ban on secondary boycotts (485 U.S. 568 [1988]). In *DeBartolo* the union peacefully distributed handbills at a shopping mall owned by DeBartolo, protesting the fact that the owner of a department store to be built at the mall had hired a contractor to do the job who paid substandard wages. The handbills asked consumers not to patronize any of the stores in the mall.

The Court held that the First Amendment protected peaceful distribution of leaflets urging a customer boycott of the mall owner and other retailers. Unions can therefore use *leaflets* to urge a consumer boycott of secondary employers in order to persuade them to cease doing business with companies that do business with nonunion employers. But unions cannot use *picketing* to achieve the same goal (*NLRB v. National Retail Store Employees, Local 1001 [Safeco]*, 447 U.S. 607 [1980]).

The law distinguishes labor picketing, which can be broadly prohibited because it is not speech protected by the First Amendment, from other peaceful forms of labor protest, which are constitutionally protected speech unless they are as coercive as picketing. The proposition that labor picketing is not pure speech was first articulated in a 1957 case involving a union picketing at a nonunion workplace with signs stating that the job used nonunion workers. The Supreme Court there emphasized the coercive (as opposed to expressive) aspects of picketing: "Picketing by an organized group is more than free speech, since it involves patrol of a particular locality and since the very presence of a picket line may induce action of one kind or another, quite irrespective of the nature of the ideas which are being disseminated" (*International Brotherhood of Teamsters, Local 695 v. Vogt*, 354 U.S. 284, 289 [1957]). The perceived power and harmfulness of picketing as a form of speech led the court to conclude that the First Amendment's protections do not extend to all forms of labor picketing.

In *DeBartolo*, however, the Court decided that consumer handbilling was noncoercive because it was only an attempt to persuade the public, not a call to action directed at workers. The Court said: "more than mere persuasion is necessary to prove a violation of Section 8(b)(4)(ii): that section requires a showing of threats, coercion, or restraints." Although the employer argued that the handbilling, if it successfully persuaded customers not to shop at the mall, would coerce the department store owner to cease doing business with the contractor, the Court replied: "The loss of customers because they read a handbill urging them not to patronize a business, and not because they are intimidated by a line of picketers, is the result of mere persuasion."

Like the handbills in *DeBartolo*, many of the JfJ tactics have focused on public support and have not called for work stoppages. Under *DeBartolo*, to the extent that the SEIU confines itself to distributing handbills appealing to the public outside office buildings, the conduct is exempt from Section 8(b)(4)(ii)(B). The question is whether the union's other, more "in-your-face" kinds of protests would be considered peaceful persuasion as opposed to illegal coercion.

In the years since *DeBartolo* was decided, the NLRB and to a lesser extent the courts have considered whether a range of labor activities that have a secondary object are protected persuasion or impermissible coercion. Two general principles have emerged. First, the protesters need to make clear with whom they have a labor dispute and that they do not seek a work stoppage. They may legally seek only a customer boycott of a neutral, not a strike by any neutral's employees. Second, when the protest involves a very large number of protesters and much noise, it is likely to be deemed coercive unless it is clearly not focused on the premises of a neutral employer. These inquiries turn on subjective judgments and fine distinctions, and there is plenty of uncertainty in the scope of the law's prohibitions.

The first principle is illustrated in a 1993 decision in which the NLRB found unlawful a rally held in the parking lot of a K-Mart store to protest K-Mart's use of nonunion construction firms in building and remodeling its stores. At the rally, protesters yelled, chanted, and performed a skit suggesting that K-Mart did not care whether the children of nonunion employees received adequate health care. Protesters distributed helium balloons with "K-Mart" inside a circle and a slash sign; on the other side the balloons said: "We are appealing only to the public, the consumer. We are not seeking to induce any person to cease work or refuse to make deliveries." They displayed banners that said: "K-Mart Ignores the Health Care Needs of Their Own Workers" (*K-Mart Corp.*, 313 NLRB 50 [1993]).

The NLRB found the conduct had an impermissible secondary object because the nonunion firms were not present at the K-Mart stores during the protests and because the union urged the customers to refuse to patronize K-Mart. The NLRB also emphasized that the banners, the skit, and the balloons did not make clear that the union's dispute was with a nonunion construction firm rather than K-Mart. The protesters did distribute handbills explaining that the union's dispute was with a construction firm, not K-Mart, but the NLRB evidently did not consider this sufficient. The NLRB then determined that the protest was coercive because the "Union's conduct during the rallies went beyond peacefully imparting their message to customers; indeed, the totality of their conduct—which might fairly be deemed picketing despite the absence of conventional picket signs—imposed economic pressure that necessarily 'threatened, coerced, or restrained' K-Mart." If the methods had not been coercive, they would have been protected under *DeBartolo*, even if they sought a total consumer boycott of K-Mart, so long as they made clear that the union's actual dispute was with the nonunion contractor rather than K-Mart.[3]

Although the NLRB did not say as much, one factor that may have influenced its conclusion that the protest was coercive was that it was loud, large, and appeared to be directed at K-Mart specifically, rather than at the public generally. In this respect, the *K-Mart* decision also reflects the second general principle, that mass protests may be deemed unlawful if they are focused too directly at the secondary employer. Consider, for example, a 1988 Advice Memorandum, in which the NLRB General Counsel declined to issue a complaint against the SEIU local based on a JfJ protest at a building in San Jose. The General Counsel emphasized that although the protest involved fifty or so people marching down the street in front of the target building wearing JfJ T-shirts, holding brooms, yelling and making noise, and in some cases carrying signs, the protest involved "general parading through large public areas" rather than confrontational "patrolling" in front of a particular building. The memo also emphasized that on those occasions when the union conducted rallies at or near the target building "there was no evidence of confrontation, blocking of ingress or egress, patrolling, or evidence that the demonstrators were there to 'signal' employees or customers not

---

3. Indeed, so long as the protest activity is limited to handbilling and other nonpicketing publicity, the union is free to urge a total consumer boycott of a neutral employer. *DeBartolo*, 485 U.S. 568, 583–84 (1988); *United Steelworkers of America (Pet, Inc.)*, 288 NLRB 1190 (1988); *International Brotherhood of Elec. Workers Local Union No. 5 (Historical Landmarks for Living)*, Case No. 6–CB-7693, Dec. 12, 1988, Advice Memorandum.

to enter the buildings" (*Service Employees' International Union Local 77, Empire Industrial Maintenance*, Case No. 32–CC-1226, May 27, 1988, Advice Memorandum).[4]

Permissible publicity becomes prohibited coercion if there is "confrontation in some form between union members and employees, customers, or suppliers who are trying to enter the employer's premises." If the activity is "not limited to the area of any individual business enterprise, [and does] not come to rest at any particular establishment, but consist[s] rather of a general parading through large public areas," it is permissible even if it appeals to the public not to patronize the secondary employer (*Chicago Typographical Union No. 16, Alden Press, Inc.*, 151 NLRB 1666, 1669 [1965]).

The size of the protest and the amount of noise it generates are important when they are focused on the secondary employer. Large and noisy demonstrations are permissible if they are perceived to be directed at generating public attention rather than being located only in front of the secondary employer. Even a protest in front of a secondary employer may be permissible if the number of protesters is reasonable. In a 1991 decision, the NLRB explicitly drew a distinction between a mass rally involving three or four hundred people who surrounded a building, which the NLRB found coercive, and the peaceful distribution of handbills by twenty to a hundred people who moved aside when people sought to enter the building, which the NLRB found permissible (*Laborers International Union, Local 232*, 305 NLRB 298 [1991]). Similarly, the NLRB's General Counsel determined that distributing balloons bearing the words "Build Unions" and "Employ Union Carpenters" during otherwise lawful secondary handbilling was not "confrontational" in part because the number of protesters involved (15) "was fully commensurate with the kind of handbilling activities directed at the large number of customers visiting the stores" (*Carpenters Local 108, Stop & Shop Co.*, Case No. 1–CC-2269, Aug. 4, 1989, Advice Memorandum).

When the noise is localized, the nature of the noise seems to matter. In a protest in Waikiki, the union had a number of Hawaiian and Pacific Island musicians perform on a flatbed truck parked in front of a secondary employer's restaurant. A large crowd gathered to listen, blocking

---

4. Similarly, in a more recent decision involving JfJ activities in San Jose, the NLRB General Counsel determined that an hour-long demonstration on public streets four blocks away from the target building was not coercive, even though the demonstration blocked an intersection and the protesters displayed large banners that said the occupants of the target building were "Enemies of Justice" *Service By Medallion*, Case No. 32–CC-1363, August 30, 1993 (decision of the General Counsel upholding the decision of the Regional Director not to issue a complaint on unfair labor practice charges).

the sidewalk and ingress and egress from the building. The union's music drowned out the restaurant's music. The NLRB found no coercion, remarking that the music was traditional entertainment in Hawaii (*Honolulu Typographical Union No. 37, Hawaii Press Newspapers,* 167 NLRB 1030, 1032 [1967]).

Even the JfJ tactic that might seem the most confrontational—following the primary employer to his home or club and protesting there to embarrass him in front of his neighbors or friends—has been held to be immune from secondary boycott challenge. The protesters must make clear that the target of the protest is the primary employer only and seek no labor stoppage or boycott of the secondary employer (*Local 1199 Drug and Hospital Employees Union, Stanford Condominium,* Case No. 2–CC-2179, Sept. 3, 1993, Advice Memorandum; *District 29, United Mine Workers v. NLRB,* 977 F.2d 1470, D.C. Circuit, 1992).

Primary Strikes and JfJ Protests

In assessing the likelihood that future JfJ activities in Los Angeles will avoid secondary boycott liability, it is important to recall that the 1990 Los Angeles JfJ campaign involved a traditional primary strike of the janitorial employees who worked at the Century City buildings. Striking employees are permitted to picket (not merely handbill) at their workplace (even when the workplace is shared by neutral employers), so long as they confine their picketing activities so as to avoid unnecessarily enmeshing neutral employers who are tenants in the building (*Sailors' Union of the Pacific, Moore Dry Dock,* 92 NLRB 547 [1950]). Most of the San Francisco protests found illegal in *West Bay,* by contrast, did not involve a strike.

However, in a 1997 decision involving protest at a building where nonunion janitors went on strike as part of the JfJ campaign, the NLRB's General Counsel in an Advice Memorandum found such picketing coercive. The employees did not confine it to the areas and entrances used by the primary employer and its employees. Rather, making excessive noise outside a neutral restaurant during the lunch and dinner hours, the union appeared to be trying to maximize the impact of the picketing by interfering with the restaurant's business. The General Counsel specifically declined to decide whether excessive noise or mass picketing alone would be coercive in the absence of an apparent effort to affect neutral tenants in the building (*Faison & Assocs., Inc.,* Case No. 5–CC-1231, April 30, 1997, Advice Memorandum). Thus the kinds of protests that the SEIU local might be able to conduct in Los Angeles or elsewhere in the future may depend on whether it is in a position to call a strike of the janitors in the target building.

Company Unions

One additional legal issue may be significant in future JfJ campaigns in southern California. Employers sometimes establish a company-controlled union to convince employees that representation by an independent union is unnecessary. Although building service contractors have not tried this in southern California, the tactic is useful when dealing with unsophisticated employees who may not be aware of the significantly greater protections offered by independent unions. Company unions were widely used in the 1930s, prior to the NLRA, and recently by a San Francisco–area building service contractor in response to JfJ organizing.

In its 1992 *Electromation* decision (309 NLRB 990 [1992], *enforced*, 35 F.3d 1148, 7th Circuit 1994; 29 U.S.C. §158(a)(2)), the NLRB emphatically reaffirmed the prohibition on company unions. In that case, the employer had established employee committees to discuss various workplace issues and to propose solutions to management. The NLRB found the establishment of the committees to be illegal, even though the employer did not call them unions. Any organization or association that exists for the purpose of dealing with the employer over the terms of employment is illegal if the employer establishes its structure, creates rules for membership in it, or controls the issues that the association considers.

Under *Electromation*, almost any organization an employer might establish or support that likely would convince employees not to support an independent union would be a prohibited company-dominated union. The employer cannot legally hold out its organization as an alternative to union representation (*Waste Mgt. of Utah, Salt Lake Div.*, 310 NLRB 883 [1993]). Employee organizations may exist to decide the validity of employee complaints or to resolve work-related problems, but if they address "grievances, labor disputes, wages, rates of pay, hours of employment, or conditions of work," they *must do so without management control* (29 U.S.C. §152(5); *NLRB v. Peninsula General Hospital Medical Center*, 36 F.3d 1262, 4th Circuit, 1994). Management can be involved in committees that address something other than conditions of work, such as those concerning safety, productivity, or efficiency. But even then, if safety issues spill over to conditions of work such as discipline, wages, or hours, management involvement is unlawful (*E. I. du Pont de Nemours*, 311 NLRB 893, 895 [1993]).

In a recent case involving Somers Building Maintenance, SEIU Local 1877 encountered an attempt by the leading nonunion building contractor in Sacramento to adopt a company-dominated union as part of its response to a prolonged SEIU effort to organize Sacramento janitors. Somers is a one-thousand-worker nonunion cleaning contractor operating in the Sacramento / Silicon Valley area. Among its clients is Hewlett-Packard. The union has employed JfJ tactics, including a variety of public demonstrations, in its dispute with Somers and the area's nonunion cleaning firms.

In the course of the dispute, Somers announced that it had recognized "Couriers and Service Employees Local 1" as the bargaining agent for its employees. Just before NLRB hearings were to commence in August 1996 on the SEIU's charge that Local 1 was a company-dominated union, the case was settled in the union's favor. The firm withdrew recognition of Local 1 and agreed to refund eight thousand dollars in dues that Local 1 had collected from Somers workers. However, the disbanding of Local 1 did not settle the overriding dispute over union recognition in the Sacramento / Silicon Valley area, which continues.

Employers widely protested the *Electromation* decision, arguing that it interfered with new-style "employee participation" systems. Since then, various bills have been introduced in Congress to overturn it, but repeal of the company union ban is unlikely. Even if the statute is amended to allow employee participation plans, the creation of a full-fledged union-like entity by management, collecting dues and nominally negotiating about wages and conditions, will likely remain an unfair labor practice. If and when Local 1877 attempts a major new organizing drive in outlying areas of Los Angeles or in Orange County, it is conceivable that it could encounter a repetition of the Somers tactic. Whether the union would easily prevail against such a tactic in the future may depend on how successful the union is in gathering evidence of company domination.

Conclusion

SEIU Local 1877, heir to the Justice for Janitors campaign in Los Angeles, has been highly successful to date, yet still faces a variety of significant challenges. One is to retain its current unionized base and to prevent nonunion inroads. In the year 2000 it must renegotiate its current backloaded contract that applies within that base, in the context of the evolving regional economy. A second challenge involves the difficult task of balancing the representation needs of existing members with the union's need to extend its reach into new centers of development.

A final challenge is to adapt JfJ tactics, whether applied to new organizing or to avoiding erosion, to be sure not to run afoul of the long-standing legal ban on secondary boycotts. In the main, this challenge requires the union to confine itself to peaceful, nonpicketing appeals to the public. The secondary boycott laws generally prevent the union from seeking sympathy strikes from other workers and from engaging in picketing as a way of communicating with the public. The genius of the JfJ campaign has been its very creative use of novel methods of engendering public support for the cause of exploited janitors, and the legal restrictions on labor protest require SEIU Local 1877 to continue to use care and imagination in publicizing the workers' cause.

These challenges are substantial. Yet at the moment, the economic and political outlook are relatively benign. The general U.S. economic expansion has spilled over into Los Angeles County, although it has benefited the surrounding (nonunion) counties even more. And the 1998 state elections put into office a Democrat as governor for the first time in sixteen years. An aggressive move against the organized janitors seems unlikely in this environment. And the fact of an expanding Latino voting population would certainly complicate any such move. Nonetheless, the strategy of focusing first on an organizing breakthrough in Sacramento before a major organizing effort resumes in Los Angeles risks a gradual erosion of unionization in the expanding southern California building service market.

The Los Angeles Manufacturing Action Project: An Opportunity Squandered?

Héctor L. Delgado

Faced with declining membership and increasingly daunting obstacles to organizing, the labor movement is searching for new and innovative strategies and tactics. One important and highly touted effort to meet this challenge was the Los Angeles Manufacturing Action Project (LAMAP), a multiunion, multiemployer, industry-wide community-based organizing project. This chapter examines the strategy proposed by LAMAP, the rationale for it, organized labor's response, and the lessons learned from the project's failure or, perhaps more to the point, the failure of unions and the AFL-CIO to support the project.

Union strategies and tactics matter, as recent studies examining the relationship between union organizing tactics and union certification election outcomes show. In her study of 261 NLRB certification elections, for example, Bronfenbrenner found that union tactics mattered more than employer tactics, the demographics of the workforce, organizer backgrounds, or organizing climate. Unions are more likely to win certification elections when they use a rank-and-file intensive organizing strategy, including a reliance on person-to-person contact; emphasize union democracy and representative participation; build the first contract during the organizing drive; employ escalating pressure tactics; and recognize the importance workers place on dignity, justice, and fairness. (Bronfenbrenner 1997, p. 209)

Similarly, Fiorito, Jarley, and Delaney(1995) found that unions that adopted new or innovative policies, practices, or services were more effective than less innovative unions. My own research on the unionization of undocumented immigrants in Los Angeles prompted me to draw the same conclusion. In my study of a waterbed factory in which 160 undocumented immigrant workers voted by a 2–1 margin to unionize and negotiated a contract with their employer, the resources invested and the tactics employed by the union were key factors in the campaign's success. The union assigned eight organizers to the effort, solicited and obtained support from community organizations and leaders, conducted a corporate campaign, utilized short-term work stoppages and slowdowns, and utilized different media effectively to win the election and secure a collective bargaining agreement (Delgado 1993).

The Los Angeles Manufacturing Action Project was founded in February 1994. It was a project born of decades of eroding union power, new opportunities in the Los Angeles basin to organize workers on a massive scale, and the recognition that immigrant workers were not only receptive to unionization but had the potential to be at the vanguard of a labor movement revival. Peter Olney, the chief architect of LAMAP and an organizer in Los Angeles for over a decade, had worked on several campaigns in which he witnessed firsthand the militancy of immigrant workers. "They were enormously exploited," Olney observed, "but also extremely willing to rise up courageously to try to improve their conditions and get involved in unions."[1] The successful Justice for Janitors, drywallers', and American Racing Equipment campaigns (described elsewhere in this volume) and the changing demographics of the labor force had already raised questions about the efficacy of traditional organizing tactics and methods.

Others involved in the early development of LAMAP had organizing resumes comparable to or surpassing Olney's. Among these were David Sickler, then the Regional Director of the AFL-CIO; Joel Ochoa, a student activist in Mexico and community and labor activist in the United States; and environmental activist Carlos Porros. Sickler's experience as a union activist had convinced him that targeting industries and adopting a more militant approach were essential to a revival of the labor movement, and Ochoa, more than anyone, understood the importance of working with grassroots organizations and communities to build a strong base for LAMAP and the labor movement.

One of Olney's earlier experiences was a stint with the International Ladies' Garment Workers' Union (ILGWU), one of the first unions in

---

1. For my primary data I relied principally on LAMAP and union materials and in-depth interviews with Peter Olney, Joel Ochoa, José de Paz, John August, David Johnson, Jon Barton, Randy Cammack, Father Pedro Villaroya, Gilda Haas, Jaime Torres, Juan de Lara, William Kramer, David Sickler, Héctor Fernandez, Jimmy Rodríguez, Brian McWilliams, and Dan Ringer.

Los Angeles to hire Latino organizers and the first to hire a Mexican, Miguel Machuca, as its Director of Organizing in the early 1980s. The ILGWU became the "union of choice" among immigrant workers in this period. Consequently, Olney recalls, "we ended up representing furniture workers, waterbed workers, machine shop workers, cookie factories, frame shops, welding shops. Not because the union had a conscious strategy of targeting those sectors, but because they were the union out there, visible on channels 52 and 34. They were the union of choice. They were active and on the streets." In a 1993 article Olney wrote that "the empirical evidence from Southern California indicates that in fact immigrant workers are the easiest of all to organize" (1993, 13). This observation is corroborated by my own research (Delgado 1993).

The other source of inspiration for LAMAP was the size of the manufacturing sector in Los Angeles and surrounding counties. LAMAP relied heavily on research by Goetz Wolff and Gilda Haas, faculty members in Urban Planning at UCLA. Both were involved in discussions with Olney early in the process. Mapping the manufacturing sector was a key task performed by Wolff. His research revealed that Los Angeles had the largest concentration of manufacturing workers in the country, approximately 700,000, and that Latino immigrants comprised a majority of the workforce in manufacturing and 75–80 percent in light manufacturing. Wolff found "a powerful geographic conjunction between those light manufacturing jobs, where those workers lived, and the ethnicity of those workers: it was the old industrial area between downtown Los Angeles and the twin ports of Long Beach and Los Angeles, better known as the Alameda Corridor" (1998, 5). Only 9 percent of manufacturing was unionized, and most of the shops involved had been organized decades earlier. In the intervening years, many other once-unionized shops had fallen victim to the decline of heavy manufacturing in the state and the erosion of organized labor's power.

Attempts to organize industrial workers in southern California have been relatively few in the past twenty years, and these culminated either in lost elections or victories in which organized labor netted few new members. "If you look at what is going on today in organizing manufacturing in L.A.—virtually nothing is going on," observes Dave Johnson, International Representative of the United Electrical Workers (UE). For organized labor to survive, he emphasizes, it has to organize manufacturing workers and reestablish a strong industry base. The importance of this base was not lost on Olney and his collaborators. They were convinced, however, that in order to organize these workers, they needed to do something bold and different.

It was clear that no one union had the resources and the history and the gumption, the vision to go it alone. We needed the creation of a social movement in that community around organizing. To do that, unions would have to surrender some of their territorialism, their short-term "quarterly-returnism" in terms of organizing, and put together a multi-union, community-based industrial organizing project that would be able to capture that potential and momentum, and break the bounds of segregated, jurisdictional "turfism" that a lot of union organizing is, and to put in its place something new and different that could tap that potential. So that was the concept of rounding up a bunch of unions to put in the resources so that we could have one organizing arm in the field, organizing workers under the rubric of an LAMAP or an immigrant workers' organizing committee, rather than having the steelworkers organizing these guys, machinists organizing those guys. The idea was to have one army of organizers working for this project, building a community base, working on immigration issues. (Olney interview, 3/98)

An essential though not entirely new component of LAMAP's strategy was a sectoral focus.

The idea behind industrial unions, Olney noted, was that "you organize the entire industry to level the playing field, so that unions don't compete around labor costs. Workers can drive wages to higher levels and not be whipsawed by employers. And that's an old concept of the CIO and before that, and certainly recaptured or given new life by the Justice for Janitors campaign...in Los Angeles." But national multiemployer, industry-wide contracts, established principally in the 1940s, had all but disappeared by the 1980s (Moody 1990, 216). LAMAP tried to incorporate what had worked in the past, both distant and recent, and its founders engaged in many conversations with experienced organizers to fine-tune the project and fit it to existing and projected economic, political, and social conditions.

Conditions in Los Angeles, as Wolff concluded from his research and Olney and others knew intuitively from their experiences as organizers, were reminiscent of the era when labor had last organized successfully on the scale LAMAP was proposing. The reemergence of ethnic community networks was particularly critical.

Another factor in the weakening of formal rank-and-file democracy has been a major population shift. Since the early 1940s Americans have been a population on the move. The old ethnic and cohesive working-class neighborhoods nearby the industrial workplaces have become all but extinct. Informal organization in the work process no longer has supplemental aid from informal organization in the neighborhood. Only as

racial and ethnic minorities in the central city cores gain more employment in city industry does the advantage return. (Weir 1983, 261)

In immigrant Los Angeles, and the Alameda corridor in particular—perhaps the densest manufacturing area in the country—the trends Weir
lamented have been completely reversed. The literature on immigrants is
replete with references to the importance of social networks in immigration, settlement, and work processes. In my own research, too, such networks played a key role in the unionization process.

In fashioning LAMAP, Olney drew on the experience and advice of
Jon Barton, then the Organizing Director of SEIU Local 1877 and the
lead organizer of the Campaign for Justice, a multiunion campaign
launched in San Jose in 1993. On the heels of a campaign in which they
organized three thousand janitors in Silicon Valley, the local targeted the
valley's thirty thousand low-wage, subcontracted manufacturing jobs and
another thirty thousand service jobs, filled principally by workers of color.
SEIU took the lead to try to organize these workers, put up the bulk of
the money, and invited others to join them. Four unions responded: the
Teamsters, Amalgamated Clothing and Textile Workers Union
(ACTWU), Communication Workers, and Hotel Employees and Restaurant Employees Union (HERE). The campaign ran for six months and at
its high point had thirty organizers on staff. They conducted a "multi-
month research and mapping exercise" to see where these workers lived,
and then proceeded to organize in neighborhoods, door-to-door, around
workplace issues, holding neighborhood meetings in which workers
shared their workplace experiences.

Although the effort was successful on the ground, especially in mobilizing workers across ethnic lines, the project failed, as Barton recalls, because of "internal relationships between different organizing directors
and unions" and the fact that "unions didn't see San Jose or the high-tech
industry as strategically important to them at the time." Despite the campaign's ultimate failure, Olney and Barton believe it underscored the potential of multiunion, community-based campaigns.

Another source of inspiration for LAMAP was the AFL-CIO's California Immigrant Workers' Association (CIWA), which had also been trying
to tap the tremendous potential of the immigrant population. CIWA was
created in 1989 by the regional AFL-CIO office to provide services to and
organize immigrant workers. The association was funded by twenty-one
AFL-CIO affiliated unions and six central labor councils (Acuña 1996,
190). José De Paz, a well-known and respected community activist in the
Latino community, was the association's Executive Director and Joel

Ochoa was one of its organizers. Prior to working with CIWA, Ochoa had gained valuable organizing experience working with Bert Corona and the Centro de Acción Social Autónomo (CASA—Center for Autonomous Social Action), an organization formed principally to organize undocumented immigrant workers.[2]

Ochoa notes that organized labor is perceived in Latino communities as an "outsider." This obstacle is not insurmountable, but requires a commitment by labor to establish and cultivate roots in Latino communities.

> In this respect it is essential that labor build and sustain a presence in the community in the form of labor / community centers with the goal of creating a real labor and community alliance. These centers should not simply be sites where unions can pick up a few organizing leads or where residents can obtain some free services. On the contrary, these centers should be sites where interests converge. Labor can learn the importance of addressing community issues, and the community can learn the importance of collective bargaining. In this sense, the centers can serve as a mutual "point of entry" for broader participation in the political, cultural, social and economic life of both immigrants and labor unions. (Ochoa 1995, 3–4)

The labor movement, LAMAP was convinced, could be invigorated by immigrants, and the community component of the project was designed to establish a presence for organized labor in these communities to build a base for future organizing (see Brecher and Costello 1990; Shostak 1991; Scipes 1991; Form 1995; Fantasia 1988).

Drawing on their own and others' experience and knowledge of immigrant communities, LAMAP's founders developed an organizing strategy for Los Angeles' vast immigrant manufacturing workforce. They had a vehicle and road map, but needed the AFL-CIO and the unions to provide the fuel. From the beginning they knew it would not be an easy sell. In September 1994, Olney pitched LAMAP at a meeting of the AFL-CIO's National Organizing Committee in Washington, D.C., attended by international union officers and their organizing directors. They were excited by and expressed interest in the project.

2. CASA was an outgrowth of La Hermandad Mexicana Nacional (Mexican National Brotherhood), formed in San Diego in 1951. The organization consisted mainly of trade unionists and Mexican immigrant workers, many of whom were members of the Carpenters' Union or the Laborers' Union. Prior to the formation of Hermandad, most unions did not believe the undocumented were receptive to unionization. Bert Corona recalls, "I think that one of the most important contributions the Hermandad has made has been to prove . . . that immigrant workers are among the most organizable, most militant, and most pro-union members of the work force" (García 1994, 296).

Two months later, Gilda Haas and her students in UCLA's Community Scholars Program made a presentation to representatives of twenty-two unions in a hotel near the Los Angeles airport on the organizing potential of several sectors in the Alameda Corridor.[3] Most of the unions present were represented by one or two organizers or business agents, but other unions had as many as five representatives, including high-ranking union officials. The Teamsters, for example, sent John August, their Organizing Coordinator, from Washington, D.C. As William Kramer recalls, the ones especially interested in the project sent "a mix of D.C. people and local people." At this meeting, unions were asked to invest in the project in order to continue the research and community work. The hope was to develop plans for a full-fledged organizing campaign in late 1995 or early 1996.

By January 1995, nine unions had agreed to contribute $25,000 each as seed money. These unions were the United Auto Workers (UAW); United Brotherhood of Carpenters (UBC); United Food and Commercial Workers (UFCW); International Ladies' Garment Workers' Union (ILGWU); International Longshoremen's and Warehousemen's Union (ILWU); International Association of Machinists (IAM); Oil, Chemical and Atomic Workers (OCAW); United Steelworkers of America (USWA); and the International Brotherhood of Teamsters (IBT). The United Electrical Workers (UE) participated through OCAW as it was not affiliated with the AFL-CIO.

On the basis of this initial funding, LAMAP's leaders began to work on establishing a presence in Latino immigrant communities. Toward that end, LAMAP set up an office in a predominantly Latino neighborhood in the Alameda Corridor. "We wanted to incorporate the project into community life," Ochoa explained. In fact, LAMAP began to develop its identity around community issues, including immigration and naturalization. It also began working with a group of parents on the education of their children, the protection of Roosevelt Park, and the development of Neighborhood Watch groups. As José De Paz summed it up, "Community is something you create."

Assisting LAMAP in these efforts was Father Pedro Villaroya, then Director of Hispanic Ministries for the Archdiocese of Los Angeles. He had read an article about LAMAP in the *Los Angeles Times* in the fall of 1995, contacted Olney, and immediately became involved. He described his involvement and the role of the church in the February 1996 issue of *Map Notes*, the LAMAP newsletter:

3. Haas had dedicated her course during the 1994–95 academic year to LAMAP-related work.

We have worked with the LAMAP research staff and have helped them locate over 50 Catholic churches in the Alameda Corridor. This is the core
of the Parish Outreach Program. The community that LAMAP seeks to
organize is largely Catholic and has great respect for the Church. I believe
that organizing is God's work and the Church has reaffirmed time and
time again that organizing is a basic human right. You cannot separate the
right for workers to join unions from this concept. The Human Person
can only be fulfilled when there is dignity and justice at work. This is what
LAMAP is all about and this is the message that the Priests and Bishops
will bring to the people.

What appealed to him most about the project, he added, was "the idea of
a multi-union project that emphasizes organizing for the people and not
just for getting members."

Overseeing the work of and making policy for LAMAP was the Organizing Policy Board (OPB), made up of participating unions and representatives from the community and academia. The OPB met on a
monthly basis beginning in early 1995 to refine the project and begin co-
ordinating the work. As Olney explained, these sessions focused principally on the idea of a new "entity into which workers would be organized
from all industries, as Latinos, to be together to capture this fever of organizing; to keep those people involved in organizing."[4] This, Olney
added, was the best way to build a movement and maintain momentum.
"We were creating what we liked to call a new 'entity,' that would serve as
a catch basin of the newly organized and that would keep them engaged
in the excitement of organizing and that would also have some type of
ethnic identity." Most of the unions, however, reacted negatively to this,
especially OCAW and UE. They believed they did a good job representing
their people and did not see how they could justify to their members recruiting workers into a different organization. Some organizers attribute
the failure of unions to support LAMAP partly to their inability or reluctance to change this aspect of their culture. As one observed:

> Each union sees its future as separate from everybody else's. We certainly
> did. To a large extent that is built into the nature of the organization. You
> have to go to the membership and explain why you spent this money.
> There was a certain narrowness of perspective that all of the unions had

---

4. Latinos were not the only workers in the corridor. The feasibility study prepared by
participants in the Community Scholars Program referred to the large number of African
Americans living and working in the corridor and noted tensions between the African
American and Latino communities (Adler et al. 1995). Gilda Haas and others questioned
whether the project should target Latinos exclusively.

and that was a big obstacle. Part of an answer to that is trying to figure out a form, a structure, another project where there is enough self-interest in it immediately, but there is also a bigger collective goal to work toward. I don't have the answer.

Olney assured UE, OCAW, and the other unions that eventually the newly organized workers would become members of their unions, but to no avail. Ultimately, LAMAP compromised on this issue and agreed to recruit workers directly into unions. In retrospect, this was one of Olney's few regrets. Had he fought harder for the "vision of the new entity," it might have stopped the project in its tracks, but had the project weathered the storm, it would have done so "with more integrity and more potential to win." Brian McWilliams of ILWU advised him not to compromise on this issue.

McWilliams recalled in an interview that compromising on this issue made it more difficult for LAMAP to "lock in" unions for the long term. "When you put a bunch of unions together to do this, there's an opportunity to force them to develop a system, so they can't get out of working together. So they have to bargain jointly in an industry, and they have to look out for each other, and they serve workers better because of that situation." He believed, as did the architects of LAMAP, that entire industries had to be targeted to level the playing field, taking wages out of the equation to force companies to compete on other bases, and that the only way to do this was by unions working together in a manner proposed by LAMAP. "None of us are big enough or have enough resources by ourselves to go out and organize an industry," McWilliams observed. When the union representatives at OPB meetings got into discussions of "who gets the pie," McWilliams said, "they missed the point." By assigning newly organized workers to individual unions, the incentive for unions to remain with and continue to fund the project after their industry was organized decreased and, ironically, the level of mistrust among them increased.

In addition to the discomfort of having to wait for their sector to be targeted, while funding campaigns in other sectors, and lacking any guarantee that by the time their number came up LAMAP would still be in existence or that the unions that had already organized would continue to fund the project, unions were uneasy with other components of the project. Some of them wondered whether the size of their sector justified the expense, as once they started organizing, each union would have to contribute $250,000 annually to LAMAP. Kramer learned subsequent to the project's demise that a number of unions did not believe they had enough of a base on which to build. As Project Director, Olney would direct the campaigns. This troubled some of the unions which were not prepared to relinquish that much control to Olney and his staff. A couple of organizers noted, in fact, that unlike Sickler, Olney was not well known outside of the Los Angeles area (although among those who knew him he enjoyed enormous respect). Others did not see clearly the connection between the community component of the project and organizing in the workplace, or at least questioned whether the return justified the investment.

As these discussions were unfolding, rebellion in the AFL-CIO ranks was spreading. In June 1995, John Sweeney declared his candidacy for the presidency of the federation. LAMAP architects believed they were positioned well with either Tom Donahue or Sweeney, both of whom had expressed support for LAMAP in their "stump" speeches during the campaign. On July 20, 1995, Olney and other LAMAP representatives presented a formal proposal to the AFL-CIO Ad Hoc Committee on the Role of the Federation in Organizing. Sweeney, then representing SEIU, was present.

The document presented at this meeting, "Organizing the Future," described LAMAP in detail as a multiunion, area-wide organizing campaign among industrial workers in the Alameda Corridor, guided by four principles. First, no one union had the resources or experience to organize these industries and workers alone. It required a "Union Goliath." Only a "single army," under a "central command," could have "the focus, discipline or firepower to make breakthroughs." Second, LAMAP would organize sectors with the goal of achieving industry-wide contracts. Third, it would rely on NLRB charges, but as part of an "array of tactical approaches" including employment law, consumer and community action, and direct worker action and civil disobedience. Fourth, the "ethnic composition and geographic concentration of the targeted workforce" meant that "the strategic involvement of community based organizations like the Catholic Church and Mexican State Federations" was crucial.

The proposal included the creation of an Organizing Committee (OC), which would be "governed" by the OPB and made up of affiliated unions, the AFL-CIO, and members of the community. The OPB and the AFL-CIO Regional Director would designate jurisdictions prior to the organizing campaign. The designated affiliate, as Olney had already conceded to the unions, would represent the newly organized workers. These workers, however, also would constitute a chapter of the OC and remain active in the project. A portion of newly elected members' union dues would go to the OC to support its work. The OC would have a council made up of newly organized sectors, sectors undergoing organization, nontargeted "hot shops," CIWA chapters, and community-based organizations and churches.

LAMAP would be responsible for hiring, training, and directing the staff and campaign, but the AFL-CIO Organizing Institute would play a central role in locating, recruiting, and training staff. LAMAP would have a staff of forty, with Peter Olney as the Executive Director. The proposed organizational chart included labor and community Field Directors; a Director to guide research, monitor bargaining and representation, and coordinate legal support; an Administrative Coordinator to supervise and direct office staff; and a Press and Media Director. The project, Olney informed the committee, had received and would continue to receive research support from UCLA faculty. Kent Wong, an LAMAP board member, Director of UCLA's Labor Center, and National President of the AFL-CIO's Asian Pacific American Labor Alliance, had already created a position in the Labor Center to coordinate academic and research support for LAMAP. The position was filled by William Kramer, a recent UCLA Master's graduate in Urban Planning.

The proposed annual operating budget was three million dollars, which participating unions and the AFL-CIO were asked to provide. Roughly two-thirds of the budget would be covered by the $250,000 annual contribution by each of the nine unions, and the AFL-CIO in Washington, D.C., was asked to invest the remaining portion. The response of the committee to the report was enthusiastic, but from this point on the project began to unravel.

Olney and the others arrived in New York for the AFL-CIO convention in October 1995, talked with delegates, and met with the LAMAP-affiliated unions. Several already had jumped ship. Still on board in October were the Steelworkers, the Carpenters, the Longshoremen, UNITE, and the Teamsters. Olney never expected all ten unions to take the second step of investing a quarter of a million dollars in LAMAP. He was happy to have the five unions. Ochoa, however, was less optimistic and believed they needed all ten and ultimately more.

After Sweeney was elected President of the AFL-CIO, LAMAP started meeting with Richard Bensinger, the federation's new Director of Organizing, about the project. The AFL-CIO had established funding criteria privileging multiunion organizing projects, based on such considerations as the strategic viability of the project, the capability of the staff, the membership involved, research support, and related criteria. Olney and the others believed they met these criteria handily and should receive money.

In April 1996, however, there was a fateful meeting in Bensinger's office. The Teamsters and Carpenters were there, but the Longshoremen and Steelworkers did not show up. The Steelworkers' representative's plane was forced to land in Baltimore and he decided to return home rather than continue to Washington, D.C. for the meeting. "The writing was on the wall," Olney said. "We saw we didn't have the support." The Carpenters started to "make noises" about pulling out, Olney recalled, and finally the "only ones left standing with us were the Teamsters." The AFL-CIO had indicated that they would support the project if the unions did. But one union was not enough.

Ochoa's assessment of what occurred in New York is one shared in considerable measure by Olney. "Something funny happened at the election," Ochoa commented. "We pretty much lost our momentum. During the prior AFL-CIO administration there was a vacuum in terms of organizing, and John Sweeney pretty much made organizing his top priority. Organizing came center stage. The vacuum we were filling disappeared." Contributing to the AFL-CIO's reluctance to support the project was that the plan had been conceived under Lane Kirkland and that Sickler was seen as a member of the "old guard." "The irony of ironies," Olney observes, "is that the Sweeney folks won and they were the apostles of organizing." Expecting to benefit from the new administration and the shift from a "death march" to a revival of organized labor through organizing, LAMAP instead became, in Olney's words, "one of its first casualties."

The Teamsters were the only ones to put money into the project after the initial seed money invested by several unions. Indeed, the Teamsters had been the most committed union from the beginning. LAMAP staff began talking with the Teamsters about scaling down the project and making it a Teamsters' project. In the summer of 1996 the Teamsters and LAMAP got involved in a strike by Mission Guerrero truck drivers who were in the throes of renegotiating their contract. LAMAP conducted research on the company and helped the union to mobilize community support. One hundred and ten drivers waged a ten-week strike and won. This victory was seen as a stepping-stone to organizing tortilla production workers on an industry-wide basis. The Teamsters and LAMAP built the project around baked goods and a multilocal approach. After the reelection of Ron Carey, they met in Lake Arrowhead in February 1997 with all of the Teamster locals in southern California and made the case for a joint approach to organizing. It looked like they were going to get both Carey and Hoffa locals and the International to contribute funds, but once again the project unraveled because of internal union politics. "They were talking organizing, but they were still playing out the Hoffa-Carey wars. We were just a political football," Olney recalled. The Teamsters did contribute enough money for a time to support a staff of ten.

The Teamsters and LAMAP continued to work on the Mission Guerrero tortilla campaign, with organizers in the two East Los Angeles plants
and the Rancho Cucamunga plant. They were making progress, but eventually, Olney lamented, the "Teamsters' internal stuff just overwhelmed
us." The International had become increasingly skittish about giving
money to outside organizations, and in the summer of 1997 the funding
was cut. The Hoffa people were always suspicious of LAMAP and its connection to the Carey camp. By June they were forced to close down, with
the exception of a parking attendants' campaign, "Parking Power" (a Justice for Janitors type of campaign), which they had been running with
Teamster Local 911 in Long Beach.

The tortilla campaign had become LAMAP's "heart and soul" and
when they were forced to end it, that killed the project. They had invested a tremendous amount of time in research and in what they believed was a very promising campaign. Olney and Dan Ringer, LAMAP's
Administrative Director, were the last to leave. Olney went off the payroll
in mid-November and Ringer at the end of January 1998. "He closed the
thing down," Olney said. "He was the undertaker."

Michael Eisenscher, who conducted research on LAMAP, observed:

> The project will...have to overcome the conflicts that frequently arise be-
> tween unions over historical jurisdictions, allocation of resources, and ri-
> valries between union leaders. Its first challenge will be to secure, then re-
> tain and increase, national union and Federation resource commitments
> over successive years. The project will have to address the inevitable ten-
> sion that will arise between local unions and LAMAP chapters as they vie
> for the commitment of newly organized workers. It will also have to resist
> efforts by national unions or the Federation to assert control or supplant
> the project's own leadership. (1996, 18–19)

The project failed to secure, let alone retain or increase, the long-term financial commitment of the unions and the AFL-CIO. More than one organizer informed me, off the record, that internal bickering contributed significantly to their unions' decisions not to buy into the project. Presidents
or organizing directors of some nonparticipating locals opposed the expenditure by the international of such large amounts of money on a project that would benefit only one, perhaps two, locals in the Alameda Corridor. Few unions were prepared to put aside self-interest, pool resources,
and act in concert with one another to develop deeper and broader ties
with workers in the communities where they lived and worked.

The "New Voice" AFL-CIO is more active, combative, and creative and
more committed to organizing than its predecessor. Sweeney's AFL-CIO

helped launch and is supporting several area-wide, sectorally based, multiunion campaigns, but within old and slowly changing structures. LAMAP had proposed new structures. Referring to the AFL-CIO's more modest multiunion campaigns, Olney commented, "Perhaps it is all they can do at this point, given where unions and institutions are at." Organizations "by their very nature" are conservative (Hall 1996, 191). They do not change easily, and the AFL-CIO, as Brecher and Costello (1996) among others note, may be especially resistant to change. But in the death of LAMAP, bureaucratic intransigence was an accomplice to factionalism within unions, competition between them, and the reluctance of the AFL-CIO's new leadership to adopt a plan conceived by the old guard they replaced.

Sickler, Olney, and others affiliated with LAMAP believed that the AFL-CIO's failure to provide the kind of leadership only *it* could provide fatally wounded the project. Mark Splain, Sickler's replacement as Regional Director, and Bob Calahan, the Steelworkers' Organizing Director at the time, both assert that what killed LAMAP was the failure of one or two unions to take the lead (Gallagher 1998), a view Jon Barton also expressed in an interview. Of course, LAMAP suffered from the failure to win direct support from unions. But this analysis underestimates the ability of the AFL-CIO to influence its affiliated unions. Since the demise of LAMAP, the AFL-CIO has supported and indeed taken the lead in multiunion campaigns in several cities. In Seattle, for example, the Federation invested over $750,000 in a multiunion campaign. Such an investment in LAMAP could have made a huge difference. Had the project been conceived on Sweeney's watch, the result might have been a different one. In fact, one union, the Teamsters, did invest over $500,000 in LAMAP, but neither the AFL-CIO nor the other unions responded in kind.

LAMAP presented organized labor with an alternative organizing model unlike anything it has attempted in recent memory. Though LAMAP failed to take root, it spawned healthy debates on the nature of the problem confronting unions and workers, and it forced many unions to reassess and defend their organizing strategies and tactics. It provided organized labor with data on the largest manufacturing sector in the country and on the workers in these factories and the communities in which they live. And, perhaps most important, it held up to organized labor a mirror for it to see what it is able and willing to do to win.

References

Abowd, John M., and Henry S. Farber. 1982. "Job Queues and the Union Status of Workers." *Industrial and Labor Relations Review* 35: 354–67.

Acuña, Rodolfo F. 1996. *Anything but Mexican: Chicanos in Contemporary Los Angeles.* London: Verso.

Adler, Susan, Ronaldo Babiera, Carolina Briones, Guadalupe Duran, Quentin Givens, Suzanne Hoffman, Edward Iny, Josefina Jimenez, William Kramer, Srithip Sresthaphunlarp, Danilo Torres, and co-authored by Angelo Adams, Mizue Aizeki, John Dominguez, Gabriel Espiritu, Kim Geron, Susan Kandel, Laura Kelly, Hany Khalil, Teresa Sanchez, Adrian Shropshire, Monica Lee Silbas, Loretta Stevens, and Arlene Williams. 1995. "Union Jobs for Community Renewal: A Feasibility Study for the Los Angeles Manufacturing Action Project." Unpublished manuscript, UCLA Graduate School of Urban Planning.

AFL-CIO Committee on the Evolution of Work. 1985. "The Changing Situation of Workers and Their Unions." Washington, D.C.: AFL-CIO.

AFL-CIO. n.d. "Organizing for Change, Changing to Organize! A Report From the AFL-CIO Elected Leader Task Force on Organizing." Washington, D.C.: AFL-CIO.

Aizeki, Mizue, Miki Fujimoto, and William Kramer. 1994."The Southern California Wheel Industry: Organizing for the Future." Unpublished manuscript, UCLA Graduate School of Urban Planning.

Aldana, Alejandro. 1992. "Trabajadores de la Construccion Pieden Hablar con Nuevo Jefe de Policia." *Union Hispana,* July 31, 1, 14.

Allen, Steven G. 1994. "Developments in Collective Bargaining in Construction in the 1980s and 1990s." In *Contemporary Collective Bargaining in the Private Sector,* edited by Paula B. Voos, 411–45. Madison, Wis.: Industrial Relations Research Association.

American Apparel Manufacturers Association (AAMA). 1998. *Focus: An Economic Profile of the Apparel Industry.* Arlington, Va.: AAMA.

Armbruster, Ralph. 1998. *Globalization and Cross-border Organizing in the Garment and Automobile Industries.* Ph.D. diss., University of California, Riverside.

Ashenfelter, Orley. 1972. "Racial Discrimination and Trade Unionism." *Journal of Political Economy* 80: 435–64.

Bailey, Eric, and Robert Shogan. 1998. "Defeat of Measure Energizes Labor." *Los Angeles Times,* June 4, A3, A28.

Bakke, E. W. 1967 (1945). "Why Workers Join Unions." *Personnel* 22: 2–11, reprinted on pp. 85–92 in *Unions, Management, and the Public*, edited by E. W. Bakke, C. Kerr, and C. W. Anrod. New York: Harcourt, Brace, Jovanovich.

Barrett, James. 1987. *Work and Community in the Jungle: Chicago's Packinghouse Workers, 1894–1922*. Urbana: University of Illinois Press.

———. 1992. "Americanization from the Bottom Up: Immigration and the Remaking of the Working Class in the United States, 1880–1930." *Journal of American History* 79: 996–1020.

Bean, Frank, and Marta Tienda. 1986. *The Hispanic-Origin Population of the United States*. New York: Russell Sage Foundation.

Blau, Peter, and Otis Dudley Duncan. 1967. *The American Occupational Structure*, New York: Wiley.

Bodnar, John E. 1985. *The Transplanted: A History of Immigrants in Urban America*. Bloomington: Indiana University Press.

Bonacich, Edna, and Richard P. Appelbaum. Forthcoming. *Behind the Label: Inequality in the Los Angeles Apparel Industry*. Berkeley: University of California Press.

Bonacich, Edna, Lucie Cheng, Norma Chinchilla, Nora Hamilton, and Paul Ong. 1994. *Global Production: The Apparel Industry in the Pacific Rim*. Philadelphia: Temple University Press.

Bourdon, Clinton C., and Raymond E. Levitt. 1980. *Union and Open-shop Construction*. Lexington, Mass.: Lexington Books.

Brecher, Jeremy, and Tim Costello, eds. 1990. *Building Bridges: The Emerging Grassroots Coalition of Labor and Community*. New York: Monthly Review Press.

———. 1996. "A 'New Labor Movement' in the Shell of the Old?" *Labor Research Review* 24: 5–25.

Brody, David. 1960. *Steelworkers in America: The Nonunion Era*. New York: Harper & Row.

———. 1993. *In Labor's Cause: Main Themes on the History of the American Worker*. New York: Oxford University Press.

———. 1995. "Criminalizing the Rights of Labor." *Dissent* (Summer): 363–67.

Bronfenbrenner, Kate. 1993. "Seeds of Resurgence: Successful Union Strategies for Winning Certification Elections and First Contracts in the 1980s and Beyond." Ph.D. diss., Cornell University.

———. 1997. "The Role of Union Strategies in NLRB Certification Elections." *Industrial and Labor Relations Review* 50: 195–211.

Bronfenbrenner, Kate, and Tom Juravich. 1994. "Seeds of Resurgence: The Promise of Organizing in the Public and Private Sectors." Working paper, Institute for the Study of Labor Organizations, George Meany Center for Labor Studies, Silver Spring, Maryland.

———. 1998. "It Takes More than Housecalls: Organizing to Win with a Comprehensive Union-building Strategy." In *Organizing to Win: New Research on Union Strategies*, edited by Kate Bronfenbrenner, Sheldon Friedman, Richard W. Hurd, Rudolph A. Oswald, and Ronald L. Seeber, 19–36. Ithaca: Cornell University Press.

Building Service Contractors Association International (BSCAI). 1996. *Financial and Operating Ratios Study, 1996–1997*. Fairfax, Va.: BSCAI.

Burnham, Rick. 1995. "Union Wants Role in House Building Industry." *Riverside Press-Enterprise*, May 7, A1, A24.

California AFL-CIO News. 1992. "AFL-CIO Aids Drywall Strikers." July 17, 4.

———. 1995. "Framer Strike Spreads." May 5, 1, 4.

California Department of Finance. 1996. *California Demographics*.

———. 1998. *California Demographics*.

California Department of Industrial Relations, Division of Labor Statistics and Research. 1957–1989. *Union Labor in California.* San Francisco.

Cheng, Lucie, and Philip Yang. 1996. "Asians: The 'Model Minority' Deconstructed." In *Ethnic Los Angeles*, edited by Roger Waldinger and Mehdi Bozorgmehr, 305–44. New York: Russell Sage Foundation.

Christensen, Kim. 1992. "Charges Eased against Drywallers." *Orange County Register,* July 21, B1, B5.

Christensen, Kim, and Jeordan Legeon. 1992. "74 Drywallers Held for Possible Deportation." *Orange County Register,* July 11, B1, B10.

Cobble, Dorothy Sue, and Michael Merrill. 1994. "Collective Bargaining in the Hospitality Industry in the 1980s." In *Contemporary Collective Bargaining in the Private Sector,* edited by Paula Voos, 447–89. Madison, Wis.: Industrial Relations Research Association.

Cohen, Lizabeth. 1990. *Making a New Deal: Industrial Workers in Chicago, 1919–1939.* New York: Cambridge University Press.

Construction Labor Report (CLR). Various issues. Bureau of National Affairs, Inc., Washington, D.C.

Cornelius, Wayne. 1992. "From Sojourners to Settlers: The Changing Profile of Mexican Immigration to the United States." In *United States-Mexican Relations: Labor Market Interdependence,* edited by Jorge Bustamante, Clark Reynolds, and Raúl Hinojosa-Ojeda, 155–95. Stanford, Calif.: Stanford University Press.

Craft, James. 1991. "Unions, Bureaucracy, and Change: Old Dogs Learn New Tricks Very Slowly." *Journal of Labor Studies* 12: 393–405.

Daily Labor Report (DLR). Various issues. Bureau of National Affairs, Inc., Washington, D.C.

DeBare, Ilana. 1997. "Labor Drive Takes New Route." *San Francisco Chronicle,* February 7, B1.

DeFreitas, Gregory. 1993. "Unionization among Racial and Ethnic Minorities." *Industrial and Labor Relations Review* 46: 284–301.

Delaney, John, Paul Jarley, and Jack Fiorito. 1996. "Planning for Change: Determinants of Innovation in U.S. National Unions." *Industrial and Labor Relations Review* 49: 597–614.

Delgado, Héctor L. 1993. *New Immigrants, Old Unions: Organizing Undocumented Workers in Los Angeles.* Philadelphia: Temple University Press.

del Pilar Marrero, María. 1992a. "Protesta Obrera Acaba en la 101 y con 68 Arrestos." *La Opinion,* July 24, A1.

———. 1992b. "Protestan Ante el Centro Parker 400 Constructores." *La Opinion,* July 29, A5.

De Paz, José. 1993. "Organizing Ourselves." *Labor Research Review* 12: 25–32.

Donato, Katharine M. 1991. "Stemming the Tide? Assessing the Deterrent Effects of the Immigration Reform and Control Act." Paper presented at the Annual Convention of the American Sociological Association.

Duncan, Greg J., and Frank P. Stafford. 1980. "Do Union Members Receive Compensating Wage Differentials?" *American Economic Review* 70: 355–71.

Eaton, Tracey. 1992. "Strike Patrols Taking Toll in Anaheim." *Orange County Register,* September 2, B1, B5.

Eisenscher, Michael. 1996. "Critical Juncture: Unionism at the Crossroads." Working paper presented at the Labor at the Crossroads Public Forum, Center for Labor Research, University of Massachusetts–Boston.

Employment Development Department. 1998. *Los Angeles–Long Beach MSA (Los Angeles County): Current Labor Force and Industry Employment.* Labor Market Information Division, Los Angeles, June 12.

Fantasia, Rick. 1988. *Cultures of Solidarity: Consciousness, Action, and Contemporary American Workers.* Berkeley: University of California Press.

Farber, Henry S., and Daniel H. Saks. 1980. "Why Workers Want Unions: The Role of Relative Wages and Job Characteristics." *Journal of Political Economy* 88: 349–69.

Fine, Janice, and Richard Locke. 1996. "Unions Get Smart: New Tactics for a New Labor Movement." *Dollars and Sense* (Sept. / Oct.): 16–19.

Fiorito, Jack, and Daniel G. Gallagher. 1986. "Job Content, Job Status, and Unionism." *Advances in Industrial and Labor Relations* 3: 261–316.

Fiorito, Jack, Daniel G. Gallagher, and Charles R. Greer. 1986. "Determinants of Unionism: A Review of the Literature." *Research in Personnel and Human Resource Management* 4: 269–306.

Fiorito, Jack, Cynthia Gramm, and Wallace Hendricks. 1991. "Union Structural Choices." In *The State of the Unions,* edited by George Strauss, Daniel Gallagher, and Jack Fiorito, 103–37. Madison, Wis.: Industrial Relations Research Association.

Fiorito, Jack, Paul Jarley, and John Thomas Delaney. 1995. "National Union Effectiveness in Organizing: Measures and Influences." *Industrial and Labor Relations Review* 48: 613–35.

Flagg, Michael. 1992a. "500 Drywall Hangers Stage Hotel Protest." *Los Angeles Times* (Orange County edition), June 12, D5, D6.

——. 1992b. "Drywallers File Complaints on Home Builders." *Los Angeles Times* (Orange County edition), July 29, D1, D3.

——. 1992c. "Drywall Strikers Make Major Breakthrough." *Los Angeles Times* (Orange County edition), September 22, D7.

——. 1992d. "Subcontractors Meet Today on Drywall Strike." *Los Angeles Times* (Orange County edition), September 24, D5–6.

——. 1992e. "Some Drywall Subcontractors OK Union Talk." *Los Angeles Times* (Orange County edition), September 25, A1, A3.

——. 1992f. "What Drywallers Want from Subcontractors." *Los Angeles Times* (Orange County edition), November 8, D3, D7.

——. 1992g. "A 'Landmark Victory' for Drywall Union." *Los Angeles Times* (Orange County edition), November 11, D1, D6.

Foner, Philip S. 1979. *Women and the American Labor Movement: From Colonial Times to the Eve of World War I.* New York: Free Press.

Form, William. 1995. *Segmented Labor, Fractured Politics: Labor Politics in American Life.* New York: Plenum Press.

Freeman, Richard. 1988. "Contraction and Expansion: The Divergence of Private Sector and Public Sector Unionism in the United States." *Journal of Economic Perspectives* 2: 63–88.

——. 1993. "How Much Has De-unionization Contributed to the Rise in Male Earnings Inequality?" In *Uneven Tides: Rising Inequality in America,* edited by Sheldon Danzinger and Peter Gottschalk, 133–63. New York: Russell Sage Foundation.

Freeman, Richard, and James Medoff. 1984. *What Do Unions Do?* New York: Basic Books.

Freire, Paulo. 1990. *Pedagogy of the Oppressed.* New York: Continuum.

Friedlander, Peter. 1975. *The Emergence of a UAW Local, 1936–1939.* Pittsburgh: University of Pittsburgh Press.

Galenson, Walter. 1983. *The United Brotherhood of Carpenters: The First Hundred Years.* Cambridge: Harvard University Press.

Gallagher, Tom. 1998. "Everybody Loved It, But ... " *Z Magazine* (Nov. 11): 13–18.

García, Mario T. 1994. *Memories of Chicano History: The Life and Narrative of Bert Corona.* Berkeley: University of California Press.

García-Irigoyen, Leticia. 1992. "Grupos Latinos Apoyan a Huelguistas de Orange." *La Opinion,* July 10, A1.

Glenn, Susan A. 1990. *Daughters of the Shtetl: Life and Labor in the Immigrant Generation.* Ithaca: Cornell University Press.

Grabelsky, Jeffrey, and Richard Hurd. 1994. "Reinventing an Organizing Union: Strategies for Change." In *Proceedings of the 46th Annual Meeting.* Industrial Relations Research Association, 95–104.

Grebler, Leo, Joan Moore, and Ralph Guzman. 1970. *The Mexican-American People: The Nation's Second Largest Minority.* New York: Free Press.

Green, James, and Chris Tilly. 1987. "Service Unionism: Directions for Organizing." *Labor Law Journal* 38: 486–95.

Greene, Julie. 1998. *Pure and Simple Politics: The American Federation of Labor and Political Activism, 1881–1917.* New York: Cambridge University Press.

Greenhouse, Steven. 1999. "In Biggest Drive Since 1937, Union Gains a Victory." *New York Times,* Feb. 26, A1, A15.

Grieder, William. 1993. "Up Against the Drywall." *Rolling Stone* (Nov. 11): 35–37, 82.

Griego, Tina. 1990. "800 Wheel Factory Workers Walk Out." *Los Angeles Times,* August 2, J1, J4.

Gutiérrez, David G. 1995. *Walls and Mirrors: Mexican Americans, Mexican Immigrants and the Politics of Ethnicity.* Berkeley: University of California Press.

———. 1998. "Ethnic Mexicans and the Transformation of 'American' Social Space: Reflections on Recent History." In *Crossings: Mexican Immigration in Interdisciplinary Perspective,* edited by Marcelo M. Suárez-Orozco, 309–35. Cambridge: Harvard University, David Rockefeller Center for Latin American Studies.

Haber, William. 1930. *Industrial Relations in the Building Industry.* Cambridge: Harvard University Press.

Hall, Len, and Michael Flagg. 1992. "Drywall Strikers Jailed En Masse in O.C. Standoff." *Los Angeles Times* (Orange County edition), July 3, A1, A28.

Hall, Richard H. 1996. *Organizations: Structures, Processes, and Outcomes.* Englewood Cliffs, New Jersey: Prentice Hall.

Hermanson, Jeff. 1993. "Organizing for Justice: ILGWU Returns to Social Unionism to Organize Immigrant Workers." *Labor Research Review* 12: 52–61.

Hirsch, Barry T., and David A. Macpherson. 1997. *Union Membership and Earnings Data Book: Compilations from the Current Population Survey.* Washington, D.C.: Bureau of National Affairs, Inc.

Hourwich, Issac A. 1912. *Immigration and Labor: The Economic Aspects of European Immigration to the United States.* New York: Putnam's.

Howard, Alan. 1997. "Labor, History, and Sweatshops in the New Global Economy." In *No Sweat: Fashion, Free Trade, and the Rights of Garment Workers,* edited by Andrew Ross, 151–72. New York: Verso.

Howley, John. 1990. "The Challenge of Organizing in Contract Services." *Labor Research Review* 9: 61–71.

Hurd, Rick. 1986. "Bottom-Up Organizing: HERE in New Haven and Boston." *Labor Research Review* 5: 5–19.

INEGI, 1990. *XI Censo General de Población y Vivienda.*

Johnston, Paul. 1994. *Success while Others Fail: Social Movement Unionism and the Public Workplace.* Ithaca: ILR Press.

Josephson, Matthew. 1956. *Union House, Union Bar: The History of the Hotel and Restaurant Employees' and Bartenders' International Union, AFL-CIO.* New York: Random House.

Kazin, Michael. 1987. *Barons of Labor: The San Francisco Building Trades and Union Power in the Progressive Era.* Urbana: University of Illinois Press.

Labor Research Review. 1991 (special issue no. 17). *An Organizing Model of Unionism.*

———. 1993 (special issue no. 20). *Building on Diversity: The New Unionism.*

———. 1993 (special issue no. 21). *No More Business as Usual: Labor's Corporate Campaigns.*

Laslett, John, and Mary Tyler. 1989. *The ILGWU in Los Angeles, 1907–1988.* Inglewood, Calif.: Ten Star Press.

Lee, Don. 1995. "Carpenters' Strike Faces Long Odds." *Los Angeles Times,* May 30, A3, A14.

Legeon, Jeordan. 1992a. "Arrests Threatened after Striking Workers Hurl Rocks." *Orange County Register,* July 31, B2.

———. 1992b. "Workers Plan Talks with Employers." *Orange County Register,* October 1, B4.

Leigh, Duane E. 1986. "Union Preferences, Job Satisfaction, and the Union-Voice Hypothesis." *Industrial Relations* 25: 65–71.

Lerner, Stephen. 1991. "Let's Get Moving: Organizing for the 90's." *Labor Research Review* 10: 1–15.

Levy, Frank. 1988. *Dollars and Dreams: The Changing American Income Distribution.* New York: W. W. Norton.

Linguistic Minority Research Institute. 1996. *LMRI News.* University of California, Santa Barbara.

Lopez, David, Eric Popkin and Edward Telles. 1996. "Central Americans: At the Bottom, Struggling to Get Ahead." In *Ethnic Los Angeles,* edited by Roger Waldinger and Mehdi Bozorgmehr, 279–304. New York: Russell Sage Foundation.

Los Angeles Times. 1992. "Drywall Boss Says He Was Held Captive." August 20, B3.

Malinic, Eric, and David Reyes. 1992. "68 Drywall Workers Seized as Protest Blocks Freeway." *Los Angeles Times,* July 24, B1, B4.

Martin, Philip L. 1996. *Promises to Keep: Collective Bargaining in California Agriculture.* Ames: Iowa State University Press.

Martinez, Gebe, and Lily Dizon. 1992. "Drywall Strike Solidarity Growing." *Los Angeles Times* (Orange County Edition), July 10, A1, A23.

Massey, Douglas, Rafael Alarcón, Jorge Durand, and Humberto González. 1987. *Return to Aztlan: The Social Processes of Mexican Migration to the United States.* Berkeley: University of California Press.

Mills, Daniel Quinn. 1972. *Industrial Relations and Manpower in Construction.* Cambridge: MIT Press.

Mink, Gwendolyn. 1986. *Old Labor and New Immigrants in American Political Development: Union, Party, and State, 1875–1920.* Ithaca: Cornell University Press.

Minkoff, Debra C. 1994. "From Service Provision to Institutional Advocacy: The Shifting Legitimacy of Organizational Forms." *Social Forces* 72: 943–69.

Moody, Kim. 1990. "Building a Labor Movement for the 1990s: Cooperation and Concessions or Confrontation and Coalition." In *Building Bridges: The Emerging Grassroots Coalition of Labor and Community,* edited by Jeremy Brecher and Tim Costello, 216–28. New York: Monthly Review Press.

Morales, Rebecca. 1986. "The Los Angeles Automobile Industry in Historical Perspective." Unpublished paper, Graduate School of Architecture and Urban Planning, University of California Los Angeles.

Moran, Julio. 1992. "Deputies Criticized over Drywall Strike." *Los Angeles Times* (Valley edition), October 8, B3.

Mouchard, Andre. 1992. "Drywall Workers' Strike Spreads." *Orange County Register*, June 12, C1.

Murray, Kathleen. 1992. "Subcontractors to Seek Solution to Drywall Dispute." *Orange County Register*, September 25, B2.

Neckerman, Kathryn M., and Joleen Kirschenman. 1991. "Hiring Strategies, Racial Bias, and Inner-city Workers." *Social Problems* 38: 433–47.

Newton, Lucy A., and Lynn McFarlane Shore. 1992. "A Model of Union Membership: Instrumentality, Commitment, and Opposition." *Academy of Management Review* 17: 275–98.

Ochoa, Joel. 1995. "A Labor and Latino Alliance: The Future is Now." California Immigrant Workers Association, AFL-CIO. Mimeo.

Oestreicher, Richard Jules. 1986. *Solidarity and Fragmentation: Working People and Class Consciousness in Detroit, 1875–1900*. Urbana: University of Illinois Press.

Olney, Peter. 1985. "Corporate Profile: Superior Industries International, Inc." L.E.A.R.N. Services, Inc., Marina del Rey, California. Mimeo.

———. 1993. "The Rising of the Million." *Crossroads* (July / Aug.): 13–15.

Orange County Human Relations Commission. 1989. *Zero Dollars per Hour: A Report on Labor Exploitation in Orange County*. Santa Ana, Calif. Mimeo.

Orange County Register. 1992. "Strikers Kidnap Worker from Construction Site, Police Say." October 4, B4.

"Organizing the Future." 1995. A Presentation to the AFL-CIO Ad Hoc Committee on the Role of the Federation in Organizing. Mimeo.

Ortiz, Vilma. 1996. "The Mexican-Origin Population: Permanent Working Class or Emerging Middle Class?" In *Ethnic Los Angeles*, edited by Roger Waldinger and Mehdi Bozorgmehr, 247–77. New York: Russell Sage Foundation.

Perry, Charles R. 1987. *Union Corporate Campaigns*. Philadelphia: Wharton School of Business.

Piore, Michael. 1979. *Birds of Passage: Migrant Labor and Industrial Societies*. New York: Cambridge University Press.

Piore, Michael J., and Charles F. Sabel. 1984. *The Second Industrial Divide: Possibilities for Prosperity*. New York: Basic Books.

Portes, Alejandro, and Robert L. Bach. 1985. *Latin Journey: Cuban and Mexican Immigrants in the United States*. Berkeley: University of California Press.

Portes, Alejandro, and Min Zhou. 1993. "The New Second Generation: Segmented Assimilation and Its Variants." *Annals of the American Academy of Political and Social Science* 530: 74–96.

Portes, Alejandro, and Ruben Rumbaut. 1996. *Immigrant America: A Portrait*. 2d ed. Berkeley: University of California Press.

Potepan, Michael J., and Elisa Barbour. 1996 (March). *San Francisco's Employment Roller Coaster: A Report on the City's Employment Economy from 1980 to 2000*. Report submitted to the mayor's Office of Community Development, City of San Francisco.

Reyes, David. 1992. "Drywall Workers Rally for Solidarity." *Los Angeles Times* (Orange County edition), July 15, B3.

Reyes, David, and Len Hall. 1992. "85 Drywall Workers Plead Guilty." *Los Angeles Times* (Orange County edition), July 21, A1, A12.

Richmond, Al. 1981. "The San Francisco Hotel Strike." *Socialist Review* 11 (May-June): 87–113.

Ross, Andrew, ed. 1997. *No Sweat: Fashion, Free Trade, and the Rights of Garment Workers.* London: Verso.

Roukis, George S., and Bruce H. Charnov. 1985. "The RICO Statute: Implications for Organized Labor." *Labor Law Journal* 36: 281–91.

Saavedra, Tony. 1992. "Drywall Contract Signed." *Orange County Register*, November 11, A1, A18.

Saavedra, Tony, and Jeff Collins. 1992. "Drywall Workers Demand Trial, Reject Freedom." *Orange County Register*, July 7, A1, A14.

Sánchez, George J. 1993. *Becoming Mexican American: Ethnicity, Culture and Identity in Chicano Los Angeles, 1900–1945.* New York: Oxford University Press.

Savage, Lydia. 1998. "Geographies of Organizing: Justice for Janitors in Los Angeles." In *Organizing the Landscape: Geographical Perspectives on Labor Unionism*, edited by Andrew Herod, 225–52. Minneapolis: University of Minnesota Press.

Schoeni, Robert, Kevin McCarthy, and Georges Vernez. 1996. *The Mixed Economic Progress of Immigrants.* Santa Monica: Rand Corporation.

Schurman, Susan, and Hal Stack. 1994. "From Strategic Planning to Organizational Change in Local Unions." In *Proceedings of the 46th Annual Meeting*, Industrial Relations Research Association, 85–94.

Scipes, Kim. 1991. "Labor-Community Coalitions: Not All They're Cracked up to Be." *Monthly Review* 43: 34–46.

Scott, James C. 1985. *Weapons of the Weak: Everyday Forms of Peasant Resistance.* New Haven: Yale University Press.

Service Employees International Union. 1996. *Many Voices, One Union: A New Voice for SEIU Members.* Report no. 5 from the Committee on the Future. Washington, D.C.: SEIU.

Service Employees International Union (SEIU). 1997. Local union publications.

Shostak, Arthur. 1991. *Robust Unionism: Innovations in the Labor Movement.* Ithaca: ILR Press.

Sipchen, Bob. 1997. "Labor of Love." *Los Angeles Times*, March 9, E1, E8.

Sisco, Eric A., and Tracy L. Thornburg. 1993. "The 1992 Southern California Drywall Strike: A Management Perspective." Paper presented at the 11th Annual Labor Law Conference, sponsored by the National Labor Relations Board, Region 21, in cooperation with the Orange County Industrial Relations Research Association, Anaheim, California.

Smith, James, and Barry Edmonston, eds. 1996. *The New Immigrants.* Washington, D.C.: National Academy Press.

Stein, Leon, ed. 1977. *Out of the Sweatshop: The Struggle for Industrial Democracy.* New York: Quadrangle.

Stinchcombe, Arthur L. 1959. "Bureaucratic and Craft Administration of Production: A Comparative Study." *Administrative Science Quarterly* 4: 168–87.

Tyler, Gus. 1995. *Look for the Union Label: A History of the International Ladies' Garment Workers' Union.* Armonk, N.Y.: M. E. Sharpe.

U.S. Bureau of Economic Analysis. Selected years. *Foreign Direct Investment in the United States: Operations of U.S. Affiliates of Foreign Companies.* Washington, D.C.: Government Printing Office.

U.S. Bureau of Labor Statistics. Selected years. *Area Wage Survey: Los Angeles–Long Beach, California, Metropolitan Area*, superseded by *Occupational Compensation Survey, Pay Only: Los Angeles–Long Beach, California, Metropolitan Area.* Washington, D.C.: Government Printing Office.

——. Selected years. *Employment and Earnings.* Washington, D.C.: Government Printing Office.

U.S. Bureau of the Census. Selected years. *County Business Patterns: California.* Washington, D.C.: Government Printing Office.

U.S. Bureau of the Census. 1996. *1992 Census of Construction Industries,* CC92–A-9, Pacific States. Washington D.C.: Government Printing Office.

Voos, Paula. 1984. "Trends in Union Organizing Expenditures, 1953–1977." *Industrial and Labor Relations Review* 38: 52–63.

Waldinger, Roger. 1997. "Black / Immigrant Competition Re-assessed: New Evidence from Los Angeles." *Sociological Perspectives* 40: 365–86.

Waldinger, Roger, and Mehdi Bozorgmehr, eds. 1996. *Ethnic Los Angeles.* New York: Russell Sage Foundation.

Waldinger, Roger, Chris Erickson, Ruth Milkman, Daniel J. B. Mitchell, Abel Valenzuela, Kent Wong, and Maurice Zeitlin. 1998. "Helots No More: A Case Study of the Justice for Janitors Campaign in Los Angeles." In *Organizing to Win: New Research on Union Strategies,* edited by Kate Bronfenbrenner, Sheldon Friedman, Richard W. Hurd, Rudolph A. Oswald, and Ronald L. Seeber, 102–19. Ithaca: Cornell University Press.

Wallace, Steven P. 1986. "Central American and Mexican Immigrant Characteristics and Economic Incorporation in California." *International Migration Review* 20: 657–71.

——. 1989. "The New Urban Latinos: Central Americans in a Mexican Immigrant Environment." *Urban Affairs Quarterly* 25: 239–64.

Weiner, Melissa Balmain, and Jonathan Volzke. 1992. "149 Drywall Strikers Arrested." *Orange County Register,* July 3, A1.

Weir, Stan. 1983. "The Conflict in American Unions and the Resistance to Alternative Ideas from the Rank and File." In *Workers' Struggles, Past and Present: A "Radical America" Reader,* edited by James Green, 251–68. Philadelphia: Temple University Press.

Wells, Miriam J. 1999. "Unionization and the Cultural Division of Labor." Unpublished manuscript.

Wolff, Goetz. 1997. "The Apparel Cluster: A Regional Growth Industry." California Community College Fashion Symposium. Los Angeles: California Mart. Mimeo.

——. 1998. "Research for Organizing: The LAMAP Experience." Unpublished manuscript.

Wolff, Goetz, and Carol Zabin. 1997. "Manufacturing Matters: A Sectoral Approach to Combating Low Wages in Los Angeles." Final report submitted to the Haynes Foundation, Lewis Center for Regional Policy Studies, UCLA.

Zabin, Carol, and Luis Escala Rabadan. 1998. "Mexican Hometown Associations and Immigrant Political Empowerment in Los Angeles." Aspen Institute working paper, Washington D.C.

Zoroya, Gregg. 1992. "Mass Arrest of Strikers Largest in OC History." *Orange County Register,* July 4, A1, A24.

Notes on Contributors

EDNA BONACICH is Professor of Sociology and Ethnic Studies at the University of California, Riverside. She has served as a volunteer with UNITE's Los Angeles Organizing Department, especially its Justice Center, for the past ten years. She is coauthor (with Richard Appelbaum) of *Behind the Label: Inequality in the Los Angeles Apparel Industry*, forthcoming from the University of California Press.

HÉCTOR L. DELGADO is Assistant Professor of Sociology and Chicano/Latino Studies at the University of California, Irvine. He is the author of *New Immigrants, Old Unions: Organizing Undocumented Workers in Los Angeles* (Temple University Press, 1993) and continues to conduct research on immigrant workers and the labor movement.

CLAUDIA DER-MARTIROSIAN has a Ph.D. in sociology from UCLA. Her dissertation examined the role of social networks in the economic adaptation of Iranian immigrants in Los Angeles. She is a statistical consultant at the Division of General and Public Health Dentistry in the UCLA School of Dentistry.

CHRISTOPHER L. ERICKSON is Associate Professor in the Human Resources and Organizational Behavior Area of the UCLA Anderson School of Management. He received his Ph.D. in economics from MIT and was previously on the faculty of the New York State School of Industrial and Labor Relations at Cornell University. He researches and writes on various aspects of industrial relations.

CYNTHIA FELICIANO is a graduate student in sociology at UCLA. Her research focuses on educational inequality among first- and second-generation immigrant youth.

CATHERINE FISK is Professor of Law and William Rains Fellow at Loyola Law School in Los Angeles, where she teaches labor and employment law. She has written on labor history, employee benefits, employment discrimination, and on ownership of employee intellectual property and human capital.

DAVID LOPEZ has a Ph.D. in sociology from Harvard University and is an Associate Professor of Sociology at UCLA. He has written extensively on language and ethnicity in the United States, with special emphasis on the Latino population. His current research is on the impact of immigration on ethnic stratification in California.

RUTH MILKMAN is Professor of Sociology and Women's Studies at UCLA. She is the author of *Gender at Work: The Dynamics of Job Segregation during World War II* (University of Illinois Press, 1987), *Japan's California Factories* (UCLA Institute of Industrial Relations, 1991), and *Farewell to the Factory: Auto Workers in the Late Twentieth Century* (University of California Press, 1997).

DANIEL J. B. MITCHELL is Ho-Su Professor at the Anderson Graduate School of Management and the School of Public Policy and Social Research, UCLA, and former director of the UCLA Institute of Industrial Relations. He is currently coeditor of the journal *Industrial Relations*. He has written extensively about such topics as wage determination, wage-price controls, concession bargaining, flexible pay plans, nonwage employee benefits, uses of labor-market data, and labor standards in international trade.

RACHEL SHERMAN is a graduate student in sociology at the University of California, Berkeley. She is the author of "From State Introversion to State Extension: Modes of Emigrant Incorporation in Mexico, 1900–1997," forthcoming in *Theory and Society*. In addition to researching the contemporary labor movement in the United States, she is currently working on a dissertation on the San Francisco hotel industry.

KIM VOSS is Associate Professor of Sociology at the University of California, Berkeley. She is the author of *The Making of American Exceptionalism: The Knights of Labor and Class Formation in the Nineteenth Century* (Cornell University Press, 1993) and coauthor of *Inequality by Design: Cracking the Bell Curve Myth* (Princeton University Press, 1996). She is currently engaged in research on the contemporary American labor movement and in a comparative project on how English, French, and American workers interpreted strike defeats in the late nineteenth century.

ROGER WALDINGER is Professor of Sociology at UCLA and has published four books, including *Still the Promised City? African-Americans and New Immigrants in Postindustrial New York* (Harvard University Press, 1996) and, with Mehdi Bozorgmehr, *Ethnic Los Angeles* (Russell Sage Foundation, 1996).

MIRIAM J. WELLS is Professor of Anthropology in the Department of Human and Community Development, University of California, Davis. Her research interests include the sociology and anthropology of work, social movements, and the political economy of rural development. Her book, *Strawberry Fields: Politics, Class, and Work in California Agriculture* (Cornell University Press) won the 1996 Theodore Saloutos Award from the Agricultural History Society.

KENT WONG is the Director of the UCLA Center for Labor Research and Education, and teaches Labor Studies and Asian-American Studies at UCLA. He previously worked for six years as staff attorney for the Service Employees International Union, Local 660. He is President of the University and College Labor Education Association, representing fifty labor centers and labor educators nationally. He also served as Founding President of the Asian Pacific American Labor Alliance, AFL-CIO, from 1992 to 1997.

CAROL ZABIN is a labor economist at the University of California, Berkeley Labor Center. Her research focuses on labor, immigration, and community economic development. She concentrates on applied research that is of direct support to labor and community organizing. She previously held faculty positions at Tulane University and UCLA.

Index